Isaac Taylor

The Spirit of the Hebrew Poetry

With a Sketch of the Life of the Author and a Catalogue of his Writings

Isaac Taylor

The Spirit of the Hebrew Poetry
With a Sketch of the Life of the Author and a Catalogue of his Writings

ISBN/EAN: 9783337280963

Printed in Europe, USA, Canada, Australia, Japan

Cover: Foto ©Thomas Meinert / pixelio.de

More available books at **www.hansebooks.com**

THE

SPIRIT OF THE HEBREW POETRY.

BY

ISAAC TAYLOR.

WITH A SKETCH OF THE LIFE OF THE AUTHOR
AND A
CATALOGUE OF HIS WRITINGS.

NEW YORK:
WILLIAM GOWANS.

1862.

PREFACE.

The title of this volume is the same as that of a course of lectures which I delivered at Edinburgh, and afterwards at Glasgow, in the winter of 1852. At the time I was asked to publish these lectures; but as in the preparation of them I had not been able to command much leisure, I felt no inclination to bring them forward, such as they were when delivered.

But in looking at the notes of those lectures, once and again in the course of these ten years, they seemed to contain some germs of thought which might be brought to bear upon the great biblical argument that has lately awakened the attention of the religious community. This biblical argument which, as to its substance, is still in progress, gives a new meaning, or an enhanced importance, to most of the questions that come within the range of Christian belief, or of biblical criticism; and it follows therefore that what might be said or written ten years ago, on any of these subjects, will need to be reconsidered, and, in fact, re-written, at the present time. So it has been that, in preparing this volume for the press—with the notes of the lectures before me—a few passages only have seemed to me entirely available for my purpose. I have indeed adopted the title of the lectures as the title of the volume; and as much perhaps as the quantity of three of the following chapters has been transferred from those notes to these pages. This explanation is due from me to any readers of the book who, by chance, might have been among the hearers of the lectures, either at Edinburgh, or at Glasgow, in the November of 1852.

A momentous argument indeed it is that has lately moved the religious mind in England. So far as this controversy has had the character of an *agitation*, it must, in the course of things, soon cease to engage popular regard:—agitations subside, and the public mind—too quickly perhaps—returns to its point of equipoise, where it rests until it is moved anew in some other manner. It would, however, be an error to suppose that the agitation will not have brought about some permanent changes in religious thought; and, moreover, if a supposition of this kind would be an error, something worse than simply *an error* would be implied if any should indulge a wish that things might be allowed to collapse into their anterior position, unchanged and unbenefited, by the recent controversy. A wish of this sort would indicate at once extreme ignorance as to the cause and the nature of the argument, and moreover a culpable indifference in relation to the progress and the re-establishment of Christian belief.

Animated, or—it may be—passionate, religious controversies are hurricanes in the world of thought, ordained of God for effecting purposes which would not be effected otherwise than by the violence of storms; and let this figure serve us a step further.—The same hurricane which clears the atmosphere, and which sweeps away noxious accumulations from the surface of the earth, serves a not less important purpose in bringing into view the fissures, the settlements, the forgotten rents in the structures we inhabit. It is Heaven's own work thus to purify the atmosphere; but it is man's work to look anew to his own house—after a storm, and to repair its dilapidations. To rejoice gratefully in a health-giving atmosphere, and a clear sky, is what is due to piety; but it is *also* due to piety to effect, in time, needed repairs at home.

As to the recent out-speak of unbelief, it is of that kind which must, in the nature of things, be recurrent, at intervals, longer or shorter. The very conditions of a Revelation that has been consigned to various records in the course of thirty centuries involve a liability to the renewal of exceptive argumentation, which easily finds points of lodgment upon so large a surface. But this periodic atheistic epilepsy (unbelief within the pale of Christianity never fails to become atheistic) will not occasion alarm to those who indeed know on what ground they stand on the side of religious belief. This ground has not, and will not, be shaken.

Looking inwards upon our Christianity—looking Churchward—there may indeed be reason for uneasiness. This recent agitation could not fail to bring into view, in the sight of all men—the religious, and the irreligious—alike, a defect, a want of understanding, a flaw, or a fault, in that mass of opinion concerning the Scriptures, as inspired books, which we have inherited from our remote ancestors. No one, at this time, well knows what it is which he believes, as to this great question; or what it is which he ought to believe concerning those conditions—literary and historical—subject to which the Revelation we accept as from God, and which is attested as such, by miracles, and by the Divine præ-notation of events, has been embodied in the books of the Canon.

There are indeed many who, not only will reject any such intimation of obscurity or doubtfulness on this ground, but who will show a hasty resentment of what they will denounce as an insidious assault upon the faith. The feelings, or say—the prejudices, of persons of this class ought to be respected, and their inconsiderateness should be kindly allowed for; their fears and their jealousies are—for the truth; nor should we impute to good men any but the best motives, even when their want of temper appears to be commensurate with their want of intelligence. But after showing all forbearance toward such worthy persons, there is a higher duty which must not be evaded:—there is a duty to ourselves, and there is a duty to our immediate successors, and there is a duty to the mass of imperfectly informed Christian persons, who, in due time, will be seen insensibly to accept, as good and safe, modes of thinking and speaking which, at one time, would have seemed to them quite inadmissible and dangerous.

The remaining defect or flaw in our scheme of belief concerning the conveyance of a Supernatural Revelation makes itself felt the most obtrusively in relation to the Old Testament Scriptures. It is here, and it is on this extensive field, that minds, negatively constituted, and perhaps richly accomplished, but wanting in the grasp and power of a healthful moral consciousness, and wholly wanting in spiritual consciousness, find their occasion. The surface over which a sophisticated reason and a fastidious taste take their course is here very large; for the events of a people's history, and the multifarious literature of many centuries, come to find a place within its area. The very same extent of surface from which a better reason, and a more healthful moral feeling gather an irresistible conviction of the nearness of God throughout it, furnishes, to an astute and frigid critical faculty, a thousand and one instances over which to proclaim a petty triumph.

So must it ever be. There is here a contrariety which is inherent in the nature of the case; and which the diverse temperaments of minds will never cease to bring into collision with religious faith. What is it then which might be wished for to preclude the ill consequences that accrue from these periodic collisions? Do we need some new theory of inspiration? Or ought there to take place a stepping back, along the whole line of religious belief? Or do we need to make a surrender of certain articles of faith? Or should we shelter ourselves under evasions? Or would it be well to quash inquiry by authority, or to make a show of terrors for intimidating assailants? None of these things are needed; nor, if resorted to, could they be of any permanent service.

The requirement is this, as I humbly think—That, on all hands, we should be willing to throw aside, as unauthentic and unwarranted, a natural prejudice; or, let it rather be called—a spontaneous product of religious feeling, which leads us to frame conditions, and to insist upon requirements, that *ought*, as we imagine, to limit the Divine wisdom in embodying the Divine will in a written Revelation. Instead of insisting upon any such conditions, ought we not rather, in all humility, to acknowledge that, in the Divine methods of proceeding toward mankind—natural, providential, and supernatural—we have everything to learn, and nothing to premise?

SANFORD RIVERS,

September, 1861.

THE

SPIRIT OF THE HEBREW POETRY.

CHAPTER I.

THE RELATION OF THE HEBREW POETRY TO THE RELIGIOUS PURPOSES IT SUBSERVES.

WHEN the Scriptures of the Old Testament are accepted, collectively, as an embodiment of First Truths in Theology and Morals, three suppositions concerning them are before us; one of which, or a part of each, we may believe ourselves at liberty to adopt. The three suppositions are these:—

1. We may grant that these writings—symbolic as they are in their phraseology and style, and, to a great extent, metrical in their structure, as well as poetical in tone—were well suited to the purposes of religious instruction among a people, such as we suppose the Israelitish tribes to have been at the time of their establishment in Palestine, and such as they continued to be until some time after the return of the remnant of the nation from Babylon.

2. More than this we may allow, namely, this—that these same writings—the history and the poetry

taken together, are also well adapted to the uses and ends of *popular* religious instruction in any country and every age, where and when there are classes of the community to be taught that are nearly on a level, intellectually, with the ancient Hebrew race:—that is to say, among those with whom philosophic habits of thought have not been developed, and whose religious notions and instincts are comparatively infantile.

3. But a higher ground than this may be taken, and it is the ground that is assumed throughout the ensuing chapters; and it is in accordance with this assumption, that whatever may be advanced therein must be interpreted. It is affirmed then, that, not less in relation to the most highly-cultured minds than to the most rude—not less to minds disciplined in abstract thought, than to such as are unused to generalization of any kind—the Hebrew Scriptures, in their metaphoric style, and their poetic diction, are the fittest medium for conveying, what it is their purpose to convey, concerning the Divine Nature, and concerning the spiritual life, and concerning the correspondence of man—the finite, with God—the Infinite.

It is on this hypothesis concerning the Hebrew Scriptures, and not otherwise, that the books of the New Testament take possession as consecutive to the books of the Old Testament—the one being the complement of the other; and the two constituting a homogeneous system. The Prophets (and they were Poets) of the elder Revelation, having fulfilled a function which demanded the symbolic style, and which could submit to no other conditions than those of this figurative utterance, the Evangelists and Apostles, whose style is wholly of another order, do not lay anew a foundation that was already well laid; but they build upon it whatever was peculiar to that later Revelation of which they were the instruments. In the Hebrew writings—poetic in form, as to a great extent they are—we are to find, not a crude theology, adapted to the gross conceptions of a rude people; but an ultimate theology—wanting that only which the fulness of time was to add to it, and so rendering the Two Collections—a One Revelation, adapted to the use of all men, in all times, and under all conditions of intellectual advancement.

If on subjects of the deepest concernment, and in relation to which the human mind labours with its own conceptions, and yearns to know whatever may be known—CHRIST and His ministers are brief and allusive, they are so, not as if in rebuke of these desires; but because the limits of a divine conveyance of the things of the spiritual world had already been reached by the choir of the prophets. All that could be taught had been taught "to them of old;" and this sum of the philosophy of heaven had been communicated in those diverse modes and styles which had exhausted the resources of human utterance to convey so much as is conveyed.

To give reality to what had been foreshown in shadows; to accomplish what had been predicted; to expound, in a higher sense, whatever is universal and eternal in morals; to authenticate anew what might have been called in question—these functions were proper to the ministers of the later Dispensation; and the books of the New Testament are the record of this work of completion, in its several kinds. Yet this is the characteristic of the Christian writings, that they abstain from the endeavour to throw into an abstract or philosophic form those first truths of theology to which the prophets of the Old Testament had given expression in symbolic terms and in the figures of the Hebrew poetry. The parables of CHRIST—symbolic as they are, but not poetic—touch those things of the new "kingdom of Heaven" which belong to the *human* development of it; or to the administration of the Gospel on earth; or within the consciousness of men singly.

Those who choose to do so may employ their time in inquiring in what *other modes* than those which are characteristic of the Hebrew Scriptures the highest truths in theology might be embodied, and whether these principles may not be, or might not have been, subjected to the conditions of abstract generalization, and so brought into order within the limits of a logical and scientific arrangement. Let these philosophic diversions be pursued, at leisure, until they reach a result which might be reported of and accepted. Meantime it is enough for us to know that no such result has hitherto ever rewarded the labours, either of oriental sages in the remotest periods, or of Grecian philosophers, or of the Alexandrian teachers, or of mediæval doctors, or of the great thinkers of the sixteenth century, or of those of the times in which we live. Metaphysic Theologies, except so far as they take up the very terms and figures of the Hebrew Scriptures, have hitherto shown a properly religious aspect in proportion as they have been unintelligible:—when intelligible they become—if not atheistic, yet tending in that direction. When this is affirmed the inference is not—that a True Theology might not be embodied in abstract terms, in an upper world; but this, that the terms and the modes of *human reason* are, and must ever be, insufficient for purposes of this kind.

This failure, or this succession of failures, may indeed affect the credit of Philosophy; but in no degree does it throw disadvantage upon the religious well-being of those who are content to take their instruction and their training from the Holy Scriptures. These writings, age after age, have in fact met, and they have satisfied the requirements of piety and of virtue in the instance of millions of the humble and devout readers of the Bible; and it has been so as well among the most highly cultured as among the unlearned; and they have imparted to such whatever it is needful and possible for man to know concerning God, the Creator, the Ruler, the Father, and concerning that life divine, the end of which is—the life eternal.

The most obvious difference between the terms and style of Speculative or Metaphysic Theology, and the Theology of the Scriptures—of the Old Testament especially—is this, that while the language of the one is reduced to a condition as remote as possible from the figurative mode of conveying thought, the language of the other is, in *every instance, purely figurative;* and that it abstains absolutely, and always, from the abstract or philosophic usage of the words it employs. Yet this obvious difference between the two is not the only dissimilarity; nor perhaps is it that which is of the highest importance to be kept in view, for these two modes of theologic teaching have different intentions; or, as we might say, the centre toward which the various materials of each system tends is proper to each, and is exclusive of the other.

Scientific Theology professes to regard the Divine Nature and attributes as its centre; and from that centre (supposed to be known) inferences in all directions are logically derived. But the very contrary of this is true of Biblical Theology; for the central area of Biblical Theism is—the human spirit, in its actual condition, its original powers, its necessary limitations, its ever varying consciousness, its lapses, its sorrows, its perils, its hopes, and its fears:—its misjudgments, its faiths, its unbelief:—its brightness, its darkness:—whatever is life-like in man, and whatever portends death. Although the two systems possess in common whatever is true concerning God, everything within each wears an aspect widely unlike the aspect which it presents in the other.

The instinctive tendency of the human mind (or of a certain class of minds) to generalize, and to pursue, to their end, the most abstract forms of thought, is not in itself blameworthy, nor must it be charged with the ill-consequences and the failures which often are its fruit. Where there is no generalization there will be no progress: where there is no endeavour to pass on from the concrete to the abstract, men individually, and nations, continue stationary in a rude civilization:—there may be mind; but it sleeps; or it is impotently active:—it is busy, but it does not travel forward. Yet it is only within the range of earth, or of things that are indeed cognizable by the human mind, that this power of abstraction—the highest and the noblest of its powers—can be productive of what must always be its aim and purpose, namely, an absolute philosophy; or a philosophy which shall be coherent in itself, and shall be exempt from internal contradictions.

It is on this ground, then, that the Hebrew writers, in their capacity as teachers of Theology, occupy a position where they are broadly distinguished from all other teachers with whom they might properly be compared, whether ancient or modern, oriental or western. Philosophers, or founders of theologies, aiming and intending to promulgate a Divine Theory—a scheme of theism—have spoken of God as the object, or as the creation of human thought. But the Hebrew writers, one and all, and with marvellous unanimity, speak of God *relatively only*; or as He is related to the immediate religious purposes of this teaching. Or if for a moment they utter what might have the aspect of an abstract proposition, they bring it into contact, at the nearest possible point, with the spiritual wants of men, or with their actual moral condition; as thus, "Great is the Lord, and of great power, and His understanding is infinite. He telleth the number of the stars: He calleth them all by their names;" but this Infinite and Almighty Being is He that "healeth the broken in heart, and bindeth up their wounds." It is the human spirit always that is the central, or cohesive principle of the Hebrew Theology. The theistic affirmations that are scattered throughout the books of the Old Testament are not susceptible of a synthetic adjustment by any rule of logical distribution; and although they are never contradictory one of another, they may seem to be so, inasmuch as the principle which would show their accordance stands remote from human apprehension:—it must be so; and to suppose otherwise would be to affirm that the finite mind may grasp the Infinite. The several elements of this Theism are complementary one of another, only in relation to the needs, and to the discipline of the human mind;—not so in relation to its modes of speculative thought, or to its own reason. Texts packed in order will not build up a Theology, in a scientific sense; what they will do is this—they meet the variable necessities of the spiritual life, in every mood, and in every possible occasion of that life. Texts, metaphoric always in their terms, take effect upon the religious life as counteractive one of another; or as remedial appliances, which, when rightly employed, preserve and restore the spiritual health.

If we were to bring together the entire compass of the figurative theology of the Scriptures (and this must be the theology of the Old Testament) it would be easy to arrange the whole in perifery around the human spirit, as related to its manifold experiences; but a hopeless task it would be to attempt to arrange the same passages as if in circle around the hypothetic attributes of the Absolute Being. The human reason faulters at every step in attempting so to interpret the Divine Nature; yet the quickened soul interprets for itself—and it does so anew every day, those signal passages upon which the fears, the hopes, the griefs the consolations of years gone by have set their mark.

The religious and spiritual life has its postulates, which might be specified in order; and under each head they are broadly distinguishable from what, on the same ground, might be named as the postulates of Speculative Thought. Indispensable, for instance, to the healthful energy of the religious life is an unsophisticated confidence in what is termed the omnipresence and omniscience of God, the Father of spirits; but on this ground, where the Hebrew writers are clear, peremptory, unfaltering, and unconscious of perplexity, Speculative Thought stumbles at its first attempts to advance; and as to that faculty by aid of which we realize, in some degree, an abstract principle, and bring it within range of the imagination, it is here utterly baffled. The *belief* in this doctrine is simple;—we may say it is natural:—but as to an intellectual realization of it, this is impossible; and as to a philosophic expression of such a belief in words, the most acutely analytic minds have lost their way in utter darkness; or they have landed themselves in Pantheism; or they have beguiled themselves and their disciples with a compage of words without meaning. The power of the human mind to admit simultaneously a consciousness of more than one object is so limited, or it is so soon quite exhausted, that a doctrine which we grant to be incontestably certain, refuses more perhaps than any other, to submit itself to the conditions of human thought:—it is never mastered. Aware, as every one who thinks must be, of this insurmountable difficulty, we ought not to except against that mode of overleaping the obstruction which the Hebrew writers offer to our acceptance:—figurative in phrase, and categorical in style, they affirm that—"The eyes of the Lord are in every place, beholding the evil and the good;" or thus again—"Thou knowest my downsitting and mine uprising; Thou understandest my thought afar off."

The longer we labour, in scientific modes, at the elements of Theism the deeper shall we plunge in an abyss; and we shall learn, perhaps too late, the wisdom of resting in a devout acknowledgment to this effect—"Such knowledge (of God) is too wonderful for me: it is high, I cannot attain unto it." But the Hebrew writers make short work of philosophic stumbling-blocks; and they secure their religious intention, which is *their sole intention*, in that one mode in which a belief which is indispensable to the religious life presents itself, on what might be called its conceivable side. They affirm the truth in the most absolute and unexceptive style, giving it all the breadth it can have; but in doing so, and in the same breath, they affirm that which serves to lodge it in the spiritual consciousness, as a caution, or as a comfort; they lodge the universal principle as near as may be to the fears, and to the hopes, and to the devout yearnings of the individual man. If we do not relish this style and this method, we should think ourselves bound to bring forward a better style, and to propound a more approvable method. At any rate, we should give a sample of some one style or method other than this, and between which and the Biblical manner we might make a choice. No alternative that is at once intelligible and admissible has ever yet been brought forward. God may be known, and his attributes may be discoursed of, as related to the needs of the human spirit;—but not otherwise:—not a span beyond this limit has ever been attained.

"Do not I fill heaven and earth? saith the Lord. Can any hide himself in secret places that I shall not see him? Am I a God nigh at hand, and not a God afar off?" We may read the 139th Psalm throughout, and be convinced that what is inconceivable as an abstraction, or as an axiom in speculative theism, has, by the Hebrew writers, been firmly lodged in the beliefs of men in the only mode in which such a lodgment could be possible. This element of the Infinite finds a coalescent surface—a point of adhesion in the individual consciousness; a consciousness towards God which removes all other beings from our view, and which leaves us, each for himself, alone with his Creator and Judge.

In the place of interminable and abstruse definitions —defining nothing, propounding doubts and solving none—in the place of this laborious emptiness, the writer of the ode above referred to so affirms the doctrine of the omniscience and the omnipresence of God as at once to expand our belief of it to the utmost, and to concentrate it also upon the experiences of the spiritual life. God is everywhere present—in the vastness of the upper heavens—in the remotest recesses of Sheol (not Gehenna) everywhere, to the utmost borders of the material universe; but these affirmations of a universal truth are advanced in apposition to a truth which is more affecting, or which is of more intimate concernment to the devout spirit:—this spirit, its faults, its terrors, its aspirations; and this animal frame, of which it is the tenant, is in the hand of God, and is dependent upon His bounty, and is cared for in whatever relates to its precarious welfare; and thus is so great a theme—the Divine Omniscience—brought home to its due culmination in an outburst of religious feeling: "How precious also are thy thoughts unto me, O God! how great is the sum of them! If I should count them, they are more in number than the sand: when I awake, I am still with Thee!"

A problem absolutely insoluble, as an abstraction, and which in fact is not susceptible of any verbal enunciation in a scientific form, is that of the Divine Eternity;—or, as we are wont to say—using terms to which perhaps an attenuated meaning may be attached—the non-relationship of God to Time, and His existence otherwise than through successive instants. This is a belief which the human mind demands as a necessary condition of religious thought, and of which it finds the need at every step of the way in systematic theism, which yet is equally inconceivable, and inexpressible. In the Mosaic Ode (the 90th Psalm) the theistic axiom is so placed in apposition with the brevity and the precarious tenure of human life that the inconceivable belief becomes, in a measure, conceivable, just by help of its coalescence with an element of every one's sense of the brevity and frailty of life. So it is that the theology and the human consciousness are made to constitute a one article of belief in that spiritual economy under which man, as mortal, is in training for immortality;—as thus—"Before the mountains were brought forth, or ever Thou hadst formed the earth and the world, even from everlasting to everlasting, Thou art God." But now, in the immediate context of an affirmation which approaches the abstract style, there is found what serves to bring the higher truth into a near-at-hand bearing upon the vivid experiences of our mortal condition. "Thou turnest man to destruction, and sayest, Return, ye children of men; for a thousand years in thy sight are but as yesterday when it is past, and as a watch in the night." Then there is conjoined with this doctrine a cautionary provision against the oriental error of so musing upon vast theologic conceptions as that the individual man forgets himself, and becomes unconscious of his own spiritual condition. It is not so with the writer of this Psalm:—"Thou hast set our iniquities before Thee; our secret sins in the light of Thy countenance. . . . . So teach us to number our days that we may apply our hearts unto wisdom."

For making sure of this amalgamation of theologic elements with those emotions and sentiments that constitute the religious life there is found, in several of the Psalms, a formal alternation of the two classes of utterances. An instance of this interchange occurs in the 147th Psalm just above referred to; for in this Psalm, with its strophe and its antistrophe, there is first a challenge to the worship of God, as a delightful employment—then an evoking of religious national sentiment—then a message of comfort and hope, addressed to the destitute, the oppressed, the sorrowful; and last, there is the interwoven theologic element in affirmation of the Providence, Power, and bounty of God; for it is said of Him who "healeth the broken in heart, and bindeth up their wounds," that "He telleth the number of the stars, and calleth them all by their names; for great is our Lord, and of great power:—His understanding is infinite."

So it is throughout the devotional and poetic portions of the Hebrew Scriptures, that the theologic and the emotional elements are counterpoised—not as if the two diverse elements might be logically compacted into a scheme of theism; nor as if they were contradictory, the one of the other; but they are so placed as to be counteractive, the one of the other, in their influence upon the human spirit. Lest the devout affections should pass off into a feeble sentimentalism (as it is their tendency to do) there is conjoined with the expression of pious emotion some reference to those attributes of the Divine Nature which inspire awe and fear; and again, lest the meditation of infinite power and purity should lead the way (as it has so often done) into pantheistic mysticism, the worshipper is quickly reminded of his individual frailty—his dependence and his unworthiness. A structure, simple in its principle, and in its *intention*, may be traced throughout these Scriptures as a method that is always adhered to, whatever those diversities of style may be which attach to the writer—whether it be Moses, or David, or one of the later prophets.

The reading and hearing of the Old Testament from the earliest childhood—at home and in church—in these Bible-reading lands, has brought us to imagine that the belief of the Personality of God—God, the Creator, the Father of Spirits—is a belief which all men, unless argued out of it by sophistry, would accept spontaneously. These early and continuous lessons in Bible learning have imbued our minds with the conception of the Infinite Being—the Creator of all things, who, in making man in His own likeness, has opened for us a ground of intercourse—warranting, on our part, the assurance that He with whom we have to do is conscious as we are conscious, and that—so far as the finite may resemble the Infinite, He is, as we are—is one with us, is communionable, and is open to a correspondence which is properly likened to that of a father with his children.

But now, whether we look abroad in antiquity—Asiatic and European—or look to the now prevalent beliefs of eastern races, or look near at hand to recent schemes of metaphysic theism, we must admit it to be true, in fact, that whatever the unsophisticated instincts of the human mind (if such could anywhere be found) might prompt men to accept and profess, their actual dispositions—perverted as these are—impel them to put, in the place of this belief, either a sensuous and debasing polytheism, or a vapid pantheism. So it has been in all time past, and so at the moment now passing:—so it has been among brutalized troglodytes;—and so is it among "the most advanced thinkers" of modern literature.

Always, and now, it is true that the Hebrew writers stand possessed of an unrivalled prerogative as the Teachers—not merely of monotheism, but of the spirit-stirring belief of God—as near to man by the nearness or homogeneousness of the moral consciousness. Near to us is He, not only because in Him "we live and move and have our being," but because He—infinite in power and intelligence—is in so true a sense one with us that the unabated terms of human emotion are a proper and genuine medium of intercourse between Him and ourselves.

To remove this Bible belief to as great a distance as possible from daily life and feeling, has been the intention of all superstitions, whether gay or terrific; and it has been the aim also of abstract speculation, and, not less so, of Art and of Poetry, with their manifold fascinations; and therefore it is that the Hebrew Scriptures are so specially distasteful to those whose convictions they have not secured, and whose faith they do not command. It is the clearness—it is the fulness—it is the unfaltering decisiveness of the Hebrew writers, from the earliest of them to the latest, on this ground, that constitutes the broad characteristic of the Old Testament Scriptures, when brought into comparison with any other literature—ancient or modern. We may reject the anthropomorphic symbolism of these writings, as repugnant to our abstract notions of the Divine Nature; but this we must grant to be their distinction —namely, a uniform consistency in the use they make of the vocabulary of human sentiment, passion, emotion, so as to bring the conception of the Personal God into the nearest possible alliance with the human consciousness, on that side of it where a return to virtue, if ever it is brought about, must take place. God is near to man—and one with him *for his recovery to wisdom and goodness.* The instances are trite;—and they will occur to the recollection of every Bible reader; yet let one or two be here adduced.

The Hebrew prophet, and poet, meets and satisfies the first requirement of the awakened human spirit, which is an assured communion with God on terms of hopefulness and amity, as well as of the profoundest awe, and of unaffected humiliation. And this assurance is so conveyed as shall intimately blend the highest theistic conceptions with the health-giving consciousness of unmerited favour.—"Thus saith the High and Lofty One that inhabiteth eternity, whose name is Holy: I dwell in the high and holy place, with him also that is of a contrite and humble spirit, to revive the spirit of the humble, and to revive the heart of the contrite ones: for I will not contend for ever, neither will I be always wrath; for the spirit should fail before me, and the souls which I have made."

The same conditions are observed—and they should be noted—in this parallel passage—"Thus saith the Lord, The heaven is my throne, and the earth is my footstool. Where is the house that ye build me? and where is the place of my rest? For all these things hath my hand made; and all these things have been, saith the Lord: but to this man will I look, even to him that is poor and of a contrite spirit, and that trembleth at my word."

These familiar passages are illustrations, and they are demonstrations, of that mode of teaching "the things of God" which distinguishes the Hebrew Scriptures from all other writings—professedly religious—ancient or modern (those of course excepted which follow this same guidance). The terms are symbolic, or figurative purely; and the Divine attributes are not otherwise affirmed than in their bearing upon the spiritual welfare of that one class of minds that needs, and that will rightly avail itself of, this kind of teaching. To minds of the metaphysic class there is no conveyance of theistic axioms:—to minds of the captious temperament there is none:—to the sensual and sordid, or the contumacious and impious, there is none. These passages are as a stream of the effulgence of the upper heavens, sent down through an aperture in a dense cloud, to rest with a life-giving power of light and heat upon the dwelling of the humble worshipper. Whether this humble worshipper be one who turns the soil for his daily bread, or be the occupant of a professor's chair, it shall be the same theology that he hence derives: the former will not think to ask—and the latter will be better trained than to ask—how it is that the Omnipresent can be said, either to be seated on a throne in an upper heaven, or to make earth His footstool:—neither the one nor the other will take offence at the solecism of "inhabiting eternity." A solecism if it be;—nevertheless it is probable that no compact of words coming within the range of language has better conveyed than this does the inconceivable idea of the Divine Existence—irrespective of Time.

Biblical utterances of the first truths in Theology possess the grandeur of the loftiest poetry, as well as a rhythmical or artificial structure; and they hold off from entanglement with metaphysic perplexities—was it because the writers were men of a nation incapable of abstract thought? If this were granted, then, on merely natural principles, we ought to find them sometimes forgetful of their purpose as religious teachers, while they wander forth, in oriental style, upon grounds of gorgeous imagination. Never do they do this. Poets as they were in soul, and in phrase too, they are strictly mindful of their function as teachers of spiritual and ethical principles. David says—as our version has it—"The Lord is in His holy temple; the Lord's throne is in heaven: His eyes behold, His eyelids try the children of men." Four affirmations meet us within the compass of these few words, and each of them has a specific meaning—inviting the religious teacher to open it out, and bring it to bear with effect upon the religious life; and in the third and the fourth of these clauses a meaning of peculiar significance is conveyed, which, instead of a vague averment of the Divine omniscience, turns this doctrine in upon the conscience with a burning intensity. No phrases could more vividly than do these, give force to the conception of this critical observation of the characters and conduct of men—singly; for in relation to a process of moral discipline, He who is the Father of spirits "beholds the children of men, and His eyelids try them." It is true of the Creator, that He "knoweth all the fowls of the mountains, and the wild beasts of the forest, and that the cattle upon a thousand hills are His;" but it is a truth of another order that is affirmed—it is a truth penetrative of the conscience—it is a truth, not metaphysic or poetic, but sternly ethical, that is here presented in metaphor. A keen scrutiny of the concealed motives and of the undeveloped tendencies of the heart on the part of One who is firmly-purposed, and who is severely exact in his observation of conduct is conveyed in these expressions: —the dropping of the eyelid for the purpose of reflective scrutiny indicates a determination to look through disguises, and rightfully to interpret whatever may wear a semblance of falseness. This is a truth to be thought of by those who accustom themselves to repeat the prayer, "Search me and try me, and see what evil way there is in me:" it is a truth for those who submit themselves willingly to the severest conditions of the spiritual discipline. As for men of another class, who desire no such schooling, it is said of them that—"The Lord knoweth them afar off"—what they are it needs no careful observation to discern.

Parallel instances are abundant in the Psalms, and throughout the prophetic books; but this is not all that should be said, for instances of a contrary kind nowhere occur. The Hebrew writers, in long series, not only teach the same theology, but they teach it always, and only so, in metaphoric terms; and more than this—it is always under the condition of connecting their affirmations of the Divine attributes with the purposes and the needs of the spiritual training of the individual soul.

There is before us then a method—invariably adhered to;—there is a rule that is never violated; but it is a method and a rule of which we become cognizant only when we look back from the latest to the earliest of a long series of writers, each of whom has his own manner, his individual characteristic style. Not one in the series gives evidence of his personal consciousness of the law which, nevertheless, he is silently obeying; and it is a law which is far from obvious in itself, and it is by no means such as would spontaneously offer itself, even to minds of the highest order; much less to the fervent and the inartificial. We—of this late age—trained as we are in, and familiar with, the habitudes and the phrases of abstract thought, easily recognize the principle which gives continuity to the writings of the Old Testament; and we are able to put an abstraction of this kind into words. But it is certain that no such enunciation of an occult law would have been intelligible to the writers themselves, who nevertheless, each in his turn, implicitly and always conforms himself to it. Here indeed—as throughout the material world—there is DESIGN—there is an *intention* which gives coherence to a complicity of parts; but it is—as in the material world, so here—an intention which was unperceived and unthought of, while it was in course of execution.

CHAPTER II.

COMMIXTURE OF THE DIVINE AND THE HUMAN ELEMENTS IN THE HEBREW POETIC SCRIPTURES.

THE mere use of any such phrase as this—The Hebrew Poetry, or the speaking of the Prophets as *Poets*—is likely to give alarm to Bible readers of a certain class, who will think that, in bringing the inspired writers under any such treatment as that which these phrases seem to imply, we are forgetting their higher claims, and thus disparage them as the Bearers of a message immediately from God to men.

Alarms of this kind arise, either from a misapprehension of the facts before us; or from absolute ignorance of those facts; or, it may be, from some inveterate confusion, attaching to our modes of thinking on religious subjects. The remedy must be found in the removal of this ignorance—in the clearing up of these confusions, and especially—and most of all—in the attainment of a thorough and deep-felt confidence in the Divine origination and authority of the Canonical writings. Those religious alarms or jealousies which impede the free course of thought on this ground—if they do not spring from stolid and incurable prejudices, are yet the indication of a shaken and variable belief in the Bible, as the medium of a supernatural Revelation.

It will be in no dread of the imputation of unbelief that we enter upon the field now in view. A tremulous tread on this ground would be sure sign, either of incertitude as to first principles, or of a treasonable cowardice; and probably of both: we here disclaim the one as well as the other of these sinister restraints. If indeed there be dangers on our pathway, let them be manfully encountered, and they will disappear, as do always the phantoms of superstition when boldly looked at. The risks to faith that haunt this subject are factitious, and have had their origin in an ill-judged modern eagerness to conform our doctrine of Inspiration to the arbitrary conditions of a logical or pseudo-scientific system. No such attempt can ever be successful; but the restless and often renewed endeavour to effect a purpose of this kind breeds perplexities—it feeds a bootless controversy, and it furnishes disbelief with its only effective weapons.

If unwarranted and unwarrantable modern schemes, as to the nature and the extent of Inspiration, are put out of view, and if interminable argumentation be cut short, then the Bible will return to its place of power and of benign authority, yielding to us daily its inestimable treasures of instruction, admonition, and comfort; but so long as we adhere to a theory of Inspiration, whether it be of better quality or of worse, we shall be open to disturbance from the inroads of textual and historical criticism, and shall be haunted by the grim suspicion that the Scriptures are confusedly constituted of heterogeneous elements—some of which are purely divine, while some are merely human: or we shall accept the comfortless hypothesis that the divine substance in Holy Scripture has become flawed or intergrained with the grit and *debris* of human inadvertence, accident, ignorance, or evil intention; and that thus the Bible is a conglomerate of materials, precious and worthless.

Under the influence of suppositions of this kind, and in proportion to our personal candour and intelligence, we shall be asking aid from any who can yield it, to inform us, at every section, and verse, and line, what it is that we may accept as "from above," and what it is that should be rejected as "from men." A Bible-reading method less cumbrous than this, and less comfortless too, and less embarrassing, is surely attainable.

When we accept a mass of writings as a gift from God, in a sense peculiar to themselves, and which is their *distinction*, as compared with all other human compositions, we do so on grounds which we think to be sufficient and conclusive. Already therefore we have given in our submission to the Book, or to the collection of books, which we are willing to regard as rightfully determinative of our religious belief, and as regulative of our conduct and temper. If it be so, then no other, or middle course can, consistently with undoubted facts, be taken than this; we must bring ourselves to think of these writings as, in one sense, *wholly human;* and read them as if they were nothing more than human; and, in another sense, as *wholly divine;* and must read them as if they were in no sense less than divine.

Endless confusions, interminable questionings, come from the mitigative supposition—That, in any given portion, page, or paragraph, certain expressions, or separate clauses, or single words—here five words, and there seven words, are of human origination; while other five words, or seven, or other clauses or sentences or paragraphs, are from heaven; and that thus a perpetual caution or marginal indication is needed, by aid of which we may, from line to line, discriminate the one species of writing from the other—sifting the particles of gold from out of the sand and clay in the midst of which we find them. It is manifest that the better instructed a Bible reader may be, and the more intelligent and conscientious he is, so much the deeper, and so much the more frequent will be his perplexities, and so much the less comfort and edification will he draw from his Bible daily: it will be so if a notion of this kind has lodged itself within him.

That in Holy Scripture which is from above is an element over and beyond, and beside, the medium of its conveyance to us, although never separated therefrom. That which we find, and which "finds us" also, is not the parchment and the ink, nor is it the writing, nor is it the Hebrew vocables and phrases, nor is it the grammatical modes of an ancient language; nor is it this or that style of writing, prosaic or poetic, or abstract or symbolical; for as to any of these incidents or modes of conveyance, they might be exchanged for some other mode, without detriment to the divine element—the ulterior intention, which is so conveyed. We all readily accept any, or several of these substitutions—and we moderns necessarily do so—whenever we take into our hands what we have reason to think is a trustworthy translation. It is not even the most accomplished Hebraist of modern times (whoever he may be) that is exempted from the necessity of taking, from out of his Hebrew Bible, a meaning—as to single words, and as to combinations of words—which is only a substitute for the primitive meaning intended to be conveyed by the Hebrew writer to the men of his times. Thought, embodied in words, or in other arbitrary signs, and addressed by one human mind to another human mind, or by the Divine mind to the human mind, is subjected to conditions which belong to, or which spring from, the limitations of the recipient mind. The question is not of this sort, namely, whether Thought or Feeling might not be conveyed from mind to mind with unconditioned purity, in some occult mode of immediate spiritual communion. This may well be supposed, and, as we are bound to believe it possible, it may be accepted as a truth, and as a truth that has a deep meaning in Religion.

But the position now assumed is this—that Thought or Feeling, *when embodied in language*, is, to its whole extent of meaning, necessarily conditioned, as well by the established laws of language, as by all those incidental influences which affect its value and import, in traversing the chasms of Time. Statements of this kind are open to misapprehensions from various sources, and will not fail to awaken debate. So far as such misapprehensions may be precluded, this will best be done in submitting actual instances to the reader's consideration.

Take, as an instance—one among many that are equally pertinent to our purpose,—the Twenty-third Psalm. This is an ode which for beauty of sentiment is not to be matched in the circuit of all literature. In its way down through three thousand years, or more, this Psalm has penetrated to the depths of millions of hearts—it has gladdened homes of destitution and discomfort—it has whispered hope and joy amid tears to the utterly solitary and forsaken, whose only refuge was in Heaven. Beyond all range of probable calculation have these dozen lines imparted a power of endurance under suffering, and strength in feebleness, and have kept alive the flickering flame of religious feeling in hearts that were nigh to despair. The divine element herein embodied has given proof, millions of times repeated, of its reality, and of its efficacy, as a *formula* of tranquil trust in God, and of a grateful sense of His goodness, which all who do trust in Him may use for themselves, and use it until it has become assimilated to their own habitual feelings. But this process of assimilation can take place only on the ground of certain assumptions, such as these—It is not enough that we read, and often repeat this composition *approvingly;* or that we regard it as an utterance of proper religious sentiments: this is quite true; but this is not enough: this Psalm will not be available for its intended purpose unless these expressions of trust in the divine beneficence be accepted as *warrantable.* May not this confident belief in God as the gracious Shepherd of souls be a vain presumption, never realized?—May it not be an illusion of self love? Not so —for we have already accepted the Psalms, of which this is one, as portions of that authentic Holy Scripture which has been given us from above. Thus it is, therefore, that throughout all time past, and all time to come, this Psalm has possessed, and will possess, a life-giving virtue toward those who receive it, and whose own path in life is such as life's path most often is.

Whoever has attained to, or has acquired this thorough persuasion of the reality of Holy Scripture, as given of God, in a sense absolutely peculiar to itself, will stand exempt—or he may so stand exempt, from alarms and suspicions, as if criticism, whether textual or historical, might rob him of his treasure, or might diminish its value to him. In its relation to the religious life, and to the health of the soul, this Psalm is *wholly divine;* and so every particle of it is fraught with the life-giving energy; nor need religious persons —or more than one in ten thousand of such persons— concern themselves in any way with any questionings or considerations that attach to it as a human composition.

But the Psalm now in view is *also* wholly human, as it is also wholly divine in another sense—every particle of it being of the same stamp as other human compositions; and therefore it may be spoken of, and it may be treated, and analysed, and commented upon, with intelligent freedom, even as we treat, analyse, and expound, whatever else has come down to us of ancient literature. Let it be remembered that neither in relation to classic literature, nor to sacred literature, does free criticism include any right or power to alter the text, or to amend it at our pleasure. The text of ancient writings, when once duly ascertained, is as fixed and as unalterable as are the constellations of the heavens; and so it is that the Canon of Scripture, if it be compared with the inconstancy and variableness of any other embodiment of religious belief or feeling, is a sure foundation—abiding the same throughout all time to the world's end.

It is not only the material writing—and the Hebrew words and phrases of this Psalm, or of any other Psalm —portions as they are of the colloquial medium of an ancient people, that are liable to the ordinary conditions of written language; for further than this it must be granted, that, as the metrical structure of the Ode is highly artificial, those rules of construction to which it conforms itself may be said to over-ride the pure conveyance of the thought;—metre ruling words and syllables. It was by these artificial adaptations to the ear and memory of the people to whom, at the first, the composition was confided, it was rendered available, in the best manner, for the purposes of the religious life. Yet this is not all that needs to be said in taking this view of the instance before us. Every phrase and allusion in this ode is metaphoric—nothing is literal; the Lord is—the Shepherd of souls; and there are the green pastures—the still waters—the paths of righteousness—the valley of the shadow of death—the rod and the staff—the table prepared—the anointing oil—the overfull cup—and that House of the Lord which is an everlasting abode. But figures and symbols are incidents of the human mind—they are adaptations to its limits—they are *the best that can be done*, in regard to the things of the spiritual life. Let us speak with reverence—DIVINE THOUGHT is not conditioned in any manner; certainly not by metaphor or symbol.

There is yet a step further that should be taken in considering this Psalm as a human composition—and it is so with other Psalms, still more decisively than with this, for it gives expression to religious sentiments which belong to the earlier stage of a progressive development of the spiritual life. The bright idea of *earthly well-being* pervades the Old Testament Scriptures; and this worldly sunshine is their distinction, as compared with the New Testament; but then there are many cognate ideas which properly come into their places, around the terrestrial idea. If earthly weal—if an overrunning cup—if security and continuance, belong to the centre-thought, then, by necessity, the antithetic ideas—not only of want and pain, but of whatever ill an enemy may do, or may intend—must come in, to encircle, or beleaguer the tabernacle of those whom God has blessed. Thus, therefore, does the Psalmist here give expression to feelings which were proper, indeed, to that time, but are less proper to this time: "Thou preparest a table before me in the presence of my enemies." A feeling is here indicated which was of that age, and which was approvable then, although it has been superseded since by sentiments of a higher order, and which draw their reason from the substitution of future for present good.

This *separableness* of the Divine element from the human element throughout the Inspired writings, the understanding of which is highly important, will make itself perspicuous in giving attention to two or three instances of different kinds.

Turn to the two astronomic Psalms—the eighth, and the nineteenth (its exordium). Quite unmatched are these Odes as human compositions:—the soul of the loftiest poetry is in them. Figurative they are in every phrase; and they are so *manifestly* figurative in what is affirmed concerning the celestial framework that they stand exempt, in the judgment of reasonable criticism, on the one hand from the childish literal renderings of superstition; and on the other hand from the nugatory captiousness of rationalism. A magnificent image is that of the sun coming forth refreshed each morning anew from his pavilion, and rejoicing as a strong man to run a race! Frivolous is the superstition which supposes that an astronomic verity is couched in these figures, and that thus the warranty of Inspiration is pledged to what is untrue in nature. Equally frivolous is the criticism which catches at this superstition, and on the ground of it labours to prove that the Bible takes part with the Ptolemaic theory, and rejects the modern astronomy! Be it so that David's own conception of the celestial system might be of the former sort, and that he would have marvelled at the latter; but, as an inspired writer, he no more affirms the Ptolemaic astronomy, than he affirms that the sun —a giant—comes forth from a tent every morning.

Look to the Eighth Psalm, and estimate its theologic value—*its inspired import*—by reading it as a bold contradiction of errors all around it—the dreams of Buddhism—the fables of Brahminism—the Atheism of the Greek Philosophy, and the malign Atheism of our modern metaphysics. Within the compass of these nine verses the celestial and the terrestrial systems, and the human economy are not only poetically set forth; but *they are truly reported of*, as the three stand related to Religious Belief, and to Religious Feeling. Grant it, that when David the Poet brings into conjunction "the moon and the stars," he thought of them, as to their respective bulks and importance, not according to the teaching of Galileo; and yet, notwithstanding this misconception, which itself has no bearing whatever upon his function as an inspired writer, he so writes concerning the Universe—material and immaterial, as none but Hebrew prophets have ever written of either. What are the facts? The astronomies of Oriental sages and of Grecian philosophers are well-nigh forgotten; but David's astronomy lives, and it will ever live; for it is true to all eternity.

A sample of another kind is presented in the Fiftieth Psalm. This Ode, sublime in its imagery and its scenic breadth of conception, is a canon of the relationship of men, as the professed worshippers of God, toward Him who spurns from His altar the hypocrite and the profligate and the malignant, but invites the sincere and the humble to His presence, on terms of favour. This Psalm is sternly moral in its tone:—it is anti-ritualistic—if rites are thought of as substitutes for virtue; and moreover, by the singularity of its phrases in three instances, it makes its way with anatomic keenness through the surface to the conscience of those who are easily content with themselves, so long as they keep clear of overt acts of sin. The man who is here threatened with a vengeance from which there will be no escape (*v.* 22) is not himself perchance the thief; but he is one whose moral consciousness is of the same order, and who would do the same—opportunity favouring. He is not himself perchance the adulterer; but he is one who, being impure in heart, is ready for guilt, and pleases himself with the thought of it. Indebted for his virtue entirely to external restraints, he thinks himself free to give vent to censorious language, and to shed the venom of his tongue upon those who are nearest to him in blood. Here, then, there is not merely a protest in behalf of virtue, but it is a deep-going commixture of spiritual and ethical truth, with a promise of grace for the condign; it is a presentation of justice and of favour:—it is a discrimination of motives and characters also:—it is such that it vindicates its own Divine origination in the court of every human conscience. In this Psalm it is the voice of God we hear; for man has never spoken in any such manner as this to his fellows.

Let it be asked, then, in what manner the Divine and the human elements, *in this one instance*, sustain each other throughout all time? In tens of thousands of copies we possess this literary monument; and it is an imperishable and *an unalterable* document: it is liable to no decay or damage; and it may yet endure ages more than can be numbered: nothing on earth's surface is more safe from destruction: none can ever pretend to have authority to substitute one word for another word; or to erase a letter. Here, then, we take our hold upon a rock. Human opinion, in matters of religion, sways this way and that way, from age to age; but it is ever and anew brought back to *its point of fixedness* in the unalterable text of the Hebrew Scriptures. Upon this Fiftieth Psalm Esra and the Rabbis of his school commented at their best, in that age when Anaximander, Anaxagoras, Thales, and their disciples, were theorising to little purpose concerning "the Infinite;" and were in debate on the question whether it is matter or mind that is "the eternal principle," and the cause of all things:—a question unsettled as yet among our "profoundest thinkers." Upon this Psalm, with its bold, outspoken, and determinate morality, its grandeur and its power, the Rabbi of a later and sophisticated time commented also, weaving around it the fine silk of his casuistry, and labouring hard in his work of screening the then-abused conscience of his race from its force; so "making void the Word of God by his traditions." Upon this Psalm the Christian theologues, in series, from the Apostolic Fathers to Jerome and Augustine, in their comments give evidence, each in his age, at once concerning those secular variations of religious and ethical thought which mark the lapse of time; and of what we must call the restraining power of the canon of

Scripture, which, from age to age, overrules these variations—calling back each digressive mood of the moment; as if with a silent, yet irresistible gravitation —a centripetal force.

"Thy word," says David, "is settled in Heaven;" —it is fixed as the constellations in the firmament; and if we would justly estimate what this undecaying force of the canon of Scripture imports, in relation to the ever-shifting variations of human thought and feeling, and in relation to the fluctuations of national manners and notions, from one fifty years to another, we should take in hand some portion of the Old Testament Scriptures—say such a portion as is this sublime Psalm—and trace its exegetical history through the long line of commentators—from the Rabbis, onward to Origen, Tertullian, Basil, Chrysostom, Jerome, Augustine, the Schoolmen, and Bernard of Clairvaux; then the pre-reformation Romanists; the Reformers, the Jesuits, the Jansenists, the Puritans of England and Scotland, the English Methodists; and so on till we reach these last times of great religious animation, and of little religious depth—times of sedulous exactitude in scholarship, and of feeble consciousness as toward the unseen future and the eternal;—times in which whatever is of boundless dimensions in Holy Scripture has passed beyond our range of vision, while our spectacled eyes are intent upon iotas.*

But the Psalms of David, and of Moses, and of others, shall live on, undamaged, to the times that are next ensuing; and far beyond those times. Our Bibles shall come into the hands of our sons, and of our

* See Note.

grandsons, who, reading Hebrew as correctly as tl most learned of their sires have read it, shall do so i a season of religious depth, and of religious conscie tiousness, and who, in such a season, shall look bac with grief, and shame, and amazement, when they s how nugatory were the difficulties which are makin so many among us to stumble, and to fall. Huma opinion has its fashion, and it shifts its ground wit each generation;—a thirty or forty years is the u most date of any one clearly definable mood or sty of religious feeling and opinion: each of such ephemer fashions being a departure, upon a radius, from tl central authority—the Canon of Scripture, accepte as from God.

But the imperishable fixedness of Holy Scripture- first, in a purely literary sense, as an ascertained a cient text, which none may now alter; and next, the vehicle or depository of the Divine Will towar mankind, does not imply or necessitate, either superstitious and blind regard to the letter of Scriptur as if it were not human, or an enchainment to th words, as if the Divine element therein contained, an thereby conveyed, might not have been otherwise wor ed, and diffused among the people in other forms of la guage than in this one—to which, as a fixed stan ard, all must in fact return. Not only is the Divin in Scripture, greater than the human, but it has a intrinsic power and vitality which renders it largel independent of its embodiment in this or that form c language. There is no version of the Psalms—ancie or modern (or none which comes within the cognizan of a European reader)—which does not competentl convey the theology and the ethical majesty, and th juridical grandeur, of the one Psalm that has here been referred to. In no version, even the most faulty—whichever that may be—does an awakened conscience fail to catch the distant sound of that thunder which —in a day future—shall shake, not the earth only, but heaven. In no such version does the contrite spirit fail to hear in it that message which carries peace to the humble in heart.

If indeed the Hebrew text had perished ages ago — say at the time of the breaking up of the Jewish religious state—and if, consequently, we could now make an appeal to nothing more authentic than to ancient versions, believed to be, on the whole, trustworthy, then the constant tendency toward deflection and aberration, in human opinion, could have received no effective check. In each age, the rise of schemes of opinion—sometimes superstitious and fanatical, sometimes philosophical and negative—would have produced successive vitiations of those unauthentic documents, until even these had lost their cohesive principle, and would have ceased to be thought of. This is not our position; and therefore versions and commentaries, some critical and exact, some popular and paraphrastic; comments wise, and comments unwise, sceptical, or imbecile, may all take their course—they may severally win favour for a day, or may retain it for a century;—all are harmless as toward the Rock —the imperishable Hebrew text, which abides—ἀπὸ τοῦ αἰῶνος καὶ ἕως τοῦ αἰῶνος—and until the human family shall have finished its term of discipline on earth.

CHAPTER III.

ARTIFICIAL STRUCTURE OF THE HEBREW POETRY, AS RELATED TO ITS PURPOSES.

THE attempt to bring the Poetry of the Hebrew Scriptures into metrical analogy with that of Greece and Rome has not been successful. This would demand a better knowledge of the quantity of syllables when the language was spoken, and of the number of syllables in words, and of its rhythm, than is actually possessed by Modern Hebraists. But that a people so pre-eminently musical by constitution should have failed to perceive, or should not have brought under rule, the rhythm of words and sentences could not easily be believed; yet to what extent this was done by them, or on what principles, it would now be hopeless to inquire.

There is, however, a metrical structure, artificial and elaborate, which gives evidence of itself, even in a translation: it does not affect the cadence, or musical adjustment of words; but it does affect the choice of words and the structure of sentences. To treat the Hebrew Poetry in any technical sense does not come within the purpose of the present work, nor indeed the qualifications of the Author. What we are concerned with is—the spirit, not the body, the soul, not the form. Yet weighty inferences are derivable from the fact that religious principles were conveyed to the Hebrew people, and through these have reached other nations, in a mode that conforms itself to arbitrary rules of composition, which determine the choice of words, the structure of sentences, and the collocation of members of sentences, and the framework of entire Odes. Even in passages which breathe the soul of the loftiest and the most impassioned poetry, a highly artificial apposition and balancing of terms and clauses prevails;—as if the Form were, in the estimation of the writer, of so much importance that it should give law even to the thought itself.

This subject stands full in our path, and demands to be considered before we pass on: it is a subject that touches, not merely the Hebrew Poetry, but also the belief we should hold to concerning the Divine origination of Holy Scripture.

The conveyance of thought through the medium of language is a *conditioned* expression of a speaker's or a writer's inmost meaning—more or less so. In a strict sense the embodiment of thought at all, *in words* and combinations of words, and in sentences, is—a conditioned, as well as an imperfect conveyance of it; for words have only a more or less determinate value, which may be accepted by the hearer—especially when involved sentences are uttered, in a sense varying from that of the speaker by many shades of difference. Thought, symbolised in words, is subjected, first, to those conditions that attach to language from the universal ambiguity, or the convertible import of language; and then to the indistinctness of the speaker's conceptions, and of the hearer's also. Yet when a perfectly intelligible and familiar fact is affirmed in words that are intended to be understood in their literal, or primitive sense, we may loosely say that such utterances ar *unconditioned;* as thus—Brutus stabbed Cæsar in th senate-house at Rome. Julius Cæsar, with his legions landed in Britain. William of Normandy did the lik with his Normans centuries later.

It is otherwise in affirmations such as the following— The main principles of political economy, as taugh by Adam Smith, rest upon a rock, and will never b overthrown. The great principles of religious liberty as embodied in Locke's First Letter on Toleration, hav hitherto, and will ever defy the utmost efforts of into lerant hierarchies to shake them. The aristocracy o England is the pillar of the British monarchy:—th throne and the aristocracy must stand or fall together In affirmations of this kind the Thought of the speake or writer—that is to say, his *ultimate intention*—i conditioned by its conveyance in terms that are wholl figurative, and which therefore must await, if it be onl an instant, the result of a mental process in the min of the hearer, who—unconsciously perhaps—render them into their well-known prosaic values. Such a they are when they meet the ear, they convey no mean ing that is intelligible in relation to the subject. Un conditioned thought may be still further conditioned if I employ, not merely *figurative* terms, but such as ar suggested at the moment of speaking by vivid emotions or by stormy passions; as if, in addressing a politica meeting from a platform, I should affirm what I inten to say in a declamatory style, as thus—"The deadl miasma of republican doctrines, rising from the swamp of popular ignorance, is even now encircling the Britis polity:—year by year is it insidiously advancing towar the very centre of the State; nor can the time be distan when it shall have destroyed all life within the sacred enclosures of our ancient institutions." In this instance, not only are the words and phrases figurative, and are such therefore as need to be rendered into their literal equivalents, but they are such also as indicate an excited state of feeling in the speaker, which a calm philosophic mood will not approve; and the exuberances of which may well bear much retrenchment. Nevertheless, thus far, this conditioning of thought—as well of the impassioned style, as of that which is simply figurative —may properly be called *natural;* for it *is* natural to the human mind to utter itself in figures; and also to indulge in that fervid style which is prompted by powerful emotions.

Beyond this stage, and quite of another sort, is that conditioning of Thought which we must designate as technical, and which is mainly *factitious*, or arbitrary; as, for instance;—let us take up the above example of political ill-augury, and bring—if not the very same words, yet their nearest equivalents,—into cadence, as blank verse: in this case some of the words must by necessity be rejected as unfit altogether for a place in verse; and substitutes must be found for others, because they are not easily reduced to cadence. Moreover, the *position* of every word must be determined by a rule which, in relation to the requirements of unconditioned thought, is arbitrary and artificial; the passage might thus run—

> E'en now this poison of the people's error
> Creeps on insidious, and from day to day
> Invades yet more the precincts of the state.
> Not long to wait, alas! All life—all soul,
> Shall cease and die within these regal courts!

Thought, in this form, submits itself to the requirements of quantity and rhythm, by means of several substitutions of word for word; and also by deflections from the simpler and the more natural order of the words. A still further yielding of the original thought to the requirements of art would be needed if, in addition to cadence, we should demand *rhyme;* for in that case not only must another law of cadence be complied with; but also the fortuitous law of a jingle in the last syllable of each line must prevail. On these conditions the same meaning might thus be conveyed—

Now while we speak comes on the noisome death—
Birth of the swamps—it poisons every breath.
Doctrine delusive! creeps it o'er the state,
And dooms its ancient glories to their fate.
Soon shall we mourn, in desolated halls,
Departed greatness—where an Empire falls.

For any purposes of political instruction, or of warning, the Thought, whether it be that of the platform speaker, or that of a philosophical writer, may be fully expressed, either when made to conform itself to the laws of cadence, or when subjected to the still more technical necessities of rhyme. Nevertheless it must be granted, that, if the utterance of the orator—figurative and impassioned as it is—be the fittest possible for conveying his meaning, and if the words he uses, and *the order* in which he arranges these words, be the best possible, then the reduction of these same thoughts to the rules of blank verse, and, still more, their reduction to the conditions of rhyme, involve a disadvantage which must be of more or less consequence.

There are, however, instances in which Thought, embodied in the language of symbols, and of material images, is of a kind which sustains no damage under these conditions; in truth, the poetic style may be *the very fittest* for giving utterance to feelings, or to moods of mind; or, as already affirmed, to truths or principles to which no abstract terms or combinations of terms can ever be adequate.

Yet there are some purely technical conditions in submitting to which the spontaneous language of feeling, or the severe utterances of abstract truth, can hardly be granted to stand wholly exempt from a real disadvantage. There may, indeed, be approvable reasons, warranting the employment of such artificial means—albeit they do involve a disadvantage; nevertheless, where we find it existing, it must be accepted as it is—it is a conditioning of Thought which, when it is admitted on occasions the most serious, indicates the extent of that adaptation of the Divine to the human of which we can never lose sight without falling into perplexities.

With the exception of two or three lines—cited by St. Paul from the Greek poets—the Scriptures of the New Testament are everywhere prosaic in form:—the intention of the writer or speaker is conveyed always in the most direct manner which the rules of language admit of—figurative terms are employed where none other are available. Thought is here unconditioned, so far as it can be—the subject-matter, considered. Not so in the Scriptures of the Old Testament. Nearly a half of the entire mass, or in the proportion of twenty-two to twenty-five, the Hebrew writings are not merely poetic, as to their diction, but they are metrical in form;—or we should better say—the Thought of the writer is subjected to rules of structure that are in the highest degree artificial. This fact—well understood as now it is—escapes the notice of the reader of modern versions; albeit, when once it has been explained to a reader of ordinary intelligence, he easily perceives it—wherever it is actually found.

We have here named what is about the proportion of prose to verse throughout the Old Testament; but, in truth, if those parts of the historical books are set off from the account which are genealogical merely, and those also which are repetitive or redundant, and those, moreover, which barely, if at all, convey any religious meaning, then it will appear that very much more than a half of the Canon of Scripture in the Hebrew takes this latter form; or, as we say, is conditioned in conformity with artificial rules of structure.

Of this structure, which of late has been carefully set forth, and illustrated, even in popular works, there can be no need in this place to give any account in detail. The fact of its existence is all we have to do with; and this, briefly stated, is this—that each separate utterance of religious thought—theological, ethical, or devotional—is thrown into an antithetical form, so making up a couplet, or a triplet; or an integral verse in four, five, or six measured lines. The second line of the two is often a repetition only of the first, in other terms:—often it is an antithetic utterance of the same thought:—sometimes it is an illustrative supplement to it:—sometimes an exceptive caution; yet everywhere the ode or lyrical composition, regarded as a whole, is thus built up of members—limbs—apposed, one to the other—balancing one the other, and finding their reason, not simply in the requirements of Thought—uttered in the prosaic form—but, beyond this, in the rules or the usages of an arbitrary system of composition.

Then, besides this kind of structure, many of the odes of the Hebrew Scriptures obey a law of *alliteration*—which is still more arbitrary, inasmuch as it requires the first word of each verse, in a certain number of verses, to begin with the same letter, and these in alphabetic order. Any one who will try for himself a few experiments, in English, will find that, in yielding obedience to requirements of *this* kind, Thought must take a turn, or must very greatly mould itself to a fashion which it would not otherwise have chosen. Thought submits to a process of *conditioning* which intimately affects it, if not in substance, yet in its modes of utterance. The second verse in Milton's Christmas Hymn stands thus:—

> Only with speeches fair
> She woos the gentle air
> To hide her guilty front with innocent snow;
> And on her naked shame,
> Pollute with sinful blame,
> The saintly veil of maiden white to throw,
> Confounded, that her Maker's eyes
> Should look so near upon her foul deformities.

Now let the requirement be this—that, without displacing the rhyme, or greatly altering the sense, every line of the eight shall begin with the same letter—shall it be W?

> With only speeches fair
> Woos she the gentle air,
> Wistful to hide her front with innocent snow;
> Wide on her naked shame,

Wasted with sinful blame
White, as a saintly maiden veil to throw:
Woe were it, that her Maker's eyes,
Wrathful, should look upon her foul deformities.

We should never accept this, or any other alliterative form of the verse, as if it were in itself preferable to its original form, constrained only by the laws of metre, and by the rhyme. Nevertheless, the sentiment, or final meaning of the original, is conveyed, with little, if any damage, in the more constrained form that is demanded by the rule of alliteration:—the injury inflicted in this instance is technical, more than it is substantial. It may easily be admitted, that, if a composition of great length were intended to subserve purposes of popular instruction, the alliterative form might be chosen for the sake of the aid it affords to the memory, and thus tending to secure a faultless transmission of the whole, from father to son, or, rather, from the religious mother to her children. It will be our part hereafter to show that *the religious intention* of the Inspired writings *is* securely conveyed under all forms, however arbitrary they may be as to their literary structure.

As to the several species of the Hebrew Poetry, it can only be in an accommodated sense that we could apply to it any of those terms that belong to the Poetry of Greece, and which had their origin in the artistic intelligence of its people. There would be little meaning in the words if we spoke of Odes, Lyrics, or Epics, in this case. The Hebrew Poetry has its kinds; but they are peculiar to itself: it has originated species of Poetry: it has conformed itself to no models: it has sprung from nothing earlier than itself; or nothing that is extant:—it has had no cognates among contemporary literatures. Through the medium of innumerable versions the Biblical literature has combined itself in an intimate manner with the intellectual existence of modern (civilized) nations. Every people has made its wealth their own: in truth, itself drawing its force from the deepest and most universal principles of human nature, the Hebrew Scriptures, when once they have thoroughly permeated the popular mind, become an undistinguishable element, not only of the religious and the moral life of the people, but, to a great extent, of their intellectual life also. With ourselves—the British people—the Inspired writings of the Old Testament have become to us the milk of infancy and childhood, and the nourishment of manhood in its most robust stage. It is to these books that we owe whatever in our literature possesses most of simple majesty and force; whatever is the most fully fraught with *feeling*; whatever is the most true to nature, when nature is truest to virtue, and to wisdom. Whatever it is that enters, as by right, the moral consciousness;—whatever it is that the most effectively draws the soul away from its cleaving to the dust, and lifts the thoughts towards a brighter sphere—all such elements of our English literature, whether avowedly so or not, must trace their rise, directly or indirectly, to the Hebrew Scriptures, and especially to those portions of them that are, in spirit and in form, poetic.

If we were to affirm that certain portions of this Poetry are descriptive, or moral, or pastoral, this would be to misunderstand the purport of the samples we might adduce of these kinds. Vividly conscious as these writers, or most of them, are to what is sublime and beautiful in the visible world, they are thus conscious toward the things around them *in one sense only*—namely, as parts of God's creation. The Hebrew poet attempts no local description:—he does not dwell upon the picturesque;—albeit our modern sense of the picturesque has sprung from tastes and habits that have had their rise in the Hebrew Scriptures; nor do they at any time stop on their way to bring before us the scenic characteristics of their country. None of them has leisure to paint particular scenes, as do our Thomson, or Burns, or Cowper. It is a glance only that they take of Nature, and it is such a glance as, from its vividness and breadth, is so much the more intelligible in all lands.

The Hebrew Poetry—artificial in structure—is not *artistic* in its purpose or intention. A work may be designated as *artistic* which, as the production of genius, manifestly has no higher aim than that of giving pleasure, and of exhibiting the artist's power to achieve this one purpose. But the Poets of the Bible not only have in view always another, and a far higher object than that of the delectation of their hearers, or the display of their personal ability; for, in every instance, they are intent upon acquitting themselves of a weighty responsibility;—they are charged with a message:—they are bearing a testimony:—they are promising blessings:—they are threatening and predicting woes. Therefore it is that those several species of composition to which the taste and genius of the Persians, or of the Greeks, have given a definite form, do not make their appearance within the compass of the Inspired writings.

It is not to win admiration by the opulence of his

imagination—it is not to charm a listening multitude by the soft graces of song, or by its sublimities, that the Hebrew bard ever utters himself. We ought not to say that a scorn of popular favour betrays itself—as if *subaudite*—in these deliverances of a message from the Almighty; yet it is almost so. We should here keep in view the distinction between the genius which contents itself with its own triumphs, in achieving an excellent work, and the ability which executes, in the best manner, a work the aim of which is loftier than that of commanding applause. It might not be easy to adduce single instances in which this important distinction obtrudes itself upon notice in a manner beyond dispute; nevertheless a comparison *at large* of the Hebrew literature, with the literature of other nations, would not fail to make its reality unquestionable.

So it is, as we shall see, that, although Pa'estine, such as then it was, abounded with aspects of nature that might well tempt description, and had many points of scenic effect, nothing of this sort is extant within the compass of the Scriptures. Why might not spots in Lebanon have been brought in picture before us?—why not the luxuriance of Cœlo-Syria, where the Jordan springs to light from an Eden of beauty?—why not the flowery plain of Esdraëlon?—why not the rugged majesty of the district bordering upon the Dead Sea? Alive to every form of natural beauty and sublimity, and quick to seize his images from among them, the Hebrew Poet never lingers in such scenes: he uses the wealth of the visible world for his purposes:—Nature he commands; but she commands not him.

It may be said that the earliest born of the poetic styles in every land has this same characteristic—namely, that of having a fixed purpose—an *intention;* but then, in the course of things this archaic directness, this primitive seriousness, gives place, in the following age, to the elaborate or artistic style—to those modes of composition that find their beginning and their end in the Poet's personal ambition. This process goes on until a national literature (of the imaginative class) which was wholly genuine in its earliest era, has become wholly factitious towards its close. Yet it is not so in the instance with which now we are concerned:—the Hebrew Poetry, in the course of a thousand years, passed through no stages of artistic sophistication. Take the instance of those of the Psalms which, on probable grounds of criticism, are of a date as early as the exodus of Israel from Egypt—compare them with those which, by their allusion to the events of a much later time, must be dated toward the years of the sealing of the prophetic dispensation: the same avoidance of whatever the Poet's own ambition might have dictated is observable throughout this lapse of ages.

Do we find an exceptive instance in that one composition which stands by itself in the canonical collection—the Canticle of Solomon? This instance may yield a confirmation of our doctrine, rather than a contradiction of it; but the anomalous character of this matchless poem, as well as its singular beauty, demands a distinct consideration of it—or, we might say, a criticism—apart.

Then, again, the Hebrew literature has no Drama; nor has it an Epic; and the reasons why it has neither of these are such as demand attention. It would be to put upon the word *Drama* a very forced meaning to apply it to the Book of Job;—and, in so doing, to allow place for a notable exception to what we here allege.

These writers treat human nature in no superficial manner;—they touch it to the quick; but they do not undertake to picture forth separately its elements, its passions, its affections, or its individual characteristics. To do this, either in the mode of the Drama, or in the mode of an Epic, would imply *invention*, or *fiction*, in a sense of which no instances whatever occur within the compass of the Canonical Scriptures. The apophthegm is not a fiction, for it puts not on the historic guise:—the allegory is no fiction, for it is never misunderstood as a truthful narrative of events. No concatenation of actual events, no course of incidents in real life, ever brings out separate passions, or sentiments, in dramatic style, or with a *unison of meaning*. The dramatic *unity*, as to the elements of human nature, must be culled, and put together, with much selective care—with artistic skill. A composition of *this* order must be a work of genius—like a group of figures in sculpture.

No actual man, no real person of history, has ever been always a hero, or has ever done and said the things that may be fitting to an Epic. Therefore it is that an Epic Poem must be *an invention;* it must be an artistic achievement: the Poem may be quite true in human nature generically; but it is never true as a real narrative:—it borrows a something from history; but it creates ten times more than it borrows. Scarcely then need we say why it is that the Hebrew literature possesses neither Drama nor Epic: the reasons, as we shall presently see, are distinctly two.

The Epic—which is history transmuted into fiction—

for a foregone purpose, or in regard to a final cause, has stood foremost in the esteem of every people that has risen above the rudest barbarism—of every people—ONE only excepted; and this one is a people whose literature, mainly poetic as it is, has taken hold of the sympathies of mankind more extensively, and more permanently, than any other. Reasons drawn from a consideration of the social condition of this one people might perhaps be brought forward in explanation of this unique fact; and there would then be room for much ingenuity in showing how we may solve the problem—in some way short of an admission which those who distaste the true reason will labour to exclude. But we take it otherwise.

This series of writers, through the many centuries of their continuous testimony, spoke not, wrote not, as if they possessed a liberty of discursive choice—now scattering the decorations of fiction over realities; and now striving to impart to fiction, in as high a degree as possible, the verisimilitude of truth. They spoke and wrote with a consciousness of their obligation to absolute Truth, and with a stern fixedness of purpose as toward an authority above them: among no other writers do we find a parallel instance of *determinate purpose.* But whether distinctly conscious of their mission, or not so; or only imperfectly conscious of it, yet they spoke as they were moved by Him who is the ἀψευδὴς Θεὸς—the "truthful God." Solemnly regardful were these "holy men of God" of the sovereignty of Truth—Truth dogmatic or theological—Truth ethical, and Truth historical. Utterly averse, therefore, were they—abhorrent, let us say—not merely as toward *falsification*, but as toward *fabrication*, or any approach toward that sort of commingling of the real with the unreal which might engender falseness; or might give rise to a dangerous confounding of the two. The Hebrew Scriptures, as compared with any other national literature, are pre-eminently—they are characteristically—they, and they alone, are throughout truthful in tone, style, and structure. Need we ask, then, why they contain neither the Drama nor an Epic? Not from the want of fitting subjects—not from poverty of materials; but as ministers of Heaven to whom a task had been assigned, did these men of genius—and they were such—fail to display their skill in the creation of romances; and it was not because they could not do it, that they have not attempted to immortalize themselves, and the heroes of their national history, in producing an Oriental Iliad, or Odyssey, or Æneid. To have done this would have been to introduce among their people an element of confusion and of ambiguity, which would have interfered with the purpose of the separation of this race from all other races.

And yet this is not all that should be said; and the second reason would be by itself sufficient in solving the problem; and, not less than the first, is it conclusively demonstrative of the Divine origination of these writings. Because they are Inspired—θεόπνευστα—and teach the things of God, and enjoin the worship of God, therefore do the writers abstain from themes which give licence to the worship of man:—they take no account of heroes; and yet it was not so that an ambitious poet, who might be thirsting for the applause of his countrymen, could find no subject in the national history adapted to his purpose. Why not, in this manner, undertake to immortalize Moses, Samuel, David, Solomon? Why not? It was because the Hebrew Scriptures, dictated from above, are constantly and sternly truthful;—and they are so whether the great men of the Hebrew polity were as faultless as national fondness would have painted them; or were indeed as faulty as men at the best ever are.

It has been the ambition—and a noble ambition, of the most highly gifted minds, in every cultured people, to give expression to a perfect ideal of humanity—to picture a godlike virtue, wisdom, valour, self-control, and temperance, according to the national conception of what these qualities should be. Among the thousand themes of poetry, this one—the imaging of a godlike magnanimity and virtue—has held the highest place.

The Hebrew literature gives the several elements of virtue and piety in precept; but nowhere is it presented in the concrete. In place of the dazzling Ideal—the romance of humanity—we find only the real human nature of history—vouched for as such by the presence of those conditions of human frailty which the Idealist would have taken care to exclude. A circumstance full of meaning it is, that, in these writings, all that we learn of the acts, and of the personal qualities of the prominent persons of the national history, is found in the narrative and prosaic books, or portions of books:—none of it appears in the poetic books, or in those passages the style of which is figurative and impassioned; and which, as to its form, is metrical. What then is the import of these facts, which have no parallels in the national poetry of other countries? It is this, that whenever the individual man comes forward in these writings—whenever it is he who draws upon himself the eyes of his fellows, whether chief or prophet, he must do so—*such as he is*:—if his virtue, his wisdom, his valour, are to attract notice, so do his sins, his weaknesses, his falls, in the moments of severest trial; all these things make their appearance also, and proclaim the veraciousness of the record.

Greatly do we often miscalculate the relative credibility or incredibility of passages in ancient writings. No logic—or no sound logic—can make it appear incredible that God should raise the dead; or that He should make the waters of the sea to stand up as a heap; or that, in any other mode, the ALMIGHTY should show ALL MIGHT. But utterly incredible would be the pretension that any congeries of events, such as are usually packed together by a poet with a definite artistic intention, has ever actually had existence in the current of the world's affairs. Utterly beyond the limits of reasonable belief would be the supposition that a man—even one of ourselves—has ever acted and spoken, from year to year, throughout his course, with unfailing consistency, or in that style of dramatic coherence which the contriver of a Romance, or of an Epic, figures for his hero. No such embodiment of the Ideal has ever, we may be sure, broken in upon the vulgar realities of human existence;—there have been good men, and brave men, and wise men, often; but there have been no living sculptures after the fashion of Phidias, no heroes after the manner of Homer or Virgil.

Then there comes before us another balancing of the incredible and the credible:—as thus. The Hebrew Poets—it is not one or two of them, but all of them in long series—have abstained from those idealizings of humanity at large upon which the poets of other nations have chosen to expend their powers. How is it that they should have been thus abstinent—should thus have held off from ground which tempts every aspiring mind? We shall find no admissible answer to this question, except this, that this series of writers followed, not the impulses of their individual genius, but each of them wrote as he was inspired from above. Nothing in any degree approaching to a worshipping of man—nothing of that sort which elsewhere has been so common—nothing which could have given a warrant to the unwise extravagances of the saint-and-martyr worship of the Church in the third century, anywhere makes its appearance within the Canonical Scriptures of the Old Testament. On the contrary—as well by solemn injunction, as by their uniform example—the Inspired writers, historians, prophets, poets, repeat the warning—as to the rendering of worship to man, or to any creature—"See thou do it not; worship God."

CHAPTER IV.

THE ANCIENT PALESTINE—THE BIRTH-PLACE OF POETRY.

Poetry will never disown its relationship to the beautiful and the sublime in the visible world; in fact it has always proved its dependence upon influences of this order. Born and nurtured, not at hazard on any spot, but only in chosen regions, it finds at hand, for giving utterance to the mysteries of the inner life, an abundance of material symbols—fit for purposes of this kind—among the objects of sense. It is the function of Poetry to effect such an assimilation of the material with the immaterial as shall produce one world of thought and of emotion—the visible and the invisible, intimately commingled.

Poetry, nursed on the lap of Nature, will have its preferences—it must make its selection; and this, not merely as to the exterior decorations of its abode, but even as to the solid framework of the country which it favours; there must be, not only a soil, and a climate, and a various vegetation, favourable to its training; but a preparation must have been made for it in the remotest geological eras. The requirements of a land that is destined to be the home of poetry have in all instances been very peculiar:—it has sprung up and thriven on countries of very limited extent—upon areas ribbed and walled about by ranges of mountains, or girdled and cut into by seas. These—the duly prepared birth-places of poetry—have been marked by abrupt inequalities of surface—by upheavings and extrusions of the primæval crust of the earth:—these selected lands have glistened with many rills—they have sparkled with fountains—they have been clothed with ancient forests, as well as decked, each spring anew, with flowers. Moreover a wayward climate, made so by its inequalities of surface, has broken up the wearisome monotony of the year—such as it is in tropical and in arctic regions—by irregular shiftings of the aerial aspect of all things; and there has been, in such countries, a corresponding variety in the animal and vegetable kingdoms; there has thus been a large store in the Poet's treasury of material symbols.

A land such as this is—or was, three thousand years ago—the country in which the Hebrew Poetry had its birth, and where it reached its maturity, and where it ceased to breathe; nor has it been under conditions very different from these that Poetry has ever sprung up and flourished. It has not been a native of Tartarian steppes, nor of savannahs, or interminable prairies, nor of trackless swamps, nor of irrigated rice-levels, nor of leagues on leagues of open corn-land, nor of Saharas. Poetry has not weathered the tempests, nor confronted the terrors of the Atlas ranges:—it has not sported on the flanks of Caucasus, or on the steeps of the Andes, or the Himalayas; nor has it breathed on the rugged vertebræ of the North American continent. In none of those regions has it appeared which oppress the spirit by a dreary sameness, or by shapeless magnitudes, or featureless sublimity. Poetry has had its birth, and it has sported its childhood, and it has attained its manhood, and has blended itself with the national life in countries such as Greece, with its rugged hills, and its myrtle groves, and its sparkling rills; but not in Egypt:—in Italy; but not on the dead levels of Northern Europe. Poetry was born and reared in Palestine—but not in Mesopotamia:—in Persia—but not in India. Pre-eminently has Poetry found its home among the rural graces of England, and amid the glens of Scotland; and there, rather than in those neighboring countries which are not inferior to the British Islands in any other products of intellect or of taste.

Exceptions—apparent only, or of a very partial kind—might be adduced in contradiction of these general affirmations. Exceptions there will be to any generalization that touches human nature; for in a true sense the human mind is superior to all exterior conditions; and its individual forces are such as to refuse to be absolutely subjected to any formal requirements: greater is the individual man than *circumstances* of any sort; and greater is he far than materialists would report him to be—according to system. A Poet there may be, wherever Nature shall call him forth; but there will not be *Poetry among a people* that is not favoured by Nature, as to its home:—the imaginative tastes and the creative genius have been, as to *the mass of the people*, indigenous to Greece; but not to Egypt: to Italy; but not to France: to the British Islands; but not to Holland. And thus too, it was the ancient people of Palestine, pre-eminently, that possessed a poetry which was quite its own. But then we must be looking back a three thousand years, as to the people; and we must be thinking of the country, such as it was in the morning hours of Biblical time. In later ages—the people fallen! and the land—mourning its hopeless desolation!

Palestine, rather than any other country that might be named, demands the presence, and needs the industry of man, for maintaining its fertility. Capable, as it has been, of supporting millions of people, those millions must actually be there; and then only will it justify its repute as a "very good land." A scanty population will starve, where a dense population would fatten. On this land, emphatically, is the truth exemplified—that "the hand of the diligent maketh rich:"—it is here that, if man fails of his duty, or if he misunderstands his own welfare, the very soil disappears under his feet. So has it been now through many dreary centuries; and here has been accomplished the warning—that the sins of the fathers are visited, not only upon the children to the third and fourth generation; but upon their remotest descendants, and to their successors, who may be masters of the land.

The desolations of Palestine have been sensibly increased, even within the memory of man;—and unquestionably so within periods that are authentically known to history. Those who have visited Palestine, at intervals of fifteen or twenty years, have forcibly received this impression from the aspect of its surface, as well as from the appearance of the people, that decay is still in progress: a ruthless and rapacious rule, dreading and hating reform, withers the industry—such as it might be—of the people, and makes the land a fit roaming ground for the Bedouin marauder. A ten years of British rule, and a million or two of British capital, might yet make this land "blossom as the rose:" the wilderness and parched land how should they be made glad for such a visitation!

Yet beside the social and political causes of decay,

some purely physical influences have been taking effect upon Palestine, as upon all the countries that skirt the eastern end of the Mediterranean. Within the lapse of what is called historic time, Libyan wastes have become far more arid than once they were, and, in consequence, they have acquired a higher mean temperature. North Africa is much less abundant in corn, and is less graced with tropical vegetation, than in ancient times it was. In the course of two or three thousand years the sand hurricanes of Libya, and of the Sahara, in sweeping over the valley of the Nile, have not only sepulchred its sepulchres, and entombed its temples and palaces in a ten, or twenty, or thirty feet of deposit—narrowing continually the green bordering of the Nile; but they have given dryness for moisture to the neighbouring countries. Dense forests once shed coolness and humidity over large tracts of northern Arabia. The countless millions of people that were subjected to the Assyrian, the Babylonian, the Median despotisms, flourished upon the fatness of the Mesopotamian corn-lands, and by their industry and their water-courses not only preserved the fertility which they created, but rendered the climate itself as temperate as its latitude should make it. Under differing conditions the same course of physical change has affected Asia Minor—once more populous, in a tenfold proportion, than in modern times these regions have been; for then, population, fertility, mildness of climate, sustained each other.

Those countries of Europe which formed the background of the ancient civilization have, in the course of twenty centuries, been denuded of their forests;—and this is, no doubt, a beneficial change; but this clearance has had great influence in affecting the climate and the productions of Greece, of Italy, of France, and of Spain.

As to Palestine, the ruins which now crown almost every one of its hill-tops, and the very significant fact of the remains of spacious theatres in districts where now human habitations are scarcely seen, afford incontestable evidence of the existence of a dense population in times that are not more remote than the Christian era. Galilee, at that time, and Decapolis, and the rich pasture-lands beyond Jordan, the Hauran, and Gerash, and Bosrah, as well as all the towns of the coast, teemed then with the millions of a population which mainly, if not entirely, was fed from the home soil. At the time of the return of the people from Babylon, and for the three centuries following, every acre supported its complement of souls; and the country, according to its quality, returned a full recompence to the husbandman, in every species proper to the latitude:—abundant it was in its dates, its olives, its vines, and its figs; in its cereals, its herds, with their milk and butter; and, not of least account, its honey. These are facts of which the evidence meets us on every page of ancient literature where this garden-land is named.

It is most of all in the hill-country of Judea, throughout which the bare limestone basement of the land now frowns upon the sky, that the negligence of the people and the misrule of their masters have wrought the greatest mischief. Throughout that region which, by its elevation as well as by its latitude, should be temperate, there was a luxuriant growth on all sides in those times when the Hebrew Poetry breathed its first notes. In that age every slope was carefully terraced, and the viscid soil was husbanded:—every swell of the land gave delight to the eye in the weeks of spring, and of an early summer, in which it was laden with a double harvest. By the multitude of its springs, and the abundance of its rains—well conserved in tanks (such as the Pools of Solomon)—drought was seldom known, or was mitigated when it occurred; and a mantle of opulence clothed the country where now a stern desolation triumphs.

Still to be traced are the vestiges of the ancient wealth, the margin of the Dead Sea only excepted. Throughout Judea human industry reaped its reward; and in the south—as about Hebron, and in Galilee, and in Samaria, and in the plains of Jericho, and on the flanks of Lebanon, and round about Banias, and throughout the east country—the Hauran and Bashan—the fertility of the soil was as great as in any country known to us. An easy industry was enough to render a sensuous existence as pleasurable as the lot of man allows. In truth, within this circuit there were spots upon which, if only they were secure from the violence of their fellows, men might have ceased to sigh for a lost Paradise. But *that* Paradise was forfeited, as well as the first, and now a doleful monotony, and a deathlike silence have established their dominion, as if for ever! As to the wealth of the hills, it has slid down into the ravines:—wintry torrents, heavy with a booty wasted, have raged through the wadys, and have left despair to the starving few that wander upon the surface.

But now this Palestine—which five English counties, Northumberland, Durham, Yorkshire, Lancashire, Lincolnshire, would more than cover—brings within its narrow limits more varieties of surface, and of aspect, and of temperature, and of produce, than elsewhere may be found in countries that have ten times its area. Palestine, in the age of its wealth, was a samplar of the world:—it was a museum country—many lands in one: the tread of the camel, in two or three hours, may now give the traveller a recollection of his own—come whence he may, from any country between the torrid zone and our northern latitudes. Not in England, not in Switzerland, nor in Greece—in no country known to us—may there be looked at, and experienced, so much of *difference* in all those external things of nature which affect the bodily sensations—the conditions of life, and in what quickens the imagination;—and all upon an area the whole of which may be seen from three of its elevations, or from four. Thus it was, therefore, that the Hebrew Poet found, always near at hand, those materials of his art which the poets of other lands had to seek for in distant travel. Imagery, gay or grave, was around him everywhere; and these materials included contrasts the most extreme: then these diversities of scenery, so near at hand, must have made the deeper impression upon minds sensible of such impressions, inasmuch as this same land was bordered on every side by mountain ranges, or by the boundless table-land desert, eastward and southward; and by the Great Sea in front. Palestine was as a picture of many and bright colours, set in a broad and dull frame.

In other lands, as in a few spots in England and at rare moments—in Greece, and its islands, often—in Italy, at a few points, and in many of the Paradisaical islets of the Eastern Ocean, and of the Pacific, there may be seen that which the eye rests upon with so much pleasure in a sultry summer's day—the deep blue or purple of the sleeping ocean, serving to give brighter splendour to a foreground of luxurious foliage, and of gay flowers. Trees, shrubs, festooning climbers —garden, and wild flowers, then most recommend themselves to the painter's eye when the background is of that deep colour—the like to which there is nothing on earth—the purple of a profound sea, shone upon by a fervent sun, under a cloudless sky. But then in none of those countries or islands do splendid landscapes of this order present themselves in contrast with stony deserts, dismal as the land of death! But in Palestine —such as it was of old—the soft graces of a rural scene —the vine-covered slopes—the plains, brilliant with flowers, the wooded glens and knolls—sparkling with springs, and where the warbling of birds invites men to tranquil enjoyment—in Palestine there is, or there was, ever at hand those material symbols of unearthly good which should serve to remind man of his destination to a world better and brighter than this.

From the lofty battlements of most of the walled towns the ancient inhabitant of Palestine looked westward upon what was to him an untraversed world of waters: the "Great Sea" was to him the image of the infinite. He believed, or he might believe, that the waves which fell in endless murmurs upon those shores, had come on—there to end a course which had begun —between the two firmaments—where the sun sinks nightly to his rest. From the opposite turrets of the same fenced city he watched for the morning, and thence beheld the celestial bridegroom coming forth from his chambers anew—rejoicing as a strong man to run a race! To those who now, for an hour, will forget our modern astronomy, the Syrian sun-rising well answers to the imaginative rendering of it by the

Poet:—the sun, as it flares up from behind the mountain-wall of Edom, seems well to bear out whatever may be conceived of it, as to its daily course through the heavens.

Again, the ranges of Lebanon might be called a sample of the aspects of an Alpine region—a specimen of sublimities, elsewhere found far apart. The loftier summits—the crown of Jebel-es-Sheikh—is little lower than the level of perpetual snow: in truth, Hermon, in most years, retains throughout the summer its almond-blossom splendour;—and as to the lower ranges, they overhang slopes, and glades, and ravines, and narrow plains, that are unrivalled on earth for wild luxuriant beauty. In ancient times these rich valleys were mantled with cedar forests; and the cedar, in its perfection, is as the lion among the beasts, and as the eagle among the birds. This majestic tree, compared with any others of its class, has more of altitude and of volume than any of them: it has more of umbrageous amplitude, and especially it has that tranquil aspect of venerable continuance through centuries which so greatly recommends natural objects to the speculative and meditative tastes. The cedar of Lebanon, graceful and serviceable while it lives, has the merit of preparing in its solids, a perfume which commends it, when dead, to the noblest uses:—this wood invites the workman's tool for every ingenious device; and its odoriferous substance is such as to make it grateful alike in palaces and in temples.

It is only in these last times—at the end of thirty centuries—that a river, which has no fellow on earth—which has poured its waters down to their rest near at hand to the civilized world, and has been crossed at many points—it is only now that it has come to be understood; and the mystery of its seventy miles of course opened up. Why it was not understood long ago is itself a mystery. The brevity of ancient authors, who touch for a moment only upon subjects the most exciting to modern curiosity, is indeed an exercise of patience to those who, for the first time, come to acquaint themselves with the mortifying fact that where pages of description are eagerly looked for—five words, or, at the most, as many lines, are what we must be content to accept at their hands. Why did not Herodotus describe to us the Al-Kuds—the Holy city which he visited? Why not tell us something of the secluded people and their singular worship? So it is as to Diodorus, and Strabo, and Pliny; and so, in many instances, is it with the prolix Josephus: who gives us so often more than we care to read; but fails to impart the very information which we are in need of, on points of importance. The Jordan—which, physically and historically alike, is the most remarkable river in the world—is mentioned by ancient authors only in the most cursory manner, as dividing the countries on its right and left bank—or as emptying itself into the Asphaltic Lake. Even the Biblical writers, although the river is mentioned by them very often, say little that implies their acquaintance with the facts of its physical peculiarities. And yet, unconscious as they seem to have been of these facts, they drew from this source very many of their images. Has there ever been poetry where there is not a river? This Jordan—rich in aspects alternately of gloom, and of gay luxuriance, sometimes leaping adown rapids, and then spreading itself quietly into basins—reaches a prison-house whence there is no escape for its waters but—upward to the skies! Within a less direct distance than is measured by the Thames from Oxford to the Nore, or by the Severn from Shrewsbury to the Estuary of the Bristol Channel, or by the Humber, or the Trent, or the Tweed, in their main breadths, the waters of the Jordan break themselves away from the arctic glaciers of Hermon, and within the compass of one degree of latitude give a tropical verdure to the plains of Jericho, where the summer's heat is more intense than anywhere else on earth —unless it be Aden. To conceive of these extraordinary facts aright, we should imagine a parallel instance, as if it were so that, in the midland counties—or between London and Litchfield—perpetual snow surrounded the one, while the valley of the Thames should be a forest of palm-trees, with an African climate!

When the traveller crosses the Ghor, and ascends the wall of the Eastern table-land, that illimitable desert spreads itself out before him in traversing which meditative minds indulge in thoughts that break away from earth, and converse with whatever is great and unchanging in an upper world. If we retrace our steps in returning from the Eastern desert, and recross the Jordan, travelling southward, we come upon that region of bladeless desolation which constitutes the wall of the Asphaltic Lake, on its western side; yet from this land of gloom a few hours' journey suffices to bring into contrast the vineyards, the olive-groves, the orangeries, of a luxuriant district—and a theatre of peaks, ravines, gorges, and broken precipices, within the circle of which the summers and the winters of all time have effected no change: it is now, as it was thousands of years ago, the land of the Shadow of Death—a land where the lot of man presents itself under the saddest aspects;—for the Earth is there a prison-house, and the sun overhead is the inflicter of torment.

Yet, near to the abodes of a people among whom powerful emotions are to find symbols for their utterance, there is found one other natural prodigy, and such as is unmatched upon the surface of the Earth;—for nowhere else is there a hollow so deep as is this hollow: there is no expanse of water that sends its exhalations into the open sky, resembling at all this lake of bitumen and sulphur. And what might that chasm show itself to be, if the caldron were quite emptied out, or if the waters of the Jordan could be turned aside for a while into the Great Sea, leaving evaporation to go on until the lowest rent were exposed to view! Unfathomed, unfathomable, is this lake at its southern end:—its mysteries, be they what they may, are veiled by these dense waters:—but the traveller, conscious as now he is of the actual depth of the surface—so far below the level of the busy world as it is—needs little aid of the imagination to persuade himself that a plunge beneath the surface would bring him upon the very roofing of Sheol.

It is the wild flowers of a land that outlive its devastations:—it is these that outlive the disasters or the extermination of its people:—it is these that outlive misrule, and that survive the desolations of war. It is these "witnesses for God"—low of stature as they are, and bright, and gay, and odoriferous—that, because they are infructuous, are spared by marauding bands. These gems of the plain and of the hill-side outlast the loftiest trees of a country:—they live on to witness the disappearance of gigantic forests:—they live to see the extinction of the cedar, and of the palm, and of the ilex, and of the terebinth, and of the olive, and of the acacia, and of the vine, and of the fig-tree, and of the myrtle: —they live to see fulfilled, in themselves, the word— "every high thing shall be brought low; and the humble shall rejoice." So has it been in Palestine: once it was a land of dense timber growths, and of frequent graceful clusters of smaller trees, and of orchards, and of vineyards, which retains now, only here and there, a remnant of these adornments. Meanwhile, the alluvial plains of the land, and its hill sides, are gay, every spring, with the embroidery of flowers—the resplendent crocus, the scented hyacinth, the anemone, the narcissus, the daffodil, the florid poppy, and the ranunculus, the tulip, the lily, and the rose. These jewels of the spring morning—these children of the dew—bedded as they are in spontaneous profusion upon soft cushions of heather, and divans of sweet thyme—invite millions of bees, and of the most showy of the insect orders:—flowers, perfumes, butterflies, birds of song, all things humble and beautiful, here flourish, and are safe—for man seldom intrudes upon the smiling wilderness!

Nevertheless, skirting the flowery plains of Palestine, in a few spots, there are yet to be found secluded glades, in which the cypress and the acacia maintain the rights of their order to live; and where, as of old, "the birds sing among the branches." And so live still, on spots, the fruit-bearing trees—the apricot, the peach, the pear, the plum, the fig, the orange, the citron, the date, the melon, the tamarisk, and—noblest of all fruits—the grape, "that maketh glad man's heart:" all still exist, as if in demonstration of what God has heretofore done for this sample land of all lands, and may do again.

A sample land, in every sense, was the ancient Palestine to be, and therefore it was so in its climate. The round of the seasons here exhibits a greater compass of meteorologic changes—there are greater intensities of cold and of heat—there is more of vehemence in wind, rain, hail, thunder, lightning, not to say earthquake, than elsewhere in any country between *the same parallels of latitude*, and within limits so narrow. Altogether unlike to this condition of aerial unquietness are the neighbouring countries—Egypt, Arabia, Persia, or Mesopotamia. To find the climate of Palestine in winter, or in summer, we must include a fifteen degrees of latitude, northward and southward of its own.

Already we have adverted to those physical changes in the surrounding countries which, in the course of thirty centuries, have very materially affected the climate. of Palestine: the reality of such changes can hardly be doubted. Throughout the Psalms, the Book of Job, and the Prophets, there are many passages, relating to variations of temperature, and the like, which agree much rather with our experience in England, than they do with what is *now* common to Syria. This is certain that throughout the ages during which the Biblical literature was produced, the climate of Palestine was such as to render its allusions to the external world easily intelligible to the people of all lands, excepting only those of the arctic circle. How much more intelligible, in this respect, are those books, than they would have been if the Poets and Prophets of the Bible had been dwellers in Mesopotamia, or in Egypt, or in Nubia, or in Libya, or in Thrace, or in Southern Tartary, or in Northern Europe, or in North, or in South America, or in any of the scattered islets of the Eastern

Ocean! Palestine, situated at the juncture of continents, at the head of seas, at the centre of travel by camel or ship, is, or it was at the time in question, as to its Fauna and its Flora, a museum land;—as to its climate, it was the congener of all climates—as it was also in its adaptation to modes of life, and to the means of subsistence. Palestine was favourable to the habits of the hunter, the herdsman, the agriculturalist, the gardener, the vinedresser, and to them that cultivate the fig, and the olive, and the date-palm. Palestine, if man be there to do his part with his hoe, and his knife, and his plough, is at once an Asiatic country, and it is European. It has its counterpart in Greece, in Italy, in France, in England, as to what is the most peculiar to each; and so it is that the Scriptures of the Old Testament are intelligible (in those allusions to Nature with which they abound) to the greater number of the dwellers on earth; and that the countries in which these allusions might not be understood are as few as they could be.

It is not possible to determine how far changes of climate throughout the surrounding countries have had influence in giving to the aerial aspect of Palestine that clear, sharp, and unpictorial visibility which is now its characteristic. This clearness does not fail to attract the eye of the traveller who visits the Holy Land, with the aerial phenomena of his own landscape scenery in his recollection: striking is the contrast that presents itself in this respect. The hill country of Judea—itself now bare, and almost treeless—is seen through a medium which throws upon its hills and rocky surfaces an aspect of hardness and poverty: so it is that the home of sacred mysteries is itself shrouded in no mystery.

In England, a distance of twenty or thirty miles is enough to impart to mountain ranges the pictorial charms of many delicate tints, and these always changing; and to give even to objects less remote a sort of unreality, grateful to the eye of the poet and the painter. But it is not so in Palestine, where, under ordinary conditions of the heavens, a range of hills, which may be forty or fifty miles distant, shows itself to be—*what it is*, and nothing more! Illusions of the atmosphere do not lend the distance any unreal charms.

Bring together from the stores of our modern English Poetry those passages which borrow their rich colouring from our fitful atmosphere and its humidity:—the soft and golden glozings of sunrise and sunset, and the pearly distances at noon, and the outbursts of sunbeam, and the sudden overshadowings, and the blendings of tints upon all distances of two or three miles: it is these atmospheric illusions, characteristic of a climate that is humid, and yet warm, which have given to the English taste in landscape its peculiarity, and which shows itself equally in the national poetry, and landscape-painting. That sense of the picturesque, which is so eminently English, must, in part, at least, be traced to those aerial illusions which we willingly admit, as compensation for the discomforts of a variable climate.

If the English temper be moody, and if its tastes are largely inclusive of the melancholic element, much of this sombreness of feeling, and its tenderness, is no doubt attributable to a climate, an atmosphere, a sky, that are too little cheered by the sun: and the national poetic feeling, with its wistfulness, and its retrospective depths of feeling, is in accordance with this want of settled fervent effulgence. Among the deeper shadows, and richer colours, and the mysteriousness of the latest autumn, the Poetry of England takes its tone.

But the English traveller, with his recollections of a home landscape—its grey gentleness of tints, and its mysteries of shadow—should prepare himself for disappointment in making his way on such a route as that from Jaffa to Jerusalem: no shadowy illusions are there! It is naked reality that surrounds him far and near in this arid land. The *feeling* that is due on this surface must be challenged to come where we know it *ought* to come: and it is not what he sees, but what he thinks of, that gives excitement to his journey. Enchantment has been dispelled; let then the gravest thoughts take the place of agreeable illusions! If English landscape be a painting in oils, the Syrian landscape is a painting in fresco: each line of hills cuts its hard outline—one range in front of another—and the most remote come upon the sky with a too rigid distinctness. At an early hour the sun drinks up all moisture from the earth's surface; and thenceforward all things are seen through a medium that is perfectly translucent. In Palestine, as now it is, Nature exhibits herself as a marble statue—colourless and motionless:—whereas at home we are used to see her less fixed in her attire, and making her toilette anew from hour to hour. Has it always been so in Palestine as now it is? No certain answer can be given to this question; yet it may be believed that, in the times of David and of Isaiah, not only was the land itself everywhere richly clad, but the atmosphere had a changeful aspect, almost as much so as with ourselves.

And yet if the transparent atmosphere of Syria, under a fervent sun, gives too much of naked reality to the landscape, vast is the advantage which is its compensation, when the sparkling magnificence of the starry heavens takes its turn, instead of the things of earth, to engage the meditative eye. Grant it that the day there (now at least it is so) offers a spectacle less rich than in our latitude of mists:—but then the Night, upon the mountains of Israel, opens a scene incomparably more sublime than we are used to witness. There—it seems so—bearing down upon our heads with power are the steadfast splendours of that midnight sky! Those only who have gazed upon the starry heavens through a perfectly transparent atmosphere can understand the greatness of the disadvantage that is thrown over the celestial field by an atmosphere that is never well purged of the exhalations of earth. In a latitude so high as ours, and which yet has a mean temperature higher than its degrees should give it, the chill of the night serves only to shed fog or mist upon the lower stratum of air; but in warmer climates,—and in no country is it more so than in Syria,—the vast burden of the watery element which the fervour of day has raised aloft becomes, quickly after sunset, a prodigious dew, breaking down upon the earth, as a mighty, yet noiseless deluge:—the aerial load is suddenly thrown off upon the lap of earth, and so it is that, almost in a moment, the veil is drawn aside from the starry fields.

The planets, and the stars upon which the shepherds of Palestine were used to gaze, and which to them were guiding lights, do not seem as if they were fain to go out from moment to moment; but each burns in its socket, as a lamp that is well fed with oil. We, in this latitude, have borrowed—for technical purposes in our Astronomy—the Chaldean groupings of the stars into contours of monsters and demi-gods; but, unless we had so borrowed these celestial romances, we should never have imagined them for ourselves. The nightly heavens in warmer climates show the celestial giants with a bold distinctness; and under those skies these imputed forms of the astral clusters look down upon the earth as if they were real beings, and as if each glowing cluster—Pleiades, Orion, Mazzaroth, and Arcturus, and their companions—were possessed of a conscious life.

The pastoral usages of Palestine greatly favoured a meditative and religious contemplation of the starry heavens; and throughout long periods of the Hebrew national life in which the land had its rest from war, and when the shepherd's enemy was not his fellow-man, but the wolf only, and the lion, and the bear: the shepherd—whose own the sheep were—passed his night abroad, taking his rest upon the hill-side; and these shepherds were often of a mood that led them to "consider the heavens," the work of the Creative hand; and to gather from those fields the genuine fruits of the highest philosophy—which is—a fervent piety. The Palestinian shepherd of that age did indeed misinterpret the starry heavens in a sense;—or, we should say, he was at fault in his measurement of the distance between the celestial roofing above him, and the earth on which he trod; yet, notwithstanding this error, much nearer did he come to the firmament of universal truth than does the modern atheist astronomer, who, after he has found, by parallax, the distance of the nearest of the stars, professes to see no glory in the heavens, but that of the inventors of his astronomic tools! The ladder which rested its foot upon earth, and lodged its uppermost round upon the pavement of heaven, was indeed of far greater height than the Syrian shepherd imagined it to be; nevertheless it was to him a firm ladder of truth; and upon it have passed those who. have kept alive the intercourse between man and his Maker through many centuries.

Always with some high prospect in view, and most often when he had a message of rebuke to deliver, the Hebrew prophet drew many of his symbols from those meteorologic violences which, as we have said, are of frequent occurrence in Palestine. Thus it was that in predicting the overthrow of empires, the fall of tyrants, the destruction of cities, the scattering of nations—the messenger of God found, ready for his use, a figurative dialect which had a colloquial import among the people; besides these deluges of rain, and these awful thunderings and lightnings, and these cataracts of hail, the people had experience of the terrors of earthquake—if not of volcanic eruptions.

It was thus, therefore, that, within limits so narrow as those of the land occupied by the Hebrew people, *provision had been made* (may we not use this phrase ?) at once for supplying to its Poets, in the greatest abundance and variety, the material imagery they would need; and for bringing within the daily experiences of the people every condition of the material world which could be made available for the purposes of a figurative literature. In these adjustments of the country to the people, and of both to the ulterior intention of A Revelation for the world, we need not hesitate to recognize the Divine Wisdom, making preparation, in a marked manner, for so great and peculiar a work. Other provisions, having the same meaning, will meet us as we go on. Yet at this point there is an inference that should be noted—namely, this—That the mode or *style* of a communication of the Will of God to the human family was to be symbolical, or figurative; and that by consequence it should not be scientific or philosophic—or such as could be interpretable in an abstract, or an absolute sense.

A question now meets us, an answer to which is important to our present line of argument. The ancient Palestine, we have said, was rich in its material garniture, as related to the needs and purposes of a figurative literature. And so are, and have been, other lands; but those who have trod the soil and tilled it may have had little or no tasteful consciousness toward the aspects of Nature, as *beautiful* or *sublime.* Poetry has not had its birth among them: the language of the people has reflected only the *primitive intention* of a colloquial medium; and therefore it has been poor in its vocabulary as to the *specific* differences of objects, and as to less obtrusive distinctions among objects of the same class.

In these respects, then, how was it with the Hebrew people? Writers of a certain class have allowed themselves to repeat, a thousand times, the unsustained allegation that this people was—"a rude and barbarous horde." Do we find it to be such? We possess portions of the people's literature; and, more than this, we have in our hands their language; or, at least, so much of it as suffices for putting us in position, on sure grounds of analogy, for filling in some of the chasms, and for safely presuming what this language must have been, in its entireness, when it was the daily utterance of the people.

A difference should here be noted, as to the inferences

that are warrantably derivable, on the one hand, from certain literary remains of an ancient people, and, on the other hand, from their *language*, so far as this may be known by means of these remains. Among a rude people there may have been instances, one in a century, of Nature's gifted spirits:—individual minds, rich and productive, working the wonders of genius in solitary self-sufficient force. In such instances—rare indeed they are —the tools, the materials of genius are wanting:—it was not a rich and copious language that was at the poet's command; for the "horde" were as indigent in thought as they were rude in their modes of life. How was it then with the ancient people of Palestine?

A people's language is the veracious record of its entire consciousness—intellectual, moral, domestic, civil, political, and technical. The people's glossary is the reflection—whether clear or confused, exact or inexact —first, of the notice it took of Nature, and of the material world; and then of its own inner life of passion, affection, emotion; and then it is the voucher for the people's rate of civilization, and of its daily observances, its occupations, and the customary accidents of these. Whatever *is* in the language *is now*, or once was, in the mind and the life of the people. The single words of the language, and its congested phrases, are tokens, or they are *checks* with which some corresponding reality duly tallied, whether or not any extant history has given it a place on its pages. Exceptive instances might here be adduced; but they are not such as would interfere with our argument in this case. Races that have fallen, in the course of ages, from a higher to a lower stage of intellectual and social advancement, may, to some extent, have retained, as an inheritance which they do not occupy, the copious glossary of their remote ancestors.

As to the extent and the richness of the Hebrew tongue at the time when it was the language of common life, or during the twelve centuries from the Exodus to the Captivity, there must be some uncertainty; not merely because the extant remains of the Hebrew literature is of limited extent, but because these remains are of two or three kinds only, and—whatever may be their kind—they have one and the same *intention.* The writers, whether historians, moralists, poets, prophets, are none of them *discursive* on the fields of thought: not one of them allows himself the liberty to wander at leisure over the regions of fancy, or of speculation. Each of them has received his instructions, and is the bearer of a message; and he hastens onward to acquit himself of his task. Inasmuch as the message should command all attention from those to whom it is delivered, so it must seem to command the whole mind of the messenger, and to rule, and to overrule, his delivery of it. Thus it is that copiousness and variety should not be looked for within the compass of books which not only have all of them a religious purpose, but which speak also in the prescribed terms of an authority. Such writings are likely to take up much less of the colloquial medium than would be found in the miscellaneous and unconstrained productions of writers whose purpose it was to entertain the idle hours of their contemporaries.

Unless the botanics of Solomon were an exception, it might be that the Hebrew people had no literature beside their religious annalists, and their prophets. Yet we may believe that the talk of common life, throughout the ancient Palestine, contained a large amount of words and phrases which have found no place in the extant Hebrew books:—*these* books have immortalized for our Lexicons perhaps not more than a third part of the spoken tongue. If, therefore, it were affirmed that the Hebrew language is not copious, or rich in synonyms, what might be understood is this (if, indeed, this be true, which it is not) that its *extant* sacred literature is not rich in words. But even if this were allowed, then the question would return upon us—whether the popular mind was not vividly conscious toward the two worlds—the material, and the immaterial—toward the outer and the inner life? There is evidence that it was so: there is evidence in contradiction of modern nugatory assertions concerning "the rude and barbarous horde." A people is not *rude* that notes all diversities in the visible world; nor is it *barbarous* if its language abounds in phrases that are the need of the social, the domestic, and the benign emotions.

Proof conclusive to this effect is contained, by necessary implication, in the fact that the Hebrew people were addressed ordinarily by their Teachers in a mode which (as to its structure) is subjected to the difficult conditions of elaborate metrical rules, and in the style of that fervid and figurative phraseology which is evidence of the existence among the people of an imaginative consciousness, and of an emotional sensibility, far more acute than that of the contemporary nations of whom we have any knowledge. The Prophets and Poets of this people use the material imagery—the bold metonyms, the transmuted phrases—of the imaginative and emotional style with an ease and a *naturalness* which indicates the existence of corresponding intellectual habitudes in the popular mind. As was the Prophet, such, no doubt, were the Prophet's hearers—obdurate and gainsaying often; nevertheless they were accessible always to those modes of address which are intelligible, even to the most obdurate, when they have belonged to the discipline and economy of every man's earliest years. Every man's better recollections were of a kind that put him in correspondence with the Prophet's style, when he rebuked the vices, and denounced the wrong-doings of later life.

The crowds assembling in the courts of the Temple, where the Inspired man took his seat, and the promiscuous clusters that surrounded the pillars whereupon the Prophet's message was placarded, found the language of these remonstrances to be familiar to their ears. The terms and the style went home to the conscience of the hearer:—these utterances did not miss their aim by a too lofty upshot: they took the level of the popular intellect; and so it was that, as well the luxurious princes of the people as the wayfaring man, though of the idiotic class, might read and understand the Divine monition.

Inasmuch as the poetic and symbolic style draws its materials from the objects of sense, it is implied that the popular mind has a vivid consciousness of these objects, and is observant of the specific diversities of the natural world. This discriminative consciousness undoubtedly belonged to the popular Hebrew mind. The proof is this—that if we take as an instance any one class of natural objects—earth, air, water, the animal orders, or the vegetable world—we shall find, in the Hebrew Glossary, as large a number—as good a choice—of distinctive terms, thereto belonging, as is furnished in the vocabularies of other tongues, one or two only excepted. We may easily bring our affirmation to the test of a sort of comparative estimate, as thus:—

England is a sea-girt land, and it is a land of rivers, and streams, and springs, and brooks, and lakes, and pools, and ponds, and canals, and ditches; it is also a land in which rural employments and out-of-doors habitudes prevail: it is a country in which the mass of the people has lived much abroad, and has dwelt amidst humidity. Nevertheless fifty or sixty words exhaust the vocabulary of the English tongue in this watery department. More than this number are not easily producible, either from our writers, or from colloquial usage. With this number our poets have contented themselves, from Chaucer to these times. France is also a sea-girt land, and it is well watered; but its vocables of this class are not more in number than our own. But now, although a portion only of the language of the Hebrew people has come down to us in the canonical books, this portion brings to our knowledge as many as fifty words of this one class: it is not to be doubted that in the colloquial parlance of the people many more words had place;—as many, probably, as would fully sustain our affirmation as to the comparative copiousness of this tongue. In allowing *sixty* words of this class to the English language, many are included which are technical or geographical, rather than natural or colloquial, and which are rarely occurrent in literature—seldom, if ever, in religious writings. Such are the words —Roadstead, Estuary, Watershed (American), Lock, Canal, Drain, Bight.

There is yet another ground of comparison on which an estimate may be formed of the relative copiousness of languages. It is that which is afforded by collating a *translation* with the *original*—in this manner—to take as an instance the class of words already referred to. The Hebrew Lexicon, as we have said, gives us as many as fifty words or phrases which are representative of natural objects of this one class; and each of these terms has—if we may take the testimony of lexicographers—a well-defined meaning of its own. We have then to inquire by how many words are these fifty represented in the Authorized English version. We find in this version twenty-five words answering for the fifty of the Hebrew—apparently because the English language, at the date of this version, did not furnish a better choice. In very many places the same English word does duty for five, six, or seven Hebrew words—each of which has a noticeable significance of its own, and might fairly claim to be represented in a translation. As for instance the three words River, Brook, Spring, are employed as a sufficient rendering of eight or ten Hebrew words, each of which conveyed its proper sense to the Hebrew ear, and might not well have given place to a more generic, or less distinctive term.

A collation of the Greek of the Septuagint—say, in any one of the descriptive Psalms—will give a result equally significant, we think more so, as evidence of what may be called the picturesque or the poetic copiousness of this ancient language; and in a note at the end of the volume the reader who may wish to pursue the suggestions here thrown out will find some further aid in doing so.

The conclusion with which we are here concerned is this—That, whereas the ancient Palestine was a land richly furnished with the materials of a metaphoric and poetic literature, so were the people of a temperament and of habitudes such as made them vividly conscious of the distinctive features of the material world, as these were presented to them in their every-day life abroad. As proof sufficient of these averments we appeal, *first*, to the obvious characteristics of their extant literature; and then, to the fact of the richness, and the copiousness, and the picturesque distinctiveness of their language, which in these respects well bears comparison with other languages, ancient or modern

CHAPTER V.

THE TRADITION OF A PARADISE IS THE GERM OF POETRY.

The golden conception of a Paradise is the Poet's guiding thought. This bright Idea, which has suffused itself among the traditions of Eastern and of Western nations in many mythical forms, presents itself in the Mosaic books in the form of substantial history; and the conception, as such, is entirely Biblical. Genuine Poetry follows where a true Theology leads the way; and the one as well as the other must have—Truth in History—as its teacher and companion. It is in the style and mode of a true history that we receive the theologic principle of a Creation which was faultless, at the first. The beginning of history thus coincides with that first axiom of Religion which affirms all things to be of God, and all perfect. A morning hour of the human system there was when man—male and female—unconscious of evil, and unlearned in suffering, was inheritor of immortality. In this belief Piety takes its rise; and in this conception of the tranquil plenitude of earthly good—a summer's day of hours unnumbered and unclouded—Poetry has its source; and toward this Idea—retained as a dim hope—it is ever prone to revert. The true Poet is the man in whose constitution the tendency so to revert to this Idea is an instinct born with him, and with whom it has become a habit, and an inspiration.

Whatever it may be, within the compass of Poetry,

that is the most resplendent, and whatever it is that awakens the profoundest emotions—whether they be joyful or sorrowful—whatever it is that breathes tenderness, as well as whatever kindles hope—draws its power so to touch the springs of feeling from the same latent conception of a perfectness and a happiness possible to man, and which, when it is set forth in words, presents itself as a tradition of Paradise. Poetry, of any class, would take but a feeble hold of the human mind—distracted as it is with cares, broken as it is with toils, sorrowing in recollection of yesterday, and in fear as to to-morrow—if it did not find there a shadowy belief, like an almost forgotten dream, of a world where once all things were bright, gay, pure, and blessed in love. The Poet comes to us in our troubled mood, professing himself to be one who is qualified to put before us, in the vivid colours of reality, these conceptions of a felicity which we vaguely imagine, and think of as lost to humanity; and which yet, perhaps, is recoverable. We turn with distaste—even with contempt or resentment—from the false professor of the noblest of arts whose creations contain no recognition, explicit or tacit, of this proper element and germ of true Poetry.

Whether or not a belief of this kind may have obtained a place in our Creed, the feeling is deep in every human spirit, to this effect—That, at some time—we know not when—in some world, or region—we know not where—the brightest of those things which the Poet imagines were realized in the lot of man. But is, then, this conception an illusion? Is it a myth that has had no warrant? It is not so, nor may we so think of it. If there had been no such reality, there could have been no such imagination. If there had been no Garden of

Eden, as a first page in human history, never should the soothings of Poetry have come in to cheer the gloom of common life, or to temper its griefs;—never should its aspirations have challenged men to admit other thoughts than those of a sensual or a sordid course.

Four words—each of them full of meaning—comprise the conceptions which we attribute to the Paradisaical state. They are these—Innocence, Love, Rural Life, Piety; and it is toward these conditions of earthly happiness that the human mind reverts, as often as it turns, sickened and disappointed from the pursuit of whatever else it may ever have laboured to acquire. The *Innocence* which we here think of is not virtue, recovered:—it is not virtue that has passed through its season of trial; but it is Moral Perfectness, darkened by no thought or knowledge of the contrary. This Paradisaical *Love* is conjugal fondness, free from sensuous taint. This *Rural Life* is the constant flow of summer days—spent in gardens and a-field—exempt from exacted toil. This *Piety* of Paradise is the grateful approach of the finite being to the Infinite—a correspondence that is neither clouded, nor is apprehensive of a cloud.

It was in the fruition of each of these elements of good that the days, or the years, or the centuries, of the Paradisaical era were passed; and it was then that those things which to their descendants are Poetry, to these—the parents of Mankind—were realities. Each of these conditions of earthly well-being was indispensable to the presence and preservation of the others; for there could be no Paradise if any one of them were supposed to be wanting or impaired. Without innocence earthly good is a debasing sensuality:—without love it is selfishness and war:—without piety earthly good, at the very best, is the dream of a day in prospect of an eternal night; and to imagine a Paradise planted in the heart of cities is a conception that is almost inconceivable.

In like manner as there could be no Paradise in the absence of these, its four elements, so neither can there be Poetry where these are not its inspiration, its theme, or its intention: or if not, we put it away as either a mockery of the sadness of human life, or as a vilifying slander. Love must be the soul of poetry: Purity must be its purpose and aim:—Nature abroad must be its desire, and its chosen enjoyment, and Piety must be its aspiration. From Poetry that has no correspondence with these conditions of a Paradise we turn in dull despair to resume the heavy task of life; for if so, then beyond its austere conditions there is nothing in prospect of humanity:—the path we tread must be a continuity of care in sullen progress to the grave.

We take, then, the Mosaic Paradise as the germ of all Poetry; and unless this first chapter of human history be regarded as real—*as true*—it could stand in no relationship to those deep-seated instincts—those slumbering beliefs of possible felicity, which this tradition has fed and conserved in the human soul. If this first chapter be a fable, then we reject this belief also as a delusion. But it is not a delusion; and as often as a group of children, with ruddy cheek and glistening eye, is seen sporting in a meadow, filling their chubby hands with cowslips—laughing in sunshine—instinct with blameless glee—then and there, if we will see it, we may find a voucher for the reality of a Paradise which has left an imprint of itself in the depth of every heart: the same truth is attested with the emphasis of a contrast when

—infancy and childhood, sporting and merry at the entrance of a city den, and still snatching from the pavement a faded handful of flowers, speaks of this instinct, and exhibits the pertinacity of a belief which no pressure of actual wretchedness can entirely dispel.

Man in the garden of God, accepting, as the gift of his Creator, the plenitude of earthly good, combined in his lot Poetry and reality, which in the experience of his descendants are always severed; and yet the first of these is not lost, although it stands aloof. In ten thousand ordinary minds there is an element latent which, in the one in ten thousand, quickens and becomes productive. The musings and the yearnings of millions of souls are so many inarticulate utterances of a dream-like conception of innocence, love, ease, leafy fragrant bowers, and shining skies, which those who have never found these things in their lot, nevertheless persist in thinking have been wanting in it only through adverse accidents and their evil stars! So long as sorrows, regrets, remorses, broken promises, broken hopes, continue to call forth sighs, and to moisten cheeks with tears—so long as blighted, or wounded, or wasted affections eat as a canker into sensitive hearts, so long as the bereaved, and the friendless, and the homeless, and the lost, continue to think themselves unblessed, though they might have been blessed, then will these many sufferers be dreaming of a lot which can never be theirs, wherein the bright conditions of a lost Paradise should have been represented, if not fully realized.

Refine these yearning beliefs—train them in artistic expression, and then the product is—Poetry; and how elaborate soever this product may be, it has had its rise in what was once as real, as are now its contraries. If it had not long ago been *real* it would have had no power to generate the *unreal*, which has ever floated before the imagination of mankind:—there are no dreams where there have been no substances.

Let it be so now that we listen to the exceptions of a captious and gratuitous criticism, and that, at its instance, we consent to remove from the book of Genesis its initial portions! Let it be that two, three, or more chapters of this book are rejected as "not historical." If so, then that which has rooted itself in human nature has itself no root! If it be so, then dreams have sprung of dreams in endless series:—if so, and if Poetry takes no rise in History, then must a deeper darkness spread itself as a pall over the abounding evils, sorrows, pains, and terrors that attend humanity. Thenceforward let it be—for who shall dare to gainsay Satan the Antiquarian!—let it be so that not only pain and toil, want, care, and grief, but also cruelty, wrong, violence, and war, shall proclaim an eternal triumph! The monster henceforward takes a firmer grasp of his victim:—if it be so—then, for aught we know, the rights of this tyranny are immemorially ancient:—they are as old as "the human period" of Geology:—for aught we know, the kingdom of Evil is from everlasting, and it shall be everlasting.

It shall not be so. Give me back that which a genuine criticism allows me to retain—the initial chapters of the Mosaic record. Give me—not as a myth, but as a history—the beginning of the human family in its Eden, and then a darkness is dispelled: then hope and peace are still mine (and Poetry also), for if this Proem of human history may stand approved, then on the skirts of the thickest gloom a brightness lingers.

If there was once a Paradise on earth, then I know how to see and acknowledge, as the gifts of God, whatever is good and fair in my actual lot, and whatever is graceful; and whatever is in nature beautiful, and whatever it is which art elaborates, and which genius exalts. In all these graces of life I see so many vouchers for the fact that this Earth once had a Paradise.

And this is not all—for, with the same Mosaic belief as my ground of speculation—my turret of observation, I may look upwards and around me upon the sparkling fields of the infinite, and then am free to surmise, what I have reason to infer from an actual instance; and thus I may assuredly believe that, upon millions of worlds, there are now, and will be, gardens of God, where all is fair and good.

CHAPTER VI.

BIBLICAL IDEA OF PATRIARCHAL LIFE.

Paradise was lost! Nevertheless, in accordance with the primæval Biblical Idea, the religious man—the chief of a family—was permitted to enjoy, through a long term of years, a terrestrial lot in which were conserved the rudiments, at least, of the forfeited felicity, and thus through the lapse of centuries a conception of Life on Earth was authenticated, in meditation upon which Piety might re-assure its confidence in the Divine wisdom and goodness.

The Patriarchal Idea is Oriental, not European; it excludes the energy, the individual development, the progress, that are characteristic of the Western races: —it is—Repose, and the fruition of unambitious well-being. The Patriarchal life, in part nomadic, in part precariously dependent upon the chase, in part agricultural and of the vine culture;—the life of the tent, more than of strongholds and walls, combines those conditions of earthly existence which are the most favourable to religious contemplative tranquillity, and under which the sanctities of the domestic relationships should be reverentially conserved. Within the precincts of this economy of unwritten obligation and of traditional veneration, piety toward God—the Invisible—was a higher species of that filial regard of which the senior and the chief was the visible centre.

The Patriarchal Idea is wholly Biblical, and as such it has suffused itself through the poetry of modern nations. And there is much in the mild domestic usages and sentiments of modern nations that is to be traced up to its rise in this conception. It is *Biblical*, not merely because it is monotheistic in doctrine; but because also it gives a most decisive prominence to the belief of the near-at-hand providence of God—of HIM that immediately orders and appoints and controls all events affecting the individual man. This ever-present ALMIGHTY—Righteous and Benign—the Hearer of prayer—the Giver of all good—the Avenger of wrong—is held forth, and is vividly brought within range of human conceptions in the incidents of the Patriarchal history. Far away from the interference of futile speculative questionings, these religious beliefs, as exemplified in the life of the servants of God, received at once an historic warranty, and a dramatic—or, it might be said, even a picturesque—realization, in the records of this era.

The Paradisaical elements are conserved in the Patriarchal life—each of them attempered by blending itself with whatever in the actual lot of man has become saddened by his sins and frailty—by his pains, his toils, his cares; and it thenceforward presents itself as if in shining fragments, commingled with the ruins of purposes frustrated—hopes shattered.

Within and around the patriarchal encampment, near to the springs and the palms of the sultry wilderness, we are to find—in the place of Innocence—Virtue—put to the proof, and not always triumphant in its conflict with temptation. Within this enclosure, instead of unsullied, uncontradicted Love, there are yet heard the deep yearnings of domestic affection, rendered intense by tearful sympathies; perhaps by resentments, that strike into the very roots of human feeling. Around this enclosure are assembled, not the wild animal orders in awe of their lord—doing homage to man; but flocks and herds, the product of his provident and laborious care. Instead of a garden, wildly luxuriant in flowers and fruits, there are trim enclosures of esculent plants—flowers and perfumes giving way to roots and fruits:—there may be heard the singing of birds;—yet this is less heeded than the lowing of kine. Human existence is in its state of transition—conserving as much of its primæval felicity as shall be the solace and excitement of a life which still may be happy, if man be wise; and the wisdom, which is to ensure his welfare, is that to which the patriarchal altar gave its sanction. The Divine favour is there pledged to the obedient and devout; but it is pledged under conditions which are, in the simplest mode, ritual, and which, while they assure the worshipper in his approach to God, restrict him also.

The Patriarchal man knew that he had forfeited terrestrial immortality, and that his years on earth were numbered; and yet, in the place of a now-undesirable endless life, there was given him—longevity; and beyond it, a far more distinct vision of the future life than modern Sadducean criticism has been willing to allow. This length of years—a stipulated reward of piety—and this more than a glimmer of the life eternal, imparted a dignity to the modes of thinking, and to the demeanour and carriage of those "Sons of God" who, each in his place, stood, toward all around him, as Chief, and Prophet, and Priest. Life under these conditions—beneath the heavens—a life, inartificial and yet regal—a course abhorrent of sordidness, and thrift, so realized itself during a lapse of centuries, as to have become a Pattern Idea, the presence and influence of which are conspicuous in the cherished sentiments and in the literature of modern and western nations.

To its rise in the Patriarchal era may be traced that *one conception*, which might be called *the Ruling Thought*, as well of Art, as of Poetry—the Idea of REPOSE. Order, symmetry, beauty, security, conscious right and power, are the constituents of this Idea. When embodied, or symbolized in Art or in Poetry, it is this repose which is the silent voucher for whatever shall be its consummation in a higher sphere—even for "the Rest that remaineth." It contradicts, and refuses to be consorted with, the ambition, the discontent, the adventure, the turmoil, the changeful fortunes, the pressure, and the progress, of that lower life which knows nothing of the past, and is mindless of the remote future.

The first man had lived—for whatever term—in the fruition of the happiness which springs from the spontaneous development of every faculty—bodily and mental. The man—wise and good in his degree—under the patriarchal scheme, enjoyed as much of the things of life as were allowed to him—individually—under the conditions of a providential scheme, divinely established and administered, in a manner which rendered the Providential Hand and Eye all but visible: the Patriarch—religious in mood and habit, and thus cared for by Him whose Name was a promise—the Patriarch eschewed ambition, he dreaded change in the modes of life—he contented himself with those simple conditions of common life which, in a warm and equable climate, are more agreeable—more sufficing, than are the far more elaborate provisions of a higher civilization in a more austere climate. Especially did this patriarchal nomad life—this following of pasturage where it might be found—greatly favour that meditative mood in which piety delights itself—entertaining the idea of terrestrial life as a pilgrimage, under tents, always onward bound towards a future, where security and repose shall be—not precarious, but perpetual.

Toward this model Idea, embodied as it has been in the early history of the human family, and authenticated as good *for its time*, by the apostolic recognition of it, religious feeling in all times has constantly shewn itself to be tending. At times and in places when and where the patriarchal well-being has been wholly unattainable, there came, in the room of it, or as its best substitute, the earlier and the less fanatical form of the monastic life—the *anchoretic*—not the conventual—the sentimental and mystical, rather than the ascetic; and it is observable that this milder style of the wandering pilgrimage life over the ruggedness of earth to heaven drew itself as near as it could to the scenes of its patriachal archetype. The commendation of this primæval piety may be this:—that it was *in place* as a preparation for a more advanced stage of the religious training of the human family;—but the condemnation of the later mood—in itself innocent, was this, that it was *out of place*—out of *date*, after the ultimate Revelation had been promulgated. The ascetic had forgotten evangelic principles:—the anchoret had retreated from evangelic obligations. The Patriarchal life was the foreshadowing of a future, wherein communion with God being the high end or intention of existence, whatever else is done will be regarded only as a means conducive to that end.

In accordance with its intention and its external conditions, the piety of the Patriarchal era was *individual*, not congregative;—it was domestic, not ecclesiastical; —it was genuine and affectionate, not formal or choral, or liturgical:—it did not emulate, or even desire, the excitements of a throng of worshippers, assembling to "keep holy day," and making the air ring with their acclamations:—more of depth was there in this ancient piety; and it may be believed that the worshipper drew much nearer to the throne of the Majesty on high than did the promiscuous crowd that, in after times, assembled to celebrate festivals and to observe national ordinances. On these conditions, namely—the renouncing of worldly ambition, and the restless imagining of a something better, supposed to be attainable by thought and labour; then the Patriarchal repose took its rest upon the hope and promise of a land—unseen—the land of souls, whereinto the servants of God are gathered, each in his turn as he fails from his place on earth. How desirable a lot might we now think this, if only its material conditions might be secured!—but they may not—this is not possible; for man is summoned to work, and to suffer; and the piety of meditative repose, and of conscious transit to the paradise of spirits, must give way to a piety that needs to be strenuous, self-denying, and martyr-like; and that must win its crown, after a conflict.

Nevertheless, this enviable lot having once been realized in the remoteness of ages, it still lives in the imaginations of men, and toward it, not poets only, but the most prosaic of the order of thrift are seen to be tending. Toil and turmoil through sixty years are endured, if only these may purchase a closing decade of rest—rural occupation—security—or, in a word, a sort of suburban resemblance of the leisure and the dignity that was long ago realized in the desert, by them of old.

The Poetry of all nations has conserved more or less of these elements of the primæval repose; and in fact we find them conserved also, and represented, in that modern feeling—the love of, and the taste for—the Picturesque. Modern, undoubtedly, is this taste, which has not developed itself otherwise than in connection with pictorial Art, in the department of landscape. What is the picturesque? A question not easily answered; yet this is certain, that any attempt that may be made to find an answer to it must bring us into contact with the very elements which already have been named; and which are assembled in the Ideal of the Patriarchal Repose. The picturesque could not belong to Paradise; for it finds its gratification in those forms of decay and disorder which bespeak damage and inaction. The picturesque is not simply—beauty in Nature;—it is not luxuriance; it is not amplitude or vastness; it is not copiousness; it is not the fruit of man's interference: but rather is it the consequence of an indolent acquiescence on his part, in things—as they are, or—as they have become. The picturesque belongs to the foreground always; or to the stage next beyond the foreground;—never does it take its range upon the horizon. The picturesque claims as its own the cherished and delicious ideas of deep seclusion, of *lengthened, undisturbed continuance*, and of the absence, afar-off, of those industrial energies which mark their presence by renovations, by removals, and by a better ordering of things, and by signs of busy industry, and of thriftiness and order.

Within the sacred precincts of the picturesque, the trees must be such as have outlived the winters of centuries, and been green through the scorching heats of unrecorded sultry summers: they stoop, and yet hold up gnarled giant branches, leafy at the extreme sprays; and their twistings are such as to look supernatural, seen against an autumnal evening sky. The fences that skirt the homestead of the picturesque must have done their office through the occupancy of three or four generations. The dwellings of man must declare themselves to be such as have sheltered the hoary quietude of sires long ago gone to their graves. Inasmuch as the picturesque abjures change, it rejects improvement; it abhors the square, the perpendicular, the horizontal; and it likes rather all forms that now are other than at first they were, and that lean this way and that way, and that threaten to fall; but so did the same building threaten a fall a century ago! In a word, the picturesque is the Conservatism of Landscape Beauty. It is where the picturesque holds undisputed sway that we shall find—or shall expect to find—secure and placid longevity—domestic sanctity and reverence; together with a piety that holds more communion with the past than correspondence with the busy and philanthropic present. Give me only the picturesque, and I shall be well content never to gaze upon tropical luxuriance, or upon Alpine sublimities; nor shall ever wish to tread the broad walks that surround palaces; shall never be taxed for my admiration of those things which wealth and pride have superadded to Nature.

CHAPTER VII.

THE ISRAELITE OF THE EXODUS AND THE THEOCRACY.

It was upon no such bright themes as those of the Paradisaical era—it was upon no subjects so well adapted to the purposes of Poetry as those of the Patriarchal era—that the Hebrew Prophets employed themselves. It was far otherwise: leaving subjects of this order open and unoccupied to the genius of distant ages, these witness-bearing men, in long succession, addressed the men of their times upon matters of more immediate concernment, and in a mood and style adapted to the people with whom they had to do. If it be so—and on this point there can be no reasonable question—then it must be true in this instance, as in every similar instance, that a correct notion of the people who were so addressed, as to their degree of culture, as to their moral condition, and their social advancement, and as to their comparative intelligence, may with certainty be gathered from these remains of their literature?—the literature being regarded as the mirror of the national mind. Yet if we so regard it, and so use it, this safe method of induction may perhaps lead the way to conclusions that materially differ from those, which, on the one side, as well as on the other side, of a controversy concerning the Old Testament History, have been advanced, and have been tacitly assented to.

To defame, by all means, the ancient Israelitish people, as a "horde of barbarians," has been the purpose of a certain class of writers; and on the other side a mistaken timidity has beguiled writers into the error of supposing that, in admitting this imputed barbarism, an extenuation, or a palliation might be found for those events and those courses of action in the history of the people which most offend our modern tastes, or which stand condemned by Christian principles. What has been wanting, and the want of which has shed confusion upon the subject, has been—we need not say—candour and truthfulness on the one side; but more of intellectual and moral courage on the other side of this modern argument.

The ancient Israelite had no peer among his contemporaries; nor do we find analogous instances on any side that might render aid in solving the problem of this race, either in its earlier or its later history. In truth, there is as much need of an admission of the supernatural element for understanding the national *character*, as there is for understanding the narrative of its fortunes and its misfortunes—the catastrophes that have overwhelmed it, and the fact of its survivance of each of them in turn. The Jew—such as we now meet him in the crowded ways of European cities—is indeed a mystery insoluble, unless we are willing to accept the Biblical explication of the problem. So understood, we do indeed yield credence to the supernatural; but then, in not yielding it, the alternative is a congeries of perplexities that are utterly offensive to reason.

Taken on the ground of ordinary historical reasoning, the earliest literary remains of the Israelitish people give evidence of a far higher range of the moral and religious consciousness than is anywhere else presented in the circle of ancient literature. The inference hence derivable is not abated in its meaning by the anomalous and remarkable fact—a fact which has no parallel—that these writings, through a great extent of them, take a form of remonstrant antagonism toward the people—toward the masses, and toward their princes and rulers. Those who take upon themselves the unwelcome and dangerous office of administering national rebuke, and of uttering denunciations, are not wont to attribute to their hearers more of intelligence and of right feeling than they find among them. We may believe, then, that there was, in fact, with these hearers that measure of mind and of virtue, the existence of which is fairly to be inferred from the language of these public censors, whose often-recurring phrases are of this order—" Ye are a stiff-necked people—a foolish nation :—as were your fathers, so are ye."

As was the country, so the people :—the country, geographically, was embraced within the circuit of the East ; nevertheless, in climate and productions it was European more than it was Asiatic. And so the people —Orientals by origin, by physiognomy, by usages, and yet in many points of mental constitution, and by its restless energy, it was more European than Oriental. Toward the trans-Euphratean races—the ultra-Orientals —the Israelite showed a decisive contrariety or alienation : he refused his sympathies toward the sun-rising ; or, if in some instances amalgamation in that direction took place, the sure and speedy consequence was loss of nationality in every sense—physical, ritual, social. The captive tribes, when carried eastward, forgot their institutions—forgot their very name.

But toward the people of the " Islands of the sea"—

the European races—the Jew, while maintaining a sullen antagonism, and continuing to rebut scorn with scorn, has done so in a manner that gave proof of his consciousness of what might be called—intellectual and moral consanguinity. By his sympathies, by his intellectual range, by his moral intensity, by his religious depth, and even by his tastes, the Jew has made good his claim to be numbered with those that constitute the commonwealth of western civilization. Intimately consorted with European nations, this integrate people has repelled commixture, as if it might serve as an alloy; but it has shown its quality, in this way, that if the Western nations, like the perfect metals, are fusible, and malleable, and ductile, and apt for all purposes of art, this race also—unlike the Oriental races—fully partakes of the same original qualities, and is apt also toward the highest civilization. Not so those races that are properly Oriental, and which, like the imperfect metals, show a sparkling surface, but are stereote in thought, in usages, in political structure—the same from the beginning to the end of millenniums. As the Jew of modern times is our equal, intellectually and morally, so has he been from the first;—such was the Israelite of the Exodus, and of the next following centuries.

Orientals—those who are such by destiny—have always, as now they do, surrendered themselves inertly to despotisms of vast geographical extent. Not so the Israelite, either of the remotest times, or of later ages. Often trampled upon and loaded with chains, he has never ceased to resent his bonds, or to vex and trouble his oppressor. Always, and notoriously, has he been a dangerous and turbulent subject. The Romans, great masters of the art of governing dependencies, learned at length this lesson—that the Jew must be indulged; —or, if not indulged, then exterminated. It is true that the kinsman of the Israelite—the Arab, has defied subjugation;—but he has done so as the roaming man of a trackless desert, whereupon he may flit until his pursuers are weary of the chase. The resistance and persistence of the Israelite, and of the Jew, has implied loftier qualities, and deeper sentiments; for it has been maintained under the far more trying conditions of city life. It is one thing to scoff the tyrant from afar upon scorched illimitable sands: it is another, to maintain moral courage, and to transmit the same spirit of heroism to sons and daughters, while buffeted and mocked in every villanous crowd of a city! So has the Jew held his own, and he has done this as the true descendant of the men with whom Jephtha, and Deborah, and Samuel, and David, had to do. The same man—man indeed we find him, in conflict with Antiochus, and when led and ruled by the Asmonean princes. Such did he show himself to the Roman proconsuls;—such was he as the problem of the imperial rule;—such toward the barbarian barons of mediæval Europe—such, from first to last (*last* we must not say of the Jewish people) the man—firmer always in principle and in passive courage than that the iron and the fire should break his resolution.

The Israelite of the earliest period—the ages elapsing from the settlement in Palestine to the establishment of the monarchy, and onward—may be regarded as the genuine representative of constitutional social order; for his rule is—submission up to a limit, and resistance at all risks beyond that limit. He had no taste for anarchy; his inmost feeling was quiescent, for it arose from his vividly domestic, and his prædial habits and sentiments. The patriarchal ancestry of the nation had given him a tradition of quietude and enjoyment—under the vine and fig tree—his wife as a fruitful vine and his children as olive plants round about his table; and thus he was not the turbulent brawling citizen, machinating revolution:—he was the sturdy yeoman, and the true conservative. A soldier, and always brave if there be need to fight—if there be an enemy on the border; but he was never ambitious or aggressive.

Enough has become known concerning the common arts of life, as practised among the Egyptians in the times of the Pharaohs, to secure for them an advanced position on the scale of material civilization: they understood, and successfully practised, as well the secondary as the primary arts which minister to the subsidiary, as well as to the more imperative requirements of the social economy. During their long sojourn in the near neighbourhood of the Egyptian civilization, the Hebrew people—slaves during the latter portion only of this period—had largely partaken of this advancement. The evidences of this culture are incidental and conclusive, as we gather them from the narrative of the forty years' wandering in the Sinaitic peninsula. The mechanic and the decorative arts were at the command of the people: there were among them skilled artificers in all lines: they possessed also a formed language,—and they had the free use and habit of a written language.

If, then, we go on to inquire concerning the intellectual and moral and social condition of the thousands of the people, the warrantable method, available for the purposes of such an inquiry, is that of seeking the indications of this condition, inferentially, in the remains of the literature of the people;—not, it may be, in treatises on abstruse subjects, composed by the learned for the learned: but in writings of whatever sort which were adapted to popular use, and in which—for this is their *mark*, as so intended—the mass of the people is challenged to listen and to respond, and is invited and provoked to contradict—if in any instance there be room for a contrary averment. Such was the Israelitish people at the moment which ended their tent-life in the wilderness, and which immediately preceded their entrance upon the land assigned them, as that they, in full Ecclesia, might properly be taught, advised, upbraided, promised, threatened, in the manner of which the closing book of the Pentateuch is the record and summary.

The Israelite of that time was such that to him might be propounded, intelligently, the sublime theology and the rightful and truthful ethics of the book of Deuteronomy; which have held their place, unrivalled, as Institutes of Religion from that age to this. What is our alternative on this ground? This book is either "from Heaven," in its own sense; or it is from man. If from Heaven, then a great controversy reaches its conclusion, by admission of the opponent;—but if from men, then the people among whom this theology, and these ethical principles, and these institutions spontaneously arose, and to whose actual condition they were adapted, were a people far advanced beyond any other, even of later times, in their religious conceptions, in their moral consciousness, in their openness to remonstrance, and their sensibility toward some of the most refined emotions of domestic and social life. It is a canon, open to no valid exceptive instance, that the spoken-to *are* as the speaker and his speech. There is an easy and warrantable means of bringing this historic canon to a test, as available in the instance before us. Our question is—What were these people, or—*what had they become*, in consequence of their Egyptian sojourn—what in consequence of the discipline of the desert:—what, upon a new generation, had been the influence of the Sinaitic Law, and of the Tabernacle worship, and of the tribune administration of social order? Prospective as were many of the Mosaic injunctions—social and ecclesiastical—the theology was ripe and entire, from the first; —so were the ethical principles, and so was the worship. The generation which then had reached maturity along with all of younger age, from infancy upward, were—*the product* of this religious and social training!

There is much more in the last book of the Pentateuch than in the preceding four—regarded as a ground or source of inferences—concerning the intellectual and moral condition of the Hebrew people of that time; for it consists of a series of popular addresses, orally delivered; and these, by the calm majesty of the style throughout, by the remonstrant tone, by innumerable allusions to events and usages, carry with them a demonstration of historic verity which no ingenuous and cultured mind will fail to admit. And withal, toward the close of these upbraiding admonitions the Heaven-instructed Lawgiver and Prophet utters, with all the amplitude and speciality of actual vision, a prediction of national woe to arrive in the remotest distance of ages —a prediction so irrefragably prescient as to have wrung —to have *wrenched*—a reluctant admission of its Divine origin from those who have schooled themselves in rebutting sufficient and reasonable evidence.

The utterance of a series of oral instructions and remonstrances, in full assembly, differs, as we say, much, as to its historical value, from the promulgation of a *written code*, or of Institutes of Morals; for these may have been the work of a sage—theorising and devising for the benefit of his contemporaries more and better things than in fact they were prepared to receive. Orations, if authentic, imply more than is implied in treatises or in systems of philosophy.

An intelligent and unsophisticated reader of the majestic speeches which constitute the book of Deuteronomy—resplendent as they are with a bright and benign theistic doctrine—translucent expressions as they are of earnest paternal affection—deep as they are in the knowledge of human nature—*humane* as they are, will never believe—would never imagine, that the speaker's audience were the chiefs and the followers, of a stupid, sensual, truculent, remorseless mob. Here, indeed, the ingenuous reader feels that—as is the speaker, such are the spoken-to. Greatly may we err, as we have already said, in parting off the credible from the incredible among the records of past ages. When the Hebrew Poet challenges an imagined respondent, and asks, in the confidence of truth—"What was it, O Sea, that thou fleddest, and thou Jordan, that thou didst turn back?"—we grant him readily his own expected answer:—it was at the presence of the Almighty that the earth then trembled, and that the sea was then moved out of its place. This is not incredible, nay, it is easy of belief, that He which formed the deep, and founded the hills, should hold them in His hand, and do with them what He wills. But now let it be considered whether, with the books of Moses before us, and the aged

Lawgiver in view, and with his people listening, as his sons around him, we can imagine them to be the savages which a malignant and perverse criticism has laboured to paint them. We may be sure it was not so:—let any instances be adduced which might give support to a supposition of that kind.

Was the Hebrew people a barbarous and sanguinary horde? The modern archetype of the ancient Israelite, if we are to take our notion of him from writers of a certain class, is to be found among the (unchristianized) tribes of Kafir-land, or among those—such as once they were, of New Zealand; or among the Red Men of the American wilderness; or we might find him among those that now roam the Arabian deserts; or we might find him among the degraded and ferocious occupants of the dens and cellars of great cities. But assemble now a ten thousand of such men—the nearest resemblances you can find of the "barbarians" of the Exodus and of the Conquest under Joshua; endeavour to gain the hearing of the savage crowd—with the painted face, and the horrid knife in the girdle, and the skull of an enemy dangling from his belt; take with you, for an experiment, the twenty-sixth chapter of the book of Deuteronomy, and with it make proof of the endeavour to find your way to the mind and heart of untutored and of unculturable and sanguinary savages. In fact, no such experiment could be attempted. Try it, then, under any other imaginable conditions. The Christian Missionary must have laboured for many years among any of the people of Asia—in China, in Thibet, in India, and he must have schooled the children of those nations from infancy to adult years, before he could hope to surround himself with an audience that might be expected to listen with intelligence to instructions and admonitions of this order. The Mosaic homilies are available as indirect, yet conclusive evidence of the existence of a true theistic habitude of mind among the people of the Exodus:—these exhortations are distinguished by a majestic simplicity, and a fervour, and a paternal warmth, which reflect, as in a mirror, the popular mind so far as is needed for completing our historic conception of the scene and its transactions:—the speaker, the listeners, and the addresses. The well-schooled and Christianized people of Protestant Europe excepted, there is not now a people on earth—Eastern or Western—among whom a hearing could be had for recitations, and advices, such as these are. If this exception be allowed for, then the popular mind anywhere among the nations of Europe must have been fused and cast in a new mould before language like that which was addressed by their Lawgiver to the Hebrew people could meet a response in the mind and heart of the multitude. The true and the safe inference is this—That the thousands of Israel, such as they were at the close of their forty years' life in the wilderness, could not be, as it is affirmed, a gross, stupid, and ferocious horde;—but on the contrary, a people—young in age, and quick in mind and feeling;—a people in seeking for analogues to whom we must look among the best trained of our modern Christianized—Bible-taught populations:—they must have been a people with whom there had been matured, a settled usage of theistic terms, a spontaneous intelligence of these terms, devout habitudes, and withal a diffused warmth of those social sentiments which are consequent upon, and which are the proper results of an expansion of the domestic affections.

It is either from the want of philosophic breadth in the mental habits of those who make great pretensions to this quality; or it is, on the other hand, from a sickly religiousness, that the terrible events and doings of the conquest, and the extermination of the Canaanitish tribes, are asserted to be at variance with the inferences which we thus derive from the later portions of the Pentateuch.

These inferences are sure and conclusive; and they are the more so because mainly they are indirect and circumstantial. Those events and transactions—as they stand recorded in the Books of Joshua and the Judges—are indeed appalling, and the perusal of them must be painful. It ought to be so:—it should not be otherwise than that from a stern necessity only we rest in imagination upon recitals of this order, let them be found where they may, whether in our Bibles, or out of them. When similar narratives are found out of our Bibles, our philosophic habits of thought easily help us to get rid of the difficulty; and we abstain from petulantly drawing conclusions, as to the manners or temperament of nations, which would be precipitate and unwarrantable. When found within our Bibles, it is only a gratuitous hypothesis, as to the methods of the Divine government in human affairs that generates, or that aggravates, the difficulty, in view of which our religious faith, or our Christianized sentiments, are staggered or offended. The remedy is to be sought—first, in a dispassionate attention to the facts; and then in a comparison of these facts with others of a like order, occurring on the common field of history.

Take in hand the Books of Joshua, Judges, Ruth, and Samuel. Rising to view at frequent intervals in these records, and always in a manner that is incidental and inartificial, there are evidences irresistible of the existence, diffused among the Hebrew people, of deep and vivid domestic affections—of individual and family piety—of humane sentiments and usages—of a high and chivalrous sense of honour and patriotism, and of a stern sense of justice, and of the rights and claims of the destitute and defenceless. These facts transpire in the course of these narratives; and the style of the prophets—even when administering their most severe rebukes—supposes the same facts. No such denunciations of the Divine displeasure toward cruelty, violence, oppression, rapacity, could have had any meaning unless there had been, on the side of the people, a consciousness of truth, justice, mercy, humanity, purity, and piety, of which consciousness the indications are frequent in the history of the people;—a history extending a four hundred years onward from the time of the passage of the Jordan. The acts of the Conquest had not *found* the Hebrew people a sanguinary horde; —nor had these acts rendered them such: to suppose otherwise would be to reject conclusive evidence bearing upon *this* instance, and to forget parallel instances elsewhere occurring.

War will be war, everywhere and always, until it shall have been "made to cease unto the ends of the earth." Horrible always, at the best, will be—slaughter—wholesale; and it ought to be revolting in the recital, let the provocations, or the reasons of necessity, be what they may: and especially is it so when, to circumstances of urgent national peril are added inveterate and aggravated antipathies of race. The future readers of the history of the British rule in India—such readers, more thoroughly Christianized than we of this time are—will be fain to put from them the page which tells of what was enacted by humane and Christian-hearted British chiefs in regaining the lost supremacy of a foreign over the native races of Hindoostan. Slaughter—not effected by the predetermined stroke of the magisterial sword—is, and ought always to be, beyond, and contrary to, rule and order. A people is indeed savage among whom slaughter could be a recognized practice: never can it come under the restraints of any sort of political or moral generalization: never can it be reasoned upon, or *instituted*, unless among a nation of fiends. Nevertheless, it is certain that a people whose history is marked by no blood-stains—deep and broad—has never yet held a place for itself upon the map of continents. The world being such as it has ever been, and is—even now in this late age—no place, unless it be that of abject servitude, is left for any race which is so inerme as that it could neither provoke nor inflict sanguinary revenges. If we resent any such allegation as this, we ought, in proof of our consistency, not only to snatch the musket from the soldier, but the bludgeon from the girdle of the policeman. This may not be questioned, that, unless the ancient Israelitish people had possessed as much of stern truculent energy as this, they could not have maintained themselves a ten years upon their soil—wedged in, as they were, among the iron-charioted millions of Amalek, and Midian, and Philistia, and of Assyria, and of Egypt. If not so, then must there, from century to century, have been pointed, eastward, northward, southward, the always visible and blazing swords of seraphim.

Already we have said that we *need* the hypothesis of

the supernatural for solving the problem of the national *character*, as well as for understanding the history of this people. And so now, again, in this critical instance, it is nothing less than an assumption of the supernatural in the history of the Exodus, and of the conquest of Canaan, that can make intelligible the facts with which we have to do—and which are these—first, That the Hebrew tribes did indeed enact the extermination of the Canaanitish races (so far as this was done), but that the work of slaughter, dire as it was, did not settle itself down upon the national temper or habits, so as to show itself upon the people as a permanent disposition. No such effects followed from the tragedy-period of their history:—it would not *necessarily* do so in any case; —it did not in this instance, because the people, and their chiefs, acted at the prompting of a command which, in their view, had received unquestionable authentication from Heaven. Thus warranted, the act of slaughter was, as we might say, screened from its impact upon the moral sentiments of the people. It was as when, shielded by a charm from the violence of fire, a man passes unharmed through a furnace seven times heated.

Besides this hypothesis of the supernatural, which we need in understanding the facts in view, there is to be remembered also the often-mentioned facts of the consummate abominations that had become inveterate among the Canaanitish races. This state of social putrescence—these destructive impurities, and these Moloch cruelties, were known to the invading people, and were understood by them as *the reason* of their destruction. Thus commissioned to exterminate those who could not be reformed, the work of slaughter did not unhumanize those who effected it:—that it did not the evidence is various and valid.

Distinctly looked at, under its actual conditions, the problem, so far as it affects the Israelitish people of the Exodus and the Conquest, stands clear—if not of perplexity, yet of any greater perplexity than such as hovers over every other national history, in this world of evil.

What, then, are the conditions of this same problem, considered in its upward-looking aspect, or as it is related to the rules and methods of the Divine government?

Our first step on this ground is—to reduce the problem, in *this* aspect of it, within the limits due to it. What we are concerned with is—a limited, that is to say, a Bible problem:—with the world-wide problem, affecting philosophic Theism, we are not here implicated. In this latter and more extensive sense the existence at all, and the long-continued existence, of nations so utterly degraded—so impure and cruel in their manners and in their institutions—is a far deeper mystery—it is a much more perplexing problem, than is their quick extermination, whether effected by plague, or deluge, or the sword. But then these dark depths in the human system, as they stand related to the Divine wisdom and beneficence, are not *Bible troubles:*—they are not abysses which might be filled in by throwing into them our Bibles—even millions of copies of Bibles:—after this were done they would still yawn upon us, as before. It is the disingenuous practice—or call it *artifice*—of a certain class of writers to throw the burden of world-wide mysteries upon the Bible, upon which, in truth, they take no bearing.

The dark colour of the problem—whether considered

in its widest import, or in its speciality, as related to the Biblical question now in view—has been derived from modern modes of feeling; and these are the fruit of Christianity itself. No such mystery troubled the meditations of philosophers who looked complacently upon the trains of wretches that graced the triumphs of Roman generals; and who relished the gladiatorial massacres of the amphitheatre. It is neither the philosophy nor the poetry of classic civilization that has schooled the modern mind in its mood of humanity. It is Bible reading that has done this: it is our Christian sensitiveness—out of which Infidelity has stolen an advantage—that converts a misunderstanding of those remote transactions into a sore trial of our faith in Scripture. Christian sensitiveness, which we should not wish to see blunted, together with a misapprehension of the facts, has conjoined itself with the besetting error of all religious speculation—namely, the framing of some hypothesis concerning the Divine motives which is *wholly gratuitous* and *unwarrantable.*

It has been on the ground of some hypothesis of this order—gratuitous and unwarrantable, that the thoughtful of every age have made for themselves infinite trouble, and great sorrow of heart. It has been thus that the large economy of the animal creation, and its stern realities, have driven many on toward the belief of an Evil Principle—the creator of the carnivora! And thus that we gloomily muse upon the course of events when these are signally disastrous; and thus that we find occasions of offence in Biblical history. To a great extent also we are governed, or rather we are tyrannized over, by the variable intensity of feelings which so often go beyond all reason in relation to the events of every day; as, for instance—It is with ungovernable anguish that we stand spectators of the foundering of an emigrant ship:—five hundred souls on board—men, women, children,—lost within a cable's length of the shore!—a shifting of the gale—one point—would have sufficed for bringing all safe into port! It is on an occasion of this sort that our religious impulses are liable to a dangerous strain, and we passionately ask—Why was this calamity permitted? Our only conclusion—which indeed brings with it very little abatement of our distress—is the theologic apophthegm—The ways of God are inscrutable. Yes, they are so; nevertheless, knowing that they are so, we have given place to an hypothesis concerning the Divine attributes which rests upon no authentic ground whatever. As if to bring before us the incoherence of our own modes of thinking, it happens that, the very next day after the shipwreck, we read listlessly the report of the Public Health; and find there the statement—that "fevers of the typhoid class, as well as scarlatina, have prevailed during the last few weeks in crowded districts, and have been fatal in as many as fifteen hundred cases." For the difference in the intensity or violence of our emotions in these two instances we can give no very satisfactory account; and yet it is the lesser woe that stirs the depths of religious meditation; while the greater woe barely moves thought at all. The difference has much more to do with scenic effect, than either with reason or piety.

Thought of *strictly*—in their theistic import, it is not the destruction of the cities of the plain of Sodom, nor the overthrow of hundreds of cities since then by earthquake, nor deluges extending over kingdoms, nor the prevalence of plagues, nor famines, nor the extermination of races by the sword, that in any way touches the theology of the Bible. These catastrophes—these miseries—fatal to millions of men, are all of them dark items in a catalogue for the contents of which no philosophy has hitherto furnished any explication, and for the explication of which Holy Scripture was not given, and will not avail.

It is but few persons, even among the educated, who have so trained themselves in the management of their own minds as to be able—unless it be for a moment—to take up a subject in which elements are commingled, and to sunder these elements, and to hold them apart, and, as in this instance is requisite, to think temperately, and *separately* of what belongs to the *human*, or *humanity* side of it, and of what is proper to its theistic aspect. This, therefore, must be our conclusion, as to sensitive and imperfectly disciplined Christian people—thoughtful and feeling as they are:—the blood-stained page of Hebrew history must continue to give pain in the perusal. Disciplined Christian minds, while perusing such narratives—wherever they may be found—will read them with *pain*, but not with *perplexity*; or with no more perplexity than that which surrounds far larger and deeper questions, and which sheds upon all an impenetrable gloom.

It is enough for our present purpose—and our intention in giving any prominence to the subject is completed—when we take with us, as unquestionable, the fact that the Israelite of those remote times was one whose religious beliefs, and whose modes of feeling, and whose social habitudes, were such as to place him far in advance of any among his contemporaries, or even of the men of much later times.

CHAPTER VIII.

POETRY IN THE BOOK OF JOB.

Nothing that is proper to the textual or the historic criticism of this book, or of any other canonical book, concerns us in relation to our subject in these pages; and we have to do with it only so far as we find therein what is illustrative of our immediate purpose. Undoubtingly we accept the claim of this book to a high antiquity; and moreover fully admit the historic reality of the persons, as well as the canonical validity of this portion of the Hebrew Scriptures.

Apart from the proper criticisms, philological and historical, which should determine the date of the composition, and the chronology of the events, and their reality, every reader who is not prepossessed on the other side finds himself carried back by the archaic majesty of the style, and by the breadth of the ground it occupies (as compared with the more strictly *national* style of the Prophets) to an age as early, at least, as that of the Israelitish settlement in Palestine. Everything in this Book shows its remoteness from the Mosaic ritualistic institutions, and from Israelitish modes of life. If, indeed, contemporaneous with those times, the usages it refers to, and the habits of thought it indicates, are wholly of another order. Nor is this all. The purpose and purport of the Book of Job is—the working out, and the bringing to an issue, a great problem of the moral system, on that ground which the patriarchal dispensation occupied, and from which the Mosaic institutions moved away, for admitting what was peculiar to a more limited economy. The patriarchal ground had been measured off with a longer radius, which swept a more comprehensive field; and within this more ample circuit there was room for the agitation of questions which, within the straiter Mosaic enclosure, had met their determination in a more formal manner, that is to say, in the mode of *decisions by authority.* Within the range of those of the Hebrew Scriptures that follow on from the Mosaic institutes, and that recognize the national law, there do not occur any open debatings of universal moral problems; for every theological, and every ethical principle is assumed as granted, or is taken up as having been already determined.

It is quite otherwise in the Book of Job, which takes its place on a free field. The ground assumed is the patriarchal ground of earthly well-being, and the principle taken for granted is that of a visible administration of human affairs, under the eye and sovereign control of the Righteous and Benign ALMIGHTY;—He who is unchangeable, just, and wise, and good, notes the ways of men—He follows the wicked with rebukes, and He rewards and blesses the good. But yet, in the actual course of events, this principle meets many apparent contradictions. Hence those perplexities which in every age distress thoughtful minds. How shall these instances of contrariety be so disposed of as shall save the faith and the hope of the servants of God? Here, then, is the purport of the Book: this the problem that is worked out in the arguments of the speakers, and in the conclusion of the history; it is indeed glanced at often in the Prophetic writings, and in several of the Psalms—the Seventy-third especially; but nowhere else is it formally debated, and brought to an issue.*

The argument of the Book of Job bears—we say—upon the visible administration of the Divine government, as related to the earthly well-being of those who fear and serve God. Little or nothing within its compass touches the inner life, or opens to view the experiences of those who are under training for a more intimate communion with God—the Father of spirits—and who freely court a discipline the intention of which goes quite beyond the range of terrestrial rewards and punishments. Here is the contrast between the Book of Job and many of the Psalms:—the order of Thought in the one is broad and ostensible; in the other it is of a more refined species:—it is more intense, it is more peculiar, it is more full-souled;—in a word—it is more *spiritual;* and we use this sacred term *never* in the modern mode of an affected accommodation; but in its proper, and its Biblical sense.

Inasmuch, then, as the ground occupied by the disputants in the Book of Job is of wider circuit than that whereupon the Israelitish Prophets take their stand, it might seem probable that, in availing themselves as they do of the figurative style, and in uttering themselves after the fashion of poets, they should also use a discursive liberty in which, as we have said, the Prophets of Israel do not indulge. But it is not so;—or it is so very partially, in the speeches and the rejoinders of Job and his three friends, or of their young reprover,

* See Note.

Elihu. These all *use* the poetic diction; yet only as a means adapted to their purpose. But then, for bringing the argument to its close, and for winding up the history in accordance with its intention, ANOTHER SPEAKER comes in—"Then the Lord answered Job out of the whirlwind," and asks—"Who is this that darkeneth counsel by words without knowledge?"

Where shall we find the grandeur of Poetry, where s majesty in language, where is boldness, fire, or descriptive force, if not in these four closing chapters of this Book? Strictly metrical in structure are these passages:—antithesis and apposition prevail throughout. Metaphoric in language—in single terms, and in combinations of phases are they throughout: thus far these compositions are in accordance with the usages of the Hebrew prophetic Scriptures; but here the resemblance fails, and the dissimilarity on other grounds is so extreme as to carry with it, or rather to force upon our notice, a *principle* which has been once and again referred to in these pages, and which should receive attention as explicative of the Spirit of the Hebrew Poetry.

Throughout the Prophetic writings allusions to the material world—the visible creation—are frequent, and they are always bold, forceful, and apt; yet they are brief, and they are, as we might say—*cursive*—the prophet hastens forward—he lingers never: the allusion, when it has subserved its purpose, is dismissed. But in these closing passages of the Book of Job, albeit a religious and a moral *intention* is kept in view, it is held in abeyance till the end; or it is left as an inference which the hearer is required to gather up for himself, and this inference, or this intention, gives a foremost place to the material subject: it is as if the visible natural object might, in its own right, challenge *principal attention*—as if it might, by itself, and irrespectively of every moral purpose in relation to the argument, be worthily retained in view, and be turned about descriptively, and be looked at on every side. The things spoken of stand in front:—the religious purpose—the doctrine—is to be sought for after.

In these notable passages it is the LORD—the CREATOR—that speaks of, and that commends, the works of His hands; and it is those of them He commends—and it is for such of their qualities—as least comport with modes of feeling that are characteristic of religiously meditative minds: these passages are not of the fine or sentimental order:—they give a bold contradiction to those oriental dreams which made the animal creation an occasion of offence to the languid, oriental devotee; and then their accordance is to be noted with those juster views of the economy of the animal system which modern science has lately brought itself to approve. In a repeated perusal of these free and vigorous descriptions—mainly of animal life as they are—one feels to have reached high ground, and to have left below the region of those delicate surmisings and those melancholic refinements that float about over the ague-levels of an over-wrought sensitiveness. We are here called out from the cloister and the cell, and are summoned abroad:—at this invitation we take an upward path—we breathe a pure air, and rejoice in sunshine. We are challenged to look far and wide over a prospect in the sight of which—at some moment far back in the remoteness of ages—"The morning stars sang together, and all the sons of God shouted for joy."

Is the Creation itself, is this material organization—

class balanced against class as it is—welfare pledged against welfare—constituting a vast antagonism for life —is it such as the tender-spirited among us would have made it? It is not such:—a robust reason, and a large acquaintance with the conditions and the structure of animal and vegetable life, and a knowledge, too, of the remote dependence of orders upon orders, are here required; and of this sort must be our seasoning if we would gain a right apprehension of the theology of the material world. Thoughtful and delicately-constituted minds need to be *acclimated* in the world of animal life before they can attain a healthful intelligence of the things around them. Let us be understood now, as always, to speak with reverence, and to keep in remembrance what we profess undoubtedly to believe. With this caution then premised, we say that, in these signal passages of this book—regarded now as human utterances—there is as much of a bold and fearless Reason, as there is of the fire and magnificence of Poetry. The pictorial vigour of these descriptions may perhaps have hidden from our view that healthful force in the treatment of subjects of this class which gives these passages their prominence in relation to other contemporary modes of thought, elsewhere occurring. Not of the Brahminical mintage are these descriptions; not of the Gnostic; not of the Manichæan; and assuredly they are of older stamp and hue than were those instincts of the Israelite which had become to him a second nature, and which were the product of the Mosaic distinctions of the "clean and the unclean." Free from trammels of every sort are these portraitures of behemoth, and the unicorn, and of leviathan, and of the ostrich, and of the wild ass, and of the war-horse. No way are they *nice:*

—they are in the very manner of the creative energy itself, such as we see it. If we do not relish these descriptions, it must be because we distaste also the creation; it must be because the crocodile and cayman, the boa-constrictor, and the vulture, and the hyæna, and the parasitical orders, are not what we would have made them:—it must be because the revelations of the microscope upturn our indoor-made theologies.

Inasmuch as these animal portraits overleap in chronology the wrong theories and the national and temporary prejudices of antiquity, and seem to comport better with modern scientific conceptions of the material system, so—and in a very striking manner—do the exordial portions of the same take on to our modern geology:—they do so in breadth or grasp of handling—in freedom of conception; and especially in that looking back to the morning time of the universe which it has been the work of recent science to school us in. These utterances are in the mode of a personal consciousness that is older than the material framework of the creation:—they sound like the Creator's recollections of an eternity past! If they contain no definite anticipations of the results of modern science, they are marvellously exempt from any approximate error, akin to the misapprehensions of later times. It is as if He who framed the world out of nothing would speak of His work to a certain limit, and not beyond it;—the truth is uttered; but not the whole truth.

The same style which bespeaks a personal consciousness, older than the material world, appears again as the mode proper to a consciousness that is as wide as the universe of stars. It is here as if the recollections of an era earlier than stellar time had brought with them the sociated thought of the clustered glories of constellaions that are infinitely remote; and thence, spanning the skies—of another, and another, and yet another, of the million groups of flaming worlds. Quick is this transit from era to era of eternity; and quick is this transit from side to side of the celestial infinitude; and quick again is the descent thence to earth, whereupon Man is to be taught that which concerns himself—his place, and his welfare!

CHAPTER IX.

POETRY IN THE PSALMS.

Neither the authorship of the Psalms—singly, nor their date—singly, comes within the limits of our subject; nor indeed, as already said, does any matter that is proper to textual criticism (unless it be incidentally) or to theological interpretation belong to our task. We are to find in these compositions—the poetical element, and are to note the conditions which attach to it, where we find it. For securing these purposes it seems needful to distribute them into classes—clearly distinguishable as most of them are, on the ground of their style, their purport, and their apparent intention.

The most obviously distinctive of these classes comprises those—they are of greater length than others—which recite the Hebrew history in its earlier acts and incidents; and which, if regarded on the ground of ordinary national poetry, are remarkable for their manifest tendency to break down, or even to mortify, the national pride, and to keep the people in mind of their often-repeated defections and apostacies. Of this sort especially, and which may be named as a sample of this class, is the 106th Psalm. The recital of national offences begins with the penitential profession—"We have sinned with our fathers, we have committed iniquity, we have done wickedly;" and its concluding stanzas (v. 40—48) suggest the supposition—apart from any critical reasons—that this ode was of a late date—probably as late as the return of the people from Babylon. The *reflective* tone of this summary of national history gives the impression of a retrospect, from a point of view the most remote from the times spoken of. A congregational Psalm it manifestly is:—it supposes, in the people, a now-matured religious feeling, abhorrent of idol-worship, and at length so thoroughly weaned from errors of that kind, as to treat them contemptuously. A Psalm of feeling and sentiment it is, metrical, but not poetical.

Seventeen of the Psalms* may be classed together under this designation—as recitals of the national history, this being regarded always in its religious aspect, and always more for purposes of penitential humiliation than of glorification. And we note in all of them the absolute avoidance of certain elements which, in national odes intended for popular use on festive occasions, is a circumstance full of significance. These wanting elements are what might promote sacerdotal, or rather, hierarchical aggrandisement:—the despotic, and also the heroic style, or the idolization of the ancient warriors and sages of the nation. In the loftiest and the purest sense these odes are theistic; and so they are, whether the times be bright or dark. Look to the 44th Psalm, and to the 46th, which breathe the sublimity of a tranquil faith, rising above the storms of earth. The return of the soul is ever to its resting-place, as in Ps. 60: "Give us help from trouble: for vain is the help of man." The 68th Psalm—if now we might imagine

* These seventeen Psalms, are Pss. 44, 46, 60, 68, 74, 75, 76, 78, 79, 80, 81, 83, 85, 105, 106, 126, 137.

the scenes, the sounds, and the circumstances, when, under management of "the chief musician," the courts of the temple shook with its chorus, and the "great congregation," keeping holiday, joined their voices with the ministers around the altar, we should have, in sounds, in feeling, all that poetry and music combines, and the depths of religious awe have ever done, or might ever do, to exalt the spirit of man; and to carry popular emotion to the highest pitch. No wonder that, in recollection of seasons such as these, the exiled wanderer in the wilderness should think "the tabernacles of God amiable," or that he should expend sighs in terms like these—"My soul longeth, yea even fainteth for the courts of the Lord: my heart and my flesh crieth out for the living God."—"A day in thy courts is better than a thousand"—spent in pavilions of luxury.

No spot on earth was there then—none has there been since—that might claim comparison with that "Hill of the Lord" whereupon, under the blue vault of heaven, these national anthems were performed, and took effect with every aid of a *composite* musical system—with the harmony of instruments and voices—with the popular acclamation—with the visible adornments of the temple and its awful sacrificial rites. In our dull perfunctory recitations of these anthems of the Hebrew nation we quite fail to estimate what was their power, their majesty, and beauty, when and where they got utterance at the first. Nor can it be within the chill gloom of our Gothic cathedrals—let modern music and the organ do its best—that an idea can be formed of the commingled sublimities of that ancient worship—true in its theology—perfect in its metrical and its musical expressions—lofty, and yet reverential in its tone—humanising in its sentiments, and withal indigenous—*homefelt*—national—near to the heart and recollections of the worshippers:—a worship homogeneous, and which was especially in accordance with every belief and every sentiment of that age, and of that people. There is more in this last condition than we may have been used to suppose. Turn now for a moment to this 68th Psalm.

Frigid, narrow, *unrealizing* is that exceptive criticism which fails to see and to feel the divine majesty—the super-human truth and greatness of that worship of which, in this instance, we have a sample. Along with these ascriptions of majesty, power, goodness, to God—the God of Israel—there are those pieties of the affections of which no instances whatever are extant anywhere—out of the circuit of the Hebrew Scriptures. God is "a Father of the fatherless, and a judge of the widows"—who also "setteth the solitary in families, and bringeth out those which are bound in chains." Verse, linked in with verse, are the images of power and majesty, wrought into one mass with ideas of beneficence and of mercy.

The chariots of God—twenty thousand-thousands of angels.
The Lord is among them (as in) Sinai, in the Holy.
Thou hast ascended on high—
Leading captivity captive:
Thou hast received gifts for men;
Yea the rebellious also, that the Lord God might dwell (among them.)

But now, in our modern recitations of this anthem, and of others of the same order, the flow of feeling is checked by the occurrence of expressions that run counter to, or that go far beyond, the range of our christianized sentiments. So it is here at the very start—"Let God arise, let his enemies be scattered." And afterwards—"The Lord shall bring his people from the depths of the sea—that thy foot may be dipped in the blood of thine enemies; and the tongue of thy dogs in the same. Undoubtedly we stay the course of our sympathies at points such as these! It could only be at rare moments of national anguish and deliverance that expressions of *this* order could be assimilated with modern feelings. What then should be our inference? It should not be of the confused or compromising sort —taking what we approve—and rejecting this verse, or that verse; nor should our inference be timid and pusillanimous, as if we were careful to shun some apprehended ill consequence; our inference should not be drawn from a theology which is *hypothetic*—which is a mixture of our own abstract notions, with Christian principles. These war-energies of the Hebrew mind, in a past time, were *proper* to the people, and to the age; and would continue to be so until that revolution in religious feeling had been brought about which, in abating *national* enthusiasm, and in bringing immortality into the place of earthly welfare, gave a wholly new direction to every element of the moral system. Difficult indeed it may be—perhaps it is quite impossible—for the modern mind, with its training, which has become to it a second nature, to go back to that "Hill of God," and to join in the loud acclamations of the people. Yet if we *could* do so, we should doubtless find that the battle-force of parts in the national worship did not in any way make discord with the loftiest and the purest religious emotions. We of this time are so schooled in amenities, we are so softened and sublimed, that a determined effort, which few of us can make, is needed for carrying us back to the place and era of these anthems—full as they are of power, as well as of piety. Always is the martial mood tempered with humiliating recollections of national sins:—never is it exalted by any flattery of chiefs or kings:—never does this martial force seek to enhance itself (as has been its tendency always among other people) by ambitious vauntings of conquests meditated—even for the spread of truth: the conversion of the heathen is never connected with conquests to be effected by the sword. Mahomet and his caliphs could find nothing in these anthems that would be available for the purposes of Islam.

The intention of these national and historical poems, and their tone and spirit, are well seen in the 78th Psalm. The intention was—the religious education of the people, from the earliest childhood upward: the tone and spirit are such as could not fail to form the Hebrew mind to greatness, to depth and soberness of feeling, and to a profound consciousness of that Providential Government which fitted the people for other and higher purposes than those of national aggrandisement. This metrical summary of the people's history —majestic in its imagery, and musical (even in a translation) and so poised in its couplets and triplets as that little of change would be needed for bringing it under the conditions of rhythm, in any translation—would, in its own Hebrew, and to the Hebrew ear, commend itself at once as poetry, as music, and as devout sentiment. Such was its purpose. The wonders of the Divine Government from the remotest times were to be fixed in the memory of children's children to the end of time.

> Showing to the generations to come the praises of the Lord,
> And his strength and his wonderful works that he hath done.

These—thus trained, should in their turn teach them to—

> The children which should be born;
> Who should arise, and declare them to their children:
> That they might set their hope in God,
> And not forget the works of God,
> But keep his commandments.

The recitations that follow have all the same purport; they are *as from God*—a remonstrance—a rebuke; and yet such as gave assurance always to the contrite and obedient. If this poem be taken as an inauguration of the monarchy under David, then should we not note the archaic majesty, and the modesty of its closing verses? The enemies of Israel had been discomfited, and put "to a perpetual reproach"—the monarchy was now established upon Zion—the city was adorned with palaces and strengthened with bulwarks, and thus peace was established by the arm, and under the rule of this David, whom God had chosen:—his servant, whom he had taken

> —— from the sheepfolds;
> From following the ewes, great with young,
> He brought him to feed Jacob his people,
> And Israel his inheritance.
> So he fed them according to the integrity of his heart;
> And guided them by the skilfulness of his hands.

It was the warrior David whose own arm had been the instrument of the victories which at length had given rest to the people, and had confirmed them in their hitherto precarious occupation of the land assigned them. To the Poet-king this composition is attributed; and if rightly so, then had he himself learned a religious humility which few indeed of his class—high-born or low-born—have understood. But if there were reasons for assigning this Psalm to a bard of a later time (not that any such reasons are pretended) then this avoidance of the magnifying of a people's ancient heroes is the more noticeable, for it is an abstinence which, as it has no parallels in other national poetry, so does it find its explication only on that ground where the history of this one people can be exempt from contradictions—which is the ground of its supernatural attestations.

Distinguishable from the above-mentioned are those of the Psalms—they may be reckoned as twenty*—which, looking at them apart from the guidance (if indeed it be guidance) of textual criticism, declare their own intention as anthems, adapted for that public worship which was the glory and delight of the Hebrew people;—a worship carrying with it the soul of the multitude by its simple majesty, and by the powers of music, brought, in their utmost force, to recommend the devotions of earth in the hearing of Heaven. Take the last of the Psalms as a sample of this class, and bring the spectacle and the sounds into one, for the imagination to rest in. It was evidently to subserve the purposes of *music* that these thirteen verses are put together: it was, no doubt, to give effect first to the human voice, and then, to the alternations of instruments—loud, and tender, and gay, with the graceful

* The Psalms here referred to are these—24, 47, 48, 87, 95, 96, 97, 98, 99, 100, 103, 114, 117, 118, 122, 132, 134, 148, 149, 150.

movements of the dance—that the anthem was composed, and its chorus brought out—

> Let every thing that hath breath praise the Lord:
> Praise ye the Lord!

and so did the congregated thousands take up their part with a shout—"even as the noise of many waters."

It is but feebly, and as afar off, that the ancient liturgies (except so far as they merely copied their originals) came up to the majesty and the wide compass of the Hebrew worship, such as it is indicated in the 148th Psalm. Neither Ambrose, nor Gregory, nor the Greeks, have reached or approached this level; and in tempering the boldness of their originals by admixtures of what is more Christian-like and spiritual, the added elements sustain an injury which is not compensated by what they bring forward of a purer, or a less earthly kind: feeble indeed is the tone of those anthems of the ancient Church—sophisticated or artificial is their style. Nor would it be possible—it has never yet seemed so—to Christianize the Hebrew anthems—retaining their power, their earth-like richness, and their manifold splendours—which are the very splendours, and the true riches, and the grandeur of God's world—and withal attempered with expressions that touch to the quick the warmest human sympathies. And as the enhancement of all there is the *nationality*, there is that fire which is sure to kindle fire in true human hearts—

> He showeth his word unto Jacob,
> His statutes and his judgments unto Israel.
> He hath not dealt so with any nation:
> As for his judgments they have not known them,
> Praise ye the Lord!

Nothing that mediæval Gothic has achieved—nothing that modern music has effected, can be sufficient for carrying the modern worshipper back to that place and age where and when these anthems "made glad the city of the Great King." As to the powers of Sacred Poetry, those powers were expanded to the full, and were quite expended too by the Hebrew bards. What are modern hymns but so many laborious attempts to put in a new form, that which, as it was done in the very best manner so many ages ago, can never be well done again—otherwise than in the way of a verbal repetition.

About thirty-three Psalms might be brought together, forming a class of odes which, although many or most of them probably, took their turn in the responsive services of the Temple, are less conspicuously liturgical, and have for their principal subject the attributes of God—His wonders of power in the creation—His providence and bounty, and His righteous government of mankind.* As samples of this class we might take the 8th Psalm, and the 19th, the 29th, the 50th, the 65th, the 90th, and the 91st. In truth a selection of specimens of this class is not easily made, for every one of those named below might well stand as a representative of the others.

With these brilliant poems before us, let us imagine the thirty-three, or we might now add to them the twenty anthems of public worship already named—fifty-three odes and anthems—printed by themselves, without note, comment, or any other literary or histori-

* These Psalms of Adoration are the following:—8, 18, 19, 20, 29, 33, 34, 49, 50, 65, 66, 67, 82, 86, 89, 90, 91, 92. 93, 104, 107, 111, 112, 113, 115, 121, 123, 125, 135, 136, 145, 146, 147.

cal information connected with them, save this only—that in some mode of indubitable transmission, these compositions had come into our hands from a remote antiquity, and that they were *the only extant remains* of a people, long since scattered and perished, concerning whose fortunes, institutions, beliefs, manners, we could know nothing more than what might be gathered from the remains now in view. The reader who will give himself the pains to do so, must put far from his thoughts the entire mass of his Bible beliefs—all his recollections of the pulpit, and the desk, and of controversies, and of his own conclusions—thereto related—whether they be orthodox or heterodox. Thus stripped of his modern self, let him read the 65th Psalm, and let him open his heart, and mind too, to admit—the largeness of its intention—the width of its look-out upon the world—the justness of its theism—if indeed a Creator is acknowledged, and if the Creator be good also—the warmth of its piety, and the gladsomeness of its temper, and the landscape freshness of its images; and withal the preparation which is made in its exordium for the outpourings of a grateful piety, by the open confession of sin, and the deep consciousness of it as the reason of the Divine displeasure. This ode supposes—it *connotes*—an instituted congregational worship—a temple, a liturgy, and a teaching!

What then were these people—what their theology—what their ethics—what their history? How can it have come about, or why, under the Providential Government of the world, that a people which was thus highly instructed—was thus immeasurably advanced beyond any others of antiquity—should have fallen from their position, and have disappeared from the muster-roll of the nations—leaving no monuments of themselves—these odes only excepted, which have drifted down upon the deluge-surface of human affairs? In its attempts to answer these, and such like questions, speculation might wander far, and find no conclusion; but whatever might be our surmises, as to the catastrophes of such a people, or their apostacies, or the gradual decay among them of their pristine virtue, nothing could destroy the evidence which is here in our own hands, to this effect, that—on some spot on earth, and in some remote age, there was once a people fully possessed of the highest truths, and so possessed of these truths as to have assimilated them with its moral sentiments, and with its tastes also; for its perceptions toward the visible world were alive to whatever is beautiful therein.

If such a perusal—if such a *digestion* of this one ode brings into view, with the vividness of vision, this lost theistic nation—then go on to peruse the other fifty of this collection; for these, in their different modes, will give evidence touching each leading principle of what we admit to be a true theology, and a true belief concerning the Creative Power, and a true belief in Providence, and the righteous government, and gracious administration of that Providence toward mankind, who are dealt with in their weakness, and their failings, and their sins. Vivid as these poems are, and full of force, and of feeling, and abounding as they do in allusions to the things of the time, it is not credible that they are mere inventions, which had no archetypes in the mind and usages of a people. This may not be thought. It is certain then that there has once been a people among the nations—there has been one among the millions of the worshippers of stocks—there has been one people—taught of God.

The 90th Psalm might be cited as perhaps the most sublime of human compositions—the deepest in feeling—the loftiest in theologic conception—the most magnificent in its imagery. True is it in its report of human life—as troubled, transitory, and sinful. True in its conception of the Eternal—the Sovereign and the Judge; and yet the refuge and hope of men, who, notwithstanding the most severe trials of their faith, lose not their confidence in Him; but who, in the firmness of faith—pray for, as if they were predicting, a near-at-hand season of refreshment. Wrapped, one might say—in mystery, until the distant day of revelation should come, there is here conveyed the doctrine of Immortality; for in this very plaint of the brevity of the life of man, and of the sadness of these, his few years of trouble, and their brevity, and their gloom, there is brought into contrast, the Divine immutability; and yet it is in terms of a submissive piety: the thought of a life eternal is here in embryo. No taint is there in this Psalm of the pride and petulance—the half-uttered blasphemy—the malign disputing or arraignment of the justice or goodness of God, which have so often shed a venomous colour upon the language of those who have writhed in anguish, personal or relative. There are few probably among those who have passed through times of bitter and distracting woe, or who have stood—the helpless spectators of the miseries of others, that have not fallen into moods of mind violently in contrast with the devout and hopeful melancholy which breathes throughout this ode. Rightly attributed to the Hebrew Lawgiver or not, it bespeaks its remote antiquity, not merely by the majestic simplicity of its style, but negatively, by the entire avoidance of those sophisticated turns of thought which belong to a late—a lost age in a people's intellectual and moral history. This Psalm, undoubtedly, is centuries older than the moralizings of that time when the Jewish mind had listened to what it could never bring into a true assimilation with its own mind—the abstractions of the Greek Philosophy.

With this one Psalm only in view—if it were required of us to say, in brief, what we mean by the phrase—"The Spirit of the Hebrew Poetry"—we find our answer well condensed in this sample. This magnificent composition gives evidence, not merely as to the mental qualities of the writer, but as to the tastes and habitudes of the writer's contemporaries, his hearers, and his readers; on these several points—*first*, the free and customary command of a poetic diction, and its facile imagery; so that whatever the poetic soul would utter, the poet's material is near at hand for his use. There is then that depth of feeling—mournful, reflective, and yet hopeful and trustful, apart from which poetry can win for itself no higher esteem than what we bestow upon other decorative arts, which minister to the demands of luxurious sloth. There is, moreover, as we might say, underlying this Poem, from the first line to the last, the substance of philosophic thought, apart from which, expressed or understood, Poetry is frivolous, and is not in harmony with the seriousness of human life: this Psalm is of a sort which Plato would have written, or Sophocles—if only the one or the other of these minds had possessed a heaven-descended Theology.

This, then, is our conclusion.—The Hebrew writers as Poets—such a writer as was the author of this Psalm

—were masters of all the means and the resources, the powers and the stores, of the loftiest poetry; but the *spirit* of this poetry is, with them always, its instrumentality—its absolute subordination and subserviency to a far loftier purpose than that which ever animates human genius.

There is a small number of the Psalms, eleven only,* of which Psalms 37 and 73 might be named as samples. The tone of these odes is meditative and ethical: they represent those balancing thoughts by aid of which the pious, in comparing their own lot, such as often it is, with the lot of the ungodly, or with the outside show of that lot, bring their mind to an even balance, and restore its hopeful confidence in the Divine favour. These Psalms are metrical, indeed, but they are not poetical; although the terms employed are all figurative, and are some of them resplendent with a mild radiance, as pictures of earthly well-being under the favour of God, and, as to their domestic quality, they are peculiarly characteristic of the Hebrew social feeling, which was at once domestic—national—pacific.

> Behold, how good and pleasant (*it is*)
> For brethren to dwell together in unity.

As if in rebuke of the turmoil, and the ambition, and the greediness of city life, the Hebrew bard commends rather the quiet enjoyments of the *home* life, and especially if home life be rural life also.

> Vain for you to rise up early, to sit up late,
> To eat the bread of sorrows:
> So he giveth his beloved sleep.
> Lo, children are (*the*) heritage of the Lord:

* These Psalms are—1, 15, 37, 53, 62, 73, 101, 127, 128, 133, 139.

The fruit of the womb (*his*) reward,
As arrows in the hand of a mighty man,
So are sons of the youth (*sons of early married life*).
Happy is the man that hath his quiver full of them.
They shall not be ashamed,
But they shall speak with the enemies in the gate.

There are here combined several elements of the Hebrew life, and more so still in the Psalm following—a song of degrees—a song in the chanting of which the fatigues of the annual journeyings to the House of the Lord were soothed.

Happy is every one that feareth the Lord:
That walks in His ways:
The labour of thy hands thou shalt eat:
It is well with thee—and (*shall be*) well with thee:
Thy wife is a fruitful vine, in the inner house:
Thy sons as olive plants round about thy table.
Behold thus shall the man be blessed,
Who fears the Lord.
The Lord will bless thee out of Zion.*
Thou shalt see the prosperity of Jerusalem all thy days.
And see thy children's children.
Yea—peace upon Israel.

These pictures are mild and bright:—humanizing are they in the best sense:—they retain certain elements of Paradise;—and yet more, the elements of the Patriarchal era; with the addition of that patriotism, and of that concentration in which the Patriarchal life was wanting. The happy religious man, after the Hebrew pattern, possessed those feelings and habitudes which, if they greatly prevail in a community, impart to it the strength of a combination which is stronger

* The meaning of this line is found in Numbers v. 22—27

than any other, uniting the force of domestic virtue, of rural (yeoman-like) agricultural occupations, of unaggressive defensive valour, and of a religious animation which is *national*, as well as authentic and true. Our modern learning in oriental modes of life, and its circumstance and scenery, may help us to bring into view either of two gay pictures—that of the Hebrew man in mid-life, at rest in his country home, with his sturdy sons about him: his wife is still young: her fair daughters are like cornices, sculptured as decorations for a palace. Or else the companion picture, with its group on their way Zion-ward, resting, for the sultry noon-hour, under the palms by the side of a stream;—and yet home—happy home, is in the recollection of the party: but the Hill of God—"whereunto the tribes of the Lord go up"—is in the fervent purpose of all; and while they rest they beguile the time with a sacred song, and with its soothing melody. Happy were the people while their mind was such as this, and such their habits, and such their piety! and this was a piety which, along with true conceptions of God, was well used to those humbling meditations that give to the soul its calmness and its strength too—

> Lord, what is man that thou takest knowledge of him!
> The son of the dying, that thou makest account of him!
> Man—like to vanity!
> His days are as a flitting shadow!

In other Psalms of this class—as in the 73rd—the *religious doctrine* takes place of the earthly sentiment. The exceptional instance, namely, that of afflicted piety, is taken up and discussed; the sufferer narrates his own experience on this ground; and yet he premises his conclusion, that, after all, the Hebrew principle holds good; for "truly, God is good to Israel, to such as are of a clean heart." In these compositions, feeling—piety—the truth of things, prevail over poetry; nevertheless, they bring into view glimpses of modes of life upon which the modern imagination may dwell with sweet and soothing satisfaction.

The class next to be named includes many of the Psalms (thirty, or more),* and they are not easily grouped under a fitting designation which may be applicable to all of them. They are individual and personal—not congregational—not liturgical. They are expressive of those alternations of anguish, dismay, hope, trust, indignation, or even of deeper resentments, which agitate the soul of one whose lot is cast among the malignant, the cruel, the unreasonable; or, in a word, the dwellers in Mesech—the ungodly. These Psalms, or most of them, are David's own, and they are to be interpreted severally, by aid of his history, in its earlier part especially. Neither with this history, nor with the quality of the emotions that give an impassioned tone to these compositions, are we here directly concerned. Fully to realize circumstances and states of mind, such as are here brought into view, we—in these easy times—must travel far away from the secure and tranquil meadow lands of ordinary life. But there have been tens of thousands, in ages past, who have trodden the rugged heaven-ward road, and have found it to be a way, not merely thorny and flinty to the foot, but beset with terrors; for spiteful and remorseless men have couched

* The Psalms of this class are—3, 4, 5, 7, 9, 10, 11, 12, 13, 14, 17, 21, 35, 36, 41, 52, 54, 55, 56, 58, 59, 64, 77, 94, 109, 120, 124, 129, 140, 141.

beside this narrow way, and have rendered it terrible to the pilgrim:—a path of anguish and of many fears it has been. In our drowsy repetitions of these Psalms—cushioned as we are, upon the safe luxuries of modern life, we fail to understand these outcries from the martyrs' field.

> O Lord, the God of vengeance—
> O God, the God of vengeance, shine forth.
> Rise up, thou Judge of the earth;
> Recompense a reward to the proud!

Let only such times return upon us, as have been of more frequency than are these times of ease, in the history of the Church, and we should quickly know how to understand a Psalm such as the 94th. *Christian* men and women, when they are called, in like manner, to suffer, are required to pay respect to a rule of suffering which is many centuries later than the time of David, but which, although it *is* indeed a higher rule, does not bring under blame the *natural*, and the *religious* emotions that were proper to the earlier dispensation. The Christian Rule which enjoins an unresisting endurance of wrong, and a Christ-like patience, would not stand, as it does, *in bold relief* upon the ground of universal morality, if it were opposed only to those malign and revengeful emotions which prompt the persecutor. The Christian martyr's rule is declared to be an *exceptional* rule, and it bespeaks its intention, as a testimony sealed in blood, in behalf of the hope of eternal life, in this very way, that it takes position as the *antithesis*, not the *contradiction*, of those emotions which, in themselves, and apart from a peculiar purpose, are not only *natural*, but are virtuous and religious. When the

Christian martyr suffers wrong to the death—in silence, or is triumphant at the stake, it is *because* he is looking for "a better resurrection"—a crown of immortality: it is, *therefore*, and it is on this newly-opened ground, that he foregoes *rightful indignation*—that he represses the instincts of resentment—that he abstains from imprecations—that he will not, no, even in the utmost severity of anguish—on the rack or in the fire, call upon God—the God of vengeance, to render a reward to the proud and the cruel. It is in thought of the life eternal, and of the judgment to come, that the Christian martyr abstains from consoling himself in the prospect of that time when his God shall bring upon his enemies "their own iniquity, and shall cut them off in their own wickedness."

There is apt to be much misunderstanding on this ground, and a consequent confusion of thought, on the part of Christian advocates, has thrown an advantage into the hands of those whose aim it has been to impugn the morality of the Hebrew Scriptures. The subject, although incidental only to the purport of this volume, comes just now in our path, and it may claim a page. We do not interfere, at all, with what may rightfully be affirmed concerning the *predictive* import of the imprecatory Psalms; for that is a subject which belongs to the theological Biblical Commentator. In these pages we are regarding these compositions from our standing on a lower level: looked at from this point of view, then there is seen to be shed upon the field of Christian martyrdom, a splendour—full of the glories of that upper world in the triumphs of which the martyr aspires to take his part. There could be no need of *martyrdoms* for bearing a testimony against dark, foul, inhuman, sanguinary passions: inasmuch as *these* receive their proper rebuke in the conduct of the virtuous, and the pious, who admit, and who give a governed expression to rightful and religious resentments, even to those emotions of anger, and to those appeals to sovereign justice, which are true elements of human nature, and which, in fact, have in them so irresistible an energy, that they overbear all contradiction, unless it spring from motives of another order.

The slow and insensible advancement of Christian motives has brought on a transfusion of the passive *martyr doctrine* into the ethics of common life. It is thus that we have come to read what are called the Imprecatory Psalms;—and then, so reading them, we are perplexed in attempting to assimilate them to the Christian rule of non-resistance; which rule in truth, we *talk of*, more than we practise it. Human nature, in its *primary constitution*, is entirely such as these very Psalms suppose it to be; nor is this structure of the emotions to be any way reprobated;—far from it —it is God's own work. As in relation to the vindictive passions, so in relation to other forces of human nature, the Gospel comes in—on *exceptive occasions*, and supervenes their operation: with a crown imperishable in view, it bridles the energies of this present life, and asks a sacrifice of the *body* and of the soul.*

It is against the abounding impiety, cruelty, wrongfulness, falseness, craftiness of the men of his times, that the writer—or writers—of these Psalms makes his passionate, or his mournful appeal to the righteousness of Heaven. His confidence in the issue of the

* See Note.

Divine Government takes its spring, and receives its force, from the vivacity of his own emotions of disapproval and of resentment too:—the one energy, that of faith, sustains itself upon the other energy, that of natural feeling: remove or weaken the one, and then the other is enfeebled, in proportion. This balancing of the one force, by the other force, must have place, unless motives derived from a higher level were brought in to take the place, and to do the office of the *natural* emotions of resentment. For a substitution of this kind the time was not yet come:—long centuries were yet to run themselves out before this revolution was to be effected. Nevertheless, inasmuch as there was to be nothing in the later economy which had not been predictively shadowed forth in the older economy, there appears, in several of these denunciatory and vengeance fraught Psalms, a glimmer, and more than a glimmer, of that light of life which was at length to bring the servants of God into a wholly new relationship toward persecutors, and the doers of wrong. These gleams of light from a brighter world give to several of the Psalms something of the poetic tone in which otherwise they are wanting.

We may take as an instance of this anticipated Christian sentiment, an expression such as the following,—the meaning of which scarcely comes to the surface in our English version.

For (*on account of*) the oppression of the poor: for the outcry of the destitute,
Now will I arise, saith Jehovah:
I will put him in safety from him that would entrap him:
Thou shalt preserve them (*take them out from*) this generation, for the age to come (*the hidden future*).

Or more distinctly in the closing verse of the 17th Psalm. Notwithstanding the short triumph of those who have their portion in this life, the servant of God is comforted in prospect of a life future.

> As for me, I shall behold thy face in righteousness:
> I shall be content, when I awake in thy likeness.

The still clearer revelation contained in the 16th Psalm might demand distinct notice under another head. Of the same import are these verses (of Psalm 36).

> They (*the servants of God*) shall be abundantly satisfied
> With the fatness of thy House;
> And (*for*) thou shalt make them drink
> Of the river of thy pleasures.
> For with thee is the fountain of life.
> In thy light shall we see light.

To take account of those of the Psalms which have most distinctly a predictive meaning, and which are prophecies of the Messiah, would not consist, on any ground, with the intention of these pages:—a due consideration of them involves what is proper to Biblical Criticism, to Biblical Exposition, and also to Christian Theology. Among such Psalms are to be reckoned, without doubt, the second, the sixteenth, the twenty-second, the forty-fifth, the seventy-second, and the hundred and tenth.

The class which is the most numerous comprises thirty-five, or, it may be, forty Psalms.* Of this num-

* The Psalms referred to are these—6, 16, 17, 23, 25, 26, 27, 28, 30, 31, 32, 38, 39, 40, 42, 43, 51, 57, 61, 63, 69, 70, 71, 84, 88, 102, 103, 116, 119, 130, 131, 138, 141, 142, 143.

ber these might be taken as samples of the rest; namely, the forty-second Psalm, the sixty-third, and the eighty-fourth.

Several of these odes bring to view what have already been named as characteristic elements of the other classes; especially that of the often-recurrent denunciation of the wickedness of the wicked—the persecutor, and the impious man—who is the enemy of God, and of His faithful servants, as well as the despoiler of the helpless, the widow, and the fatherless. But passages of this order occupy a less conspicuous place in the Psalms now referred to, and are incidental to the principal intention of them. This principal intention is—whatever relates to individual piety, and the experiences of the spiritual life. In these devotional compositions the soul, with its own *spiritual* welfare immediately in view—its intimate emotions of love, trust, hope, humiliation, sorrow, joy—spreads itself out, as toward God, communion with whom, on terms of filial affection, is, in its esteem, a blessedness rather to be chosen than all the goods of the present life—a greater treasure is it than "thousands of gold and silver." The key to these compositions is this *settled preference* of the welfare, the health, of the soul, as compared with any worldly and sensual enjoyments. It is this fixed purpose of the heart which determines the conduct; it is this which sheds a glow upon a lot of destitution, bodily suffering, or persecution:—it is *this*, and not any expanded, or distinctly uttered hope of immortality, which sustains the wounded spirit, imparting strength and courage to the broken in heart. And it is this preference which gives its charm to the public worship of God. Witness the eighty-fourth Psalm, a better version of which than that of the English Bible is much to be desired.

The prevailing feeling—the ruling sentiment of these Psalms may be shown in sample, in passages such as this.

Many say—who will show us good?
Lord, lift thou up the light of thy countenance upon us.
Thou hast put gladness in my heart,
More than in the time their corn and their wine increased.
I will both lay me down in peace and sleep;
For thou, Lord, only makest me to dwell in safety.

Or in the impassioned utterances of the forty-second, or, still more strikingly so, in the sixty-third Psalm.

O God, thou art my God; early will I seek thee.

These two odes, by the beauty and fitness of the imagery, and the warmth and tenderness of the emotions expressed in them, stand as exceptive instances to the rule that *Poetry*, throughout the Psalms, is inversely as the *Piety* to which they give utterance: or we should say—the piety of *individual feeling*. It is otherwise with what may be called congregational, or collective piety; for the anthems already spoken of are many of them in the highest sense poetical.

There is another rule which presents itself, in looking to the verbal *structure* of these devotional Psalms—those especially which have the most decisively an individual meaning;—it is this—That the *composition* submits itself, in a more formal manner than in other instances, to metrical and arbitrary conditions—as to apposition of verses, in twos, in threes; and also, by obeying the rule of alliteration. Take the 119th Psalm as an instance. In every age has this Psalm met the requirements of individual piety: it has been a chosen portion of Scripture, to spiritually minded persons. Never wearied by its repetitions, or its apparent redundancies, each verse has given direction anew to pious meditation — each verse has supplied its aliment of devout feeling. Fraught throughout with religious feeling, and wanting, almost absolutely, in *Poetry*, it stands before us as a sample of conformity to *metrical limitations.** In the strictest sense this composition is *conditioned;* nevertheless, in the highest sense is it an utterance of the spiritual life; and in thus finding these seemingly opposed elements intimately commingled, as they are, throughout this Psalm, a lesson full of meaning is silently conveyed to those who will receive it— that the conveyance of the things of God to the human spirit is in no way damaged or impeded, much less is it *deflected* or *vitiated*, by its subjugation to those modes of utterance which most of all bespeak their adaptation to the infirmity and the childlike capacity of the recipient.

This same 119th Psalm opens also a subject which might well engage careful consideration. Some of the Psalms just above referred to contain allusions, not obscure, to that better world—that "more enduring substance"—that "inheritance unfailing," upon which the pious in all times have kept the eye of faith steadily fixed. But now in all the 176 couplets of this Psalm there are not more than two or three phrases, and these of ambiguous meaning, which can be understood as having reference to the future life, and its blessedness;

* See Note.

and so it is in other Psalms of this same class. One such expression, susceptible of an extended meaning, there is in the 23d Psalm: none in the 25th, nor in the 30th, where it might naturally be looked for, nor in the 32d, the 42d, the 63d, the 84th, the 103d; and these are the Psalms which might be singled out from the class they belong to, as samples of the deepest utterings, the most intense yearnings, of individual devotion—the loving communion of the soul with God. Can any explanation be given of this apparent defectiveness, in the instances adduced, which seem to demand the very element that is *not* found in them?

We are not called to seek for an explication of this difficulty among groundless conjectures concerning what might be the Divine intention, in thus holding back from these devotional odes the element which might seem the most eminently proper to find a place among them: what we have before us is the incontestable fact, that these Psalms—and these by preference—have actually fed the piety of the pious—have sufficed for giving utterance to the deepest and most animated religious emotions, throughout all time, since their first promulgation; and it has been as much so since the time of the Christian announcement of immortality, as before it; we might say, much more so. During all these ages, these many generations of men who have sought and found their happiness in communion with God, there has been in use, *by the Divine appointment, a liturgy of the individual spiritual life*, which, abstinent of the excitements of immortal hope—unmindful of, almost, as if ignorant of, the bright future, takes its circuit, and finds its occasions, in and among the sad and changeful and transient experiences of the present life. Here is before us a daily ritual of fervent, impassioned devotion, which, far from being of an abstracted or mystical sort, is acutely sensitive towards all things of the passing moment. This metrical service of daily prayer, praise, intercession, trust, hope, contrition, revolves within the circle of the every-day pains, fears, and solaces, of the religious man's earthly pilgrimage. Pilgrimage it is, for the devout man calls himself "a stranger, a sojourner on earth;" and yet the land whereunto he is tending does not in any such manner fill a place in his thoughts, as that it should find a place in the language of his devotions!

What is the inference that is properly derivable from these facts? Is it not this, that the training or *discipline* of the soul in the spiritual life—the forming and the strengthening of those habits of trust, confidence, love, penitence, which are the preparations of the soul for its futurity in a brighter world—demands a concentration of the affections upon the Infinite Excellence —undisturbed by objects of another order? If this be a proper conclusion, then we find in it a correspondent principle in the abstinence, throughout the Christian Scriptures, of descriptive exhibitions of the "inheritance" that is promised. The eternal life is indeed authentically propounded; but the promise is not opened out in any such manner as shall make meditation upon it easy. Pious earnestness presses forward on a path that is well assured; but on this path the imagination is not invited to follow. The same purpose here again presents itself to notice—a purpose of *culture*, not of excitement.

There can be little risk of error in affirming that the New Testament itself furnishes no liturgy of devotion, for this reason that a liturgy, divinely originated, had already been granted to the universal Church; and it was such in its subjects, and in its tone, and in its modes of expression, as fully to satisfy its destined purposes. Devout spirits, from age to age of these later times, since "light and immortality were brought to light," have known how to blend with the liturgy of David the promises of Christ: these latter distinguished from those long before granted to Patriarchs and Prophets, more by their authoritative style, and their explicit brevity, than by any amplifications which might satisfy religious curiosity.

CHAPTER X.

SOLOMON, AND THE SONG OF SONGS.

In search, as we now are, of the *Poetry* of the Hebrew writings, and of that only, two inferences are unquestionable—namely, first, that on *this* ground the "Song of Songs" possesses a very peculiar claim to be spoken of; and secondly, that, inasmuch as the alleged religious or spiritual meaning of these beautiful idyls must be made to rest upon considerations quite foreign to any indications of such a meaning, found in themselves, we might abstain from taking any note of this—their superinduced spiritual significance. We might stand excused from asking any questions thereto relating; nor need we perplex ourselves with difficulties therewith connected; and might think ourselves free to abstain from any expression of opinion upon a question which belongs so entirely to the theological expositor. Yet, although it be so, there may be reasons sufficient for adverting to this very instance—quite peculiar as it is, and illustrative as it is, of what was affirmed at the outset, concerning the relation of the Divine element toward the human element in the canonical Scriptures.

Just now we are proposing to look at these eclogues as remarkable samples of the poetry of the Hebrews, in this class;—and in no other light.

By themselves they deserve to be considered on the

ground of their striking unlikeness to the mass of the Hebrew literature;—one other book of the Canon—the book of Esther, stands on the same ground of negative theistic import. In neither of these compositions does the Divine Name so much as once occur: in neither of them does there occur a single religious or spiritual sentiment of any kind:—the one—so far as appears on the surface of it—is as purely amatory, as the other is purely national—Jewish—political. Yet this absence of the religious element is not the only, nor, indeed, is it the *principal* distinction which sets the Canticles *in contrast* with the other constituents of the Old Testament. These all, as we have already said (Chapter II.) exhibit a religious intention, which is so constant, and is of such force, as to prevail over what might have been the impulses of the individual writer's genius. Poet as he may be by constitution of mind, and using freely for his purpose the materials and the symbols of poetry, yet he is never the poet-artist:—he is never found to be devising and executing, in the best manner, a work of art:—he is never the workman who has in view the tastes, wishes, and commands, of those for whom he writes.

It is on this ground, as much as upon that of the avoidance of religious expressions, or of moral sentiments, that the "Song of Songs" stands quite alone in the "goodly fellowship of the prophets." These Canticles are compositions, *apparently* on a level with compositions the purpose of which is only that of providing delectation for the reader. The author of the Canticles has done, in his way, what Theocritus and Hafiz have done—each in his way. This is what must be said—reading what we read, apart from an hypothesis which sustains itself altogether on other grounds.

Thus regarded, and thus brought forward to stand in a light of contrast with the mass of the Hebrew Scriptures, these delicious compositions carry us back, in imagination, to, or *towards*, that primæval hour of human history, a tradition of which is (as we have said) the very germ, or *inner reason* of all poetry. The author—and we need not doubt it—Solomon—the monarch of an era of peace, and of plenary terrestrial good, breaks away, as if from underneath the thick clouds and storms of centuries past:—he leaves behind him even the tranquil patriarchal ages:—he draws near to that first garden of love, and of flowers, and of singing-birds, and of all sensuous delights—even to the paradise of innocence:—he looks along the flowery alleys of that garden:—he finds his subject there, and his images; and yet not entirely so; for he takes up the paradisaical elements in part; and with these he mingles elements of another order. Himself lord of a palace, and yet alive to the better delights, and the simple conditions of rural life, he is fain to bring love and flowery fields into unison with luxurious habits. In song, this may be done: in reality, never. The Canticle is therefore a poem: it is an artistic work, because it brings into combination those ingredients of an imaginary felicity for which earth has no place.

Yet is this poem quite true to nature, if only man were innocent, and if woman were loving only, and lovely always. The truthfulness of the work is found in that primæval alliance of love and nature—of love and rural life—which imparts to the warmest of emotions its simplicity and its purity—its *healthfulness*, and to the rural taste, its animation and its vividness of enjoyment. Upon this association human nature was at the first constructed; and toward it will human nature ever be tending. Love, and fields, and flowers, and the trim graces of the garden, and the free charms of the open country, and the breathing hillside, and the sparkling stream, are—what they severally may be—as ingredients of human felicity, when they are found together. How far they may go toward realizing earthly well-being has been known to many who have been the contented dwellers beneath a thatched roof, and whose paradise was a rood or two of land, hedged off from a cornfield or meadow.

If a half-dozen heedlessly rendered passages of our English version were amended, as easily they might be, then the Canticle would well consist, throughout, with the purest utterances of conjugal fondness. Happy would any people be among whom there was an abounding of that conjugal fondness which might *thus* express itself. A social condition of this kind is—or it would be—at once the opposite of licentiousness, and its exclusion, and its proper remedy; yet it must rest upon sentiments and usages far less factitious than are those of modern European city life: marriage, entered upon early enough to secure for itself the bloom of the affections, on both sides; and so early as to have precluded the withering and the weltering of loving hearts that once were warm, pure, and capable of an entire abnegation of the individual selfism. Where, and when, shall the social system return upon its path, and become healthful, and bright, with warm emotions, and content with the modest sufficiency of rural life! Who would not willingly accept for himself the lot of the lover-husband—first out in the moist morning of May, in this climate of ours, and who thus calls his love—his wife abroad—

Rise up, my love, my fair one, and come away;
For lo, the winter is past,
The rain is over—is gone;
The flowers appear on the earth,
The time of the singing is come,
And the voice of the turtle is heard in our land;
The fig-tree hath ripened her green figs;
And the vines—the tender grape—give fragrance.
Arise, my love, my fair one, and come away!

Conjugal fondness, if true-hearted, will not make it a condition of earthly happiness that it should be able to take its leisure in gardens of oriental fragrance; but will joyfully accept very much less than this:—

A garden shut in—my sister—my spouse;
A spring shut up—a fountain sealed.
Thy plants—an orchard of pomegranates, with pleasant fruits;
Camphire, with spikenard—spikenard and saffron;
Calamus and cinnamon, with all trees of frankincense;
Myrrh and aloes, with all chief spices:
A fountain—gardens—a well of living waters,
And streams from Lebanon.

Albeit we, of a latitude so high, dare not go on, and say, in *our* early spring—

Awake, O north wind; and come, thou south;
Blow upon my garden,
The spices thereof to flow out.

But the later summer time has come when the loving wife takes up the invitation:—

Let my beloved come into his garden,
And eat his pleasant fruits.

And he replies:—

I am come into my garden, my sister—spouse:
I have gathered my myrrh with my spice;
I (*will*) eat my honeycomb with my honey;
I (*will*) drink my wine with my milk.

Although the allusions in these poems are to rural scenes, and also to the incidents of shepherd-life, there is nothing—there is not a taint of *rusticity*;—there is no coarseness—nothing of the *homeliness* of the Sicilian cattle-keepers*—nothing of the factitiousness, the affectation, of Virgil's Eclogues. The persons speak at the impulse of real and passionate emotions; but, in the utterance of these genuine and fond affections, there is always elegance, and there are the ornate habitudes of an advanced oriental civilization. There is also the genuine and inimitable *oriental self-possession*, and the consciousness of personal dignity; in these love-dialogues, and in these fond soliloquies, there is everything that may be permitted to amorous endearment; yet there is no taint of licentiousness:—these are the loves of the pure in heart. An indication at once of simplicity and of the refinement of tastes, and of purity of temperament in both lovers, appears at every turn of this abrupt composition: for ever and again is there the commingling of the language of tender fondness with the sense of the beauty and sweetness of nature—the field, the vineyard, the garden, the flowers, the

* See Note.

perfumes, the fruits, are not out of sight, from hour to hour, of these pastimes of love.

My beloved is gone down into his garden,
To the beds of spices.
To feed* in the gardens, and to gather lilies.
I am my beloved's, and my beloved is mine:
He feedeth among the lilies.
Come, my beloved, let us go forth into the field,
Let us lodge in the hamlets.
Let us get up early to the vineyards;
Let us see if the vines flourish,
Whether the tender grape appear, and the pomegranates bud forth.
There will I give thee my loves.
The mandrakes give a smell,
And at our gates all kinds of pleasant (fruits) new and old,
I have laid up for thee, O my beloved.

Fervid fondness, tenderness, and elegance—and it is an elegance which is peculiarly oriental, and which the western races with their refinements have never realized—attach to, and are characteristic of, these Canticles; and the spirit of them brings to view, at every pause, at every strophe, whatever is the most bright and graceful in nature; and it is in this same style that the enamoured one ends her plaints; for this is the last challenge of her love:—

Make haste, my beloved, and be thou like to a roe,
Or to a young hart upon the mountain of spices.

The reason is not obvious why there should be no allusion, of any sort, in these pastorals—these songs of

* Not, to *eat*; but, *ποιμαίνειν ἐν κήποις*.

love, to music—vocal, or instrumental. Music elsewhere has ever done its part in soothing, and in refining emotions of this order; why, then, is it absent from these eclogues? Not because music had not, in that age, and long before, taken its place—and a chief place —among those means of enjoyment which exalt human nature. This is abundantly certain, apart from the explicit affirmation of the royal preacher, "I gat me men-singers, and women-singers, and the delights of the sons of men—musical instruments, and that of all sorts." Why, then, is there not heard in these songs the soft breathings of the flute, or the chimes of the lyre or harp, so proper to the fragrant bowers where the royal bridegroom, and his love, spend their summer hours? Unless it should appear that the passage just now cited from the book of Ecclesiastes carries with it the weight of historical authority to the contrary,* it might be conjectured that, in the age of David and Solomon, and perhaps until a late period of the Israelitish people, music, instrumental and vocal, still observant of its primæval mood, and of its heavenly origin, reserved its powers, in trust, for religious purposes, and that to bring it into the service of emotions of a lower order would have been deemed a sacrilege, and would grievously have offended the sense of religious propriety. Might it not be so at a time when the dance was a consecrated pleasure, and when, on the most solemn occasions, persons of the highest rank, leaping and moving at the bidding of the cymbal and pipe (and probably the fiddle) took their part in these devout festivities? Oriental were these outbreakings of animated religious feeling;

* See Note.

and they were ante-Christian too; for Christianity, in setting the religious emotions at a far loftier pitch, and in connecting all such emotions with thoughts of an awful futurity, and in combining them with the dread infinitude of the unseen world, has imposed upon sacred music a character which it had not at the first; and which did not belong to it till some while after the age when the martyr Church, with its torrents of faithful blood, and its tortures, and its desolations, had come in to shed a sombre glory even upon the brightest prospects of immortality: thenceforward Church-music, wholly changed in its tones, was the music of low plaintive voices, and of the Cecilian organ. Not such was it in those remote times when the very law and reason of piety rested upon, or allied itself with, conceptions of earthly well-being; in that age the gayest music was held to be not the less *sacred*, because it was *gay*;—but, then, the consequence was this—that the music of soft delights was a *dedicated* pleasure, and was not to be held at the service of human loves.

Conjectures, more or less probable, are all that we can bring to bear upon this endeavour to show why music takes no part in these songs of love. Yet something more than conjecture we seem to need when we are endeavouring to find a probable reason for the more perplexing absence, throughout these poems, of the Divine Name, and of a religious sentiment of any kind. An explanation of the problem is not supplied by the supposition that these songs of love belong to the dark period of Solomon's religious apostacy, or of his guilty complicity in the polytheism of his wives; for in that case there would not have failed to appear—at some turn of passion—a sudden, incidental allusion to the demon worships of the Harem:—there would have been visible some foul stain of lascivious rites. No mark, no blot of *this* kind anywhere blemishes the natural brightness of this poetry; a blemish of this sort would, undoubtedly, have sufficed for excluding the Canticle from the Hebrew Canon.

Abstaining, as we do, from any argument which must be properly theological and expository, we now accept the (almost) unanimous belief of the Jewish doctors, and the (almost) unanimous concurrence therein of the Christian Church, concerning the Canticle; on the ground of which belief it was admitted into the canon of Scripture, and maintains its place there—that it is mythical throughout; and has been divinely given to illustrate, or to teach, that which St. Paul affirms to be a truth, and "a great mystery." This granted, then it would follow that the purely mystical import of this sacred poem would be interfered with—would be quite damaged and broken up—by the introduction of any of those expressions of piety which are proper to the religious man, and the religious woman—representatives as these are of piety—in an unsymbolical sense. Expressions of *this* order, whatever they might mean, have already been embraced within the range of *the mythical import* of the Poem. On the part of the celestial Bridegroom, his regard toward his mystic bride comprehends all elements of religion, as proceeding from the divine toward the human nature; and, on the part of the mystic bride, her fond love to her Lord contains, or conveys, all elements of human devotion—adoration, praise, prayer, and yearning affection. There is nothing proper to fervent piety remaining as a residue that has not been included in these mythic utterances. If on this ground—hypothetic as it is—we touch the truth of the problem, then it is manifest that the language of *unmythic piety* would be utterly out of place, would be out of harmony, in this Canticle. Might not an argument in favour of the canonicity, and of the religious intention of this Poem be warrantably made to rest upon this very circumstance of the absence, throughout it, of those religious expressions, the want of which has seemed to contravene the general belief of the Church concerning it?

Accepted, then, as a portion of inspired Scripture, and regarded as fraught throughout with a religious meaning—mystically conveyed—then does the "Song of Songs" occupy the very front place among all other instances which might be adduced in exemplification of that coexistence of the divine and of the human elements in Scripture, an understanding of which is always important,—and is, at this moment, peculiarly needed.

In this instance—signal beyond comparison as it is—the Divine element *subsists* at a remote depth below the surface; which surface might be passed over and trodden, by a thousand of the wayfarers of literature, with an utter unconsciousness of the wealth hidden beneath. Like is this divine riches to the "treasure hidden in a field," concerning which an intimation must first be granted to any one who, for the sake of it—if he knew it—would willingly sell all that he hath of this world's goods. This Poem, with its bright images of *earthly delights*—with its empassioned utterances of human fondness—its abandonment of soul, and its absorption of heart, and its emphasis of human love, if it had come down to modern times apart from all connection with a body of religious writings, would so have been read and admired, throughout all time; nor would ever a surmise of any deeper purpose have suggested itself to the modern European reader. Such an interpretation—let us grant it—might have been caught at by oriental dervishes;—for a similar use is made by them, in the East, of similar materials. The inference duly derivable from an instance so remarkable should be carefully noted, and it is of this sort:—

That we ought not to open the Bible with any predetermined notions, as to those conditions within which the divine element, in Scripture, must be expected to confine itself, in its connection with the human element, through which it conveys itself. On this unknown ground we must not theorise; we must not speculate *à priori;* for when we do this, and as often, and as far, as we do it, we surround ourselves with occasions of offence, and we provide the materials of endless doubts and perplexities. On this ground we have everything to learn:—we have nothing to stipulate; we must postulate nothing; we must quite abstain from the perilous endeavour to circumscribe the area within the limit of which, and not beyond it, the Divine Wisdom shall take its course in conveying to men the mysteries of the spiritual economy.

It may be well to look distinctly at the instance now before us, and to gather from it in full the lesson which it suggests. The theological expositor, whether of the ancient Jewish Church, or of the early Christian church, or of the modern Church, has accepted the "Song of Songs" as a divinely-inspired myth, conveying the deepest and most sacred elements of the spiritual economy in the terms, and under the forms, of instinctive human feeling and passion. The exterior medium of this conveyance is so entire, so absolute, that, until the occult meaning of the poem has been suggested, or is declared *on sufficient authority*, no reader would surmise it to be there. No religious person would have conjectured as probable, the insertion of *this* poem within the compass of the inspired Scriptures. But *it is there*, and not only is it there, but it has, if so we might speak, justified its presence in the canon by the undoubtedly religious purposes it has served, in giving animation, and depth, and intensity, and warrant, too, to the devout meditations of thousands of the most devout, and of the purest minds. Those who have no consciousness of this kind, and whose feelings and notions are all "of the earth—earthy," will not fail to find in this instance that which suits them, for purposes, sometimes of mockery, sometimes of luxury, sometimes of disbelief. Quite unconscious of these perversions, and happily ignorant of them, and unable to suppose them possible, there have been multitudes of unearthly spirits to whom this—the most beautiful of pastorals, has been—not indeed a beautiful pastoral, but the choicest of those words of truth which are "sweeter than honey to the taste," and "rather to be chosen than thousands of gold and silver."

CHAPTER XI.

THE POETRY OF THE EARLIER HEBREW PROPHETS.

Two subjects, quite distinct and separable, present themselves for consideration when the "goodly fellowship of the Prophets" comes in view. The first of these subjects embraces what belongs of right to the function of the Biblical expositor, whose office it is to examine and illustrate, *in series*, those predictions which, in their fulfilment, give evidence of a divinely-inparted prescience as to future events. The second of these subjects has a less definite aspect; for it has to do with that *Prophetic mood*—that hopeful, forward-looking habit, which is the prerogative, as it is the marked characteristic also, of the Hebrew prophetic writings, at large: it is so generally, although not in each instance, or in equal degrees in each of them; but each, without exception, is true to great Theistic principles; yet it is not all that display this far-seeing, and this world-wide anticipation of good things, on the remote horizon of the human destinies—the destinies, not of the one people, but of all nations.

This benign hilarity—this kindly catholicism—this glowing cosmopolitan prescience of a far-distant age of universal truth, righteousness, and peace, is indeed the prophetic glory, and its prerogative: it is the glory of the Hebrew poets—for poetry without hopefulness is inane and dead. On this ground these ancient Seers occupy a position where they have no competitors. On this ground they are, in a true sense, the masters of Modern Thought; for it is they who have suggested, and who have supplied the text for, those forecastings of the destiny of the nations which, in these times especially, have been prevalent in the writings, not of divines merely, but of philosophers. We all, in these days of great movements, have learned to think hopefully of every philanthropic enterprise; and our teachers in this line have been—the "goodly fellowship of the Prophets."

If it were required to mention a one feature which would be the most characteristic of our modern modes of thinking, as contrasted with ancient classical modes of thinking, we should not find a better than this:—the philosophers, and the statesmen, and the poets, and the orators, of classical antiquity, thought and spoke of the past; and their look-out was *contemporaneous only*. But the philosophers, and the statesmen, and the poets, and the orators of modern Europe, although they are not unmindful of the past, and are occupied with the present, show—all of them—this ἀποκαραδοκία—this "earnest expectation"—this hopeful faith in the future—this never-to-be-baffled confidence in a yet coming morning time, and a noon too, for the nations—savage and civilized. Subjects apparently the most remote from the region of philanthropic enthusiasm—speculations the most thriftlike and dry—show this tendency to work themselves round towards this sunshine—the sunshine of universal well-being—industry—safety—peace—wealth, which is in store for every continent. It is so that the economist, in calculating next year's prices, ruled by the probable supply of indigo—of cotton—of tobacco—of sugar—of coffee—of tea, is quite likely to come near to the very subjects which, at the same moment, platform philanthropists are propounding to crowded meetings: nay, it is likely that this same economist shall be working up, in his tables of imports, the very evidence that has lately been brought home by the wan Missionary from India, or from Africa. And so near, on this ground, do we often come to an actual collision, that the astute mercantile speculist shall be heard quoting the very man —who is quoting Isaiah!

This now established usage of the modern mind was never the usage of antiquity—Grecian or Roman. We owe this revolution, we owe this shifting about toward a better, and a brighter, and a hopeful futurity, mainly to the Hebrew Prophets. Certain luminous passages have been made use of—we might say—to *jewel* the machinery of modern society—especially in this country, and have, these seventy years past, been the centre-points of schemes of distant civilization; and so it is that, at the very time when a nugatory criticism is questioning the superhuman prescience of this or that single prediction, in the Old Testament, we are all of us in group—philanthropists—missionaries—ship-owners—dealers in merchandises of all sorts, we are all of us risking our lives—risking lives dear to us—risking our fortunes—we are sending out merchant navies, and are building mills, and are doing a half of all that is done in this busy world, on a belief that keeps itself alive by aid of those passages of far-looking brightness which illumine the pages of the Hebrew Scriptures.

This catholic mood of hopefulness has been derived much more from the Hebrew, than from the Christian Scriptures; in truth, scarcely at all from *these* (as we shall have occasion to show). But with the Prophets, the future so governed them that they seem oblivious of those materials in their own archaic literature of which, if it had been at hand, in the same distinct and authentic form, the Poets of Greece would have made no sparing use. A phrase or two recollective of the golden paradise, or of the silvery patriarchal era, is all they can afford :—they were intent upon the future :—the brightness they thought of was that of an inheritance in reversion; not that of a paradise lost. These Seers—or some of them—had been led up in spirit to the summit of the Nebo of universal history; the Seer had thence caught a glimpse of ridges illumined in the remotest distance; and the reflection rests now upon the pages of our Bibles.

It is greatly this steadfast confidence in a bright future for all nations that gives unity and coherence to this series of Hebrew prophecy, and which blends into a mass the various materials of which it consists. It is this hope for the world that has welded into one the succession of the Old Testament writers. The Patriarch of the race received this very promise, that in him should all nations hereafter be made happy. David and the Psalmists take up this same large assurance, and say—"All nations whom Thou hast made shall come, and worship before Thee." Isaiah rests often upon this theme, and kindles as he expands it; and one of the last of this company foresees the setting up of a kingdom which should have no end, and which should embrace "all people, nations, and languages." It is true that Palestine was always the Hebrew Prophet's foreground, and the Holy City his resting-place; but he looked out beyond these near objects, and with the remoteness of place he connected the remoteness of time, and dwelt, with fervent aspirations, upon the promise of an age when, "from the rising of the sun to the going down of the same," the anthems of a universal worship shall ascend from earth to heaven.

So far as the Israelitish people may be represented by the series of their writers, then it may be affirmed that these obdurate Hebrews—this stubborn repellant mass—this knot at the core among the nations, were, in fact, the most resolutely hopeful of all people, and beyond compare they were wont to look a-head toward the future. The Israelite—if the prophet speaks in his name—was, notwithstanding his nationality, and his hot patriotism, the one man upon earth who entertained thoughts concerning a remote mundane renovation, and who anticipated a time of peace and truth and justice and good-will, for all men. The august fathers of the Roman State were not more steadfast in hope for the republic, in seasons of dismay, than were the Hebrew people—if we are to gather their mood from their Prophets. This people was elastic in temper, and resolved, even when in the furnace of affliction, and when the feet were bleeding on the flints in exile, still to reserve its inheritance in a remote futurity; and this futurity embraced a wide area. Whatever the Jew of later times may have become, as the subject of centuries of insult and outrage, his ancestors of the prophetical era were well used to the hearing of passages that breathed, not only justice and mercy, but an unrestricted philanthropy.

The Prophets, never forgetful of the prerogatives of the descendants of Abraham, and never relaxing their grasp of the land which had been granted in fee simple, and forever, to their race, give expression to sentiments which are quite unparallelled in classic literature. Broad hopes and generous wishes for the world took a place also in the daily liturgies of the temple-worship; and thus, in whatever manner passages of a different aspect might come to be reconciled with these expressions, these stood as a permanent testimony, bearing witness on the behalf of universal good-will; and thus did they avail to attemper the national mind. There may take place a balancing of influences—a counteraction of motives, where there neither is, nor could be, a logical adjustment of the apparent contrariety of the two kinds of moral force. Intensely national were the Hebrew people—concentration was the rule; but largeness of feeling co-existed therewith, and it did so, not as a rare exception; and it has embodied itself in passages (as we have said) which have come to be the text and stimulants of modern philanthropy.

If at this very time such an event might be supposed, as a final and formal abandonment of whatever it is in the Hebrew prophetical writings that is predictive of the ultimate triumph of justice and benevolence, throughout the world, and of a happy issue of human affairs—if we were so resolved as to cut off the entail of hope, consigned to all nations in the Old Testament, we should quickly be brought into a mood of despair, and should learn to look in sullen apathy at those things which Hebrew Prophets regarded with healthful hope. Any such abnegation of good in the future would give a mortal chill to useful enthusiasm; it would be as a poison shed upon patriotism—confirming it in its selfishness, and depriving it of its leaven of benevolence. Such an excision of the predictive philanthropy from our Bible would bring every self-denying and arduous enterprise for the benefit of others to a speedy end: it would be death, in a moral sense, to the teacher of the ignorant, and to the champion of the oppressed. When we shut off forever, from our modern civilization, the genial glow of the Hebrew predictive writings, we let in upon the nations—Atheism in matters of religion—Despotism in politics—Sensuality, unbridled, in morals, and a dark despair for the poor and the helpless all the world over.

An expectation of the ultimate triumph of justice and peace—an expectation unknown to classical antiquity—has operated as a yeast, leavening the mass of the modern social system, just so far as Bible-teaching has prevailed among any people. This expectation has drawn its warrant from the prophetical books of the Old Testament; and from these much rather than from the Christian Scriptures. It is a fact deserving notice, that the narrow and unphilanthropic, if not the misanthropic, mood—the sullenness which modern Judaism has assumed—has been contemporaneous with the rabbinical practice of excluding the Prophets from the ordinary routine of public worship in the synagogue; while the books of Moses and portions of the Psalms, almost exclusively, have supplied the Sabbath lessons. Whether or not the reasons usually alleged for this restricted use of the Hebrew Scriptures by the Jewish rabbis be the true reasons, it is certain that the consequence, as affecting the *temper* of the Jewish mind, must have been every way much to its disadvantage. The modern Jewish nation—the rabbis and the people alike—have known very little of those incandescent passages which we Christian Bible-readers listen to with never-failing delight. Christian philanthropy, whether wisely or unwisely developed in particular instances, undertakes its labours for the benefit of the wretched, or for the deliverance of the slave, in assured prospect of a reign of righteousness which shall bless the nations, when an Iron Sceptre shall be wielded by Him "who shall spare the poor and needy, and shall save the souls of the needy; and shall redeem their souls from deceit and violence, and in whose sight their blood shall be precious."

It is on this very ground (a ground which they occupy alone) as prophets of good things *for all nations*—good things far off in the distance of ages,—that the claim of inspiration, in the fullest sense, may with peculiar advantage be affirmed and argued. It is on this ground that the Old and New Testament Scriptures are seen to stand toward each other in their proper relationship, as constituents of the one scheme or system which was ordered and planned from the beginning of time, and which extends to its close. Unless we thus believe the Hebrew Prophets to have been inspired of God, it will not be possible to show a reason for the avoidance of the same buoyant and hopeful style, as well in Christ's discourses and parables, as in the Apostolic epistles. If the question be this—Why has not Christ—or, why did not His ministers, predict a future golden age for the world at large?—we find no answer that can easily be accepted, unless we take this—That the function of predicting the triumph of reason and of peace upon earth had been assigned to the prophets of the olden time, who have well acquitted themselves in this respect. How stands it in a comparison of the older and the later Scriptures, on this very ground?

Promises addressed to the individual believer, assuring to him his daily bread, and other things that are needful for this life, do occur in the Gospels, and also in the Epistles, and the Divine faithfulness is pledged to this extent—"I will never leave thee—no, never forsake thee;" and the rule of Christian contentment is thus conditioned,—"Having nourishment and shelter, let us therewith be content." Not only are the ancient promises of earthly wealth, as the reward of individual piety, not reiterated in the New Testament, but there is an abstinence—most remarkable, as to any predictions of secular welfare for the nations of the world, and even as to the future universality of the Gospel: what we actually find has, for the most part, a contrary meaning, and a sombre aspect. (The Apocalypse demands a distinct rule of exposition.)

Throughout the ancient prophetical Scriptures the rule is this:—The things of earth, religiously considered, are spoken of, such as they appear when seen from the level of earth, and under the daylight of the present life: the prophets speak of things "seen and temporal"—piously regarded. Throughout the Christian Scriptures the things of earth—the things "seen and temporal" —are again spoken of, and again they are religiously regarded as before; but now it is as they appear when looked at from the level of the things that are unseen and eternal. From the one level the very same objects wear an aspect of gladsomeness and exultation, which, as they are seen from the other level, appear under an aspect that is discomfiting and ominous. But besides this difference of *aspect* only, it is objects of a different class that appear to be in view, severally, by the prophets, and by Christ and His ministers. The contrast, as exhibited in a few instances among many, is very suggestive of reflection.

The Hebrew Prophet is—the man of hope; he looks on through the mists of long ages of turmoil and confusion:—immediately in front he sees the rise and the ruin of neighbouring kingdoms; but he sees, in the remoter distance, a bright noon for humanity at large—"When the wolf and the lamb shall feed together, and the lion eat straw like the ox—when dust shall be the serpent's meat: and when none shall hurt or destroy in the mountain of the Lord." The Christian Seer—his eye turned off from the course of this world's affairs—thinks only of the future of the Christian commonwealth, and thus he forecasts this future—"For I know that after my departing shall grievous wolves enter in among you, not sparing the flock. Also of your ownselves shall men arise, speaking perverse things, to draw away disciples after them." The ancient Seer, expectant of good—good for the wide world—says,—"It shall come to pass in the last days that the mountains of the Lord's house shall be established on the top of the mountains, and shall be exalted above the hills, and all nations shall flow unto it." But the Christian Prophet foretells such things as these, and says—"Now the Spirit speaketh expressly that in the latter times some shall depart from the faith;" and another affirms that "in the last days perilous times shall come;" for in those latter days men generally, retaining a form of piety, shall abandon themselves to the sway of every evil passion—having the "conscience seared, as with a hot iron."

The Hebrew Prophet, from his watch-tower upon Zion, affirms that "in that mountain the Lord of Hosts should make *unto all people* a feast of fat things,"—and that *there* "He will destroy the face of the covering cast over all people, and the veil that is spread over all nations:"—the Lord—the God of Israel—"shall swallow up death in victory, and wipe away tears from off all faces: and the rebuke of His people shall He take away from off all the earth." It was many centuries later in the world's life-time, and therefore it was so much the nearer to the predicted break of day for all nations, that the Christian Prophet foresaw a thick gloom, out of the midst of which the "wicked one" should arise, who should sit in the temple of God, and there should blasphemously demand for himself the worship that is due to God, and actually receive it from the deluded dwellers upon earth—even the multitude of the nations.

These contrasts, other instances of which may be adduced, are not *contradictions:* they are not contrary affirmations, relating to the same objects, or to objects seen from the same level; but they bring into view, in a manner that should fix attention, the harmonious structure of the Scriptures—the Old and the New Covenant. The latter is ruled by its purpose to reveal and confirm the hope of immortality, which must be *individual immortality*, inasmuch as communities have no hereafter. The former, spiritual also in its intention, not less so than the latter, is yet concerned with mundane welfares, in relation to which nations and communities are regarded in mass; and therefore these Prophets look on to the very end of the secular period:—they have in view the longevity of nations and they foretell the remote benefits in which all people shall be partakers. It is the life everlasting, which Christ and His ministers have in prospect, while, as to the things of earth, they see only those changes which shall bring into peril the welfare of immortal souls.

Easily we may grant it—even if we fail to open up the reason of the fact—that it must be always, and only, with mundane objects, and with what belongs to the now visible course of things—"the things that are seen and temporal"—that poetry may and should concern itself. So it is that, while the ancient Prophets are poets, and, as such, kindle emotion, and illumine the path on which they tread, no quality of this sort can (truthfully) be alleged in commendation of Evangelists or Apostles. The encomium of these takes another, and a far higher ground. Poetry became mute at the moment when immortality was to be proclaimed: known to the Patriarchs and Prophets, and pondered and desired by them, and by the pious always, even from the first, yet an authentic announcement of it had been held in reserve to a later age; but when that fulness of time had come, and when the true light shone out, then, in the blaze of it, the things of earth assumed another aspect; and even the perspective of them underwent a change, when they were seen from a higher level. In passing from the "fellowship of the Prophets" to the "company of the Apostles," it is true that we tread the same solid earth, and we take with us the same human nature, and, as to what concerns the spiritual life, we breathe the same atmosphere; but we leave behind us the flowery plains of earthly good, and ascend to heights where the awful realities of another life banish all thought of whatever is decorative, or of those objects that awaken the tastes and the imagination. Poetry, abounding as it does in the Old Testament, finds no place at all in the New. On *this* ground of comparison the difference between Isaiah, Hosea, Joel, and Paul, Peter, John, or James, is absolute. So it must appear in bringing into comparison some passages which, at a glance, might seem to be of the same order.

As, for instance, there occur, in the Epistles of Peter, James, and Jude, some passages which not only take up the archaic phraseology, and are, in a marked manner, of the Hebrew mintage, but which are also of that denunciatory kind which gives them an exceptional aspect, as related to the evangelic strain, and brings them to be of a piece rather with the stern manner of the ancient Seers, in protesting against the wrong-doings of their contemporaries, and in predicting the judgments of God upon guilty nations. Nevertheless, while in these instances there are some points of accordance, the points of contrast are of a more important and noticeable kind.

In the first place, these Apostolic samples are sternly and ruggedly prosaic:—they have no rhythm, and, although figurative in terms, they are graced by no decorations:—they demand the deepest regard, they strike into the conscience, they awaken terror; but with the prediction of wrath they commingle no element upon which the imagination might be inclined to rest: in a word, the Apostolic message, whether it be of hope or of dread, is in no sense—poetry. Turn to those well-remembered passages which might recall the style of Amos, Joel, Nahum:—"For if God spared not the angels that sinned" . . . "these (wicked men) are wells without water, clouds that are carried with a tempest." . . . "Go to now, ye rich men, weep and howl for your miseries that shall come upon you." . . . "Ungodly men, crept in among you, raging waves of the sea, foaming out their own shame." . . . .* Wanting in poetry, but

* 2 Peter ii. 4. James v. Jude.

explicit in moral intention, are the Apostolic denunciations; and nearly combined are they always with the Christian assurance of immortality:—this is the Apostolic mark. So it is with Jude, who, in the very breath, which has given utterance to the message of wrath, and when he has made his protest for charity and mercy, commends his brethren to the Divine regard in that signal doxology,—"Now to Him that is able to keep you from falling" . . . . And, in like manner, James quickly releases himself from his stern obligation as a Prophet of judgment, and exhorts the Christian sufferer to be patient—"for the coming of the Lord draweth nigh;" and thus also Peter, who enjoins his brethren, under any extremity of suffering, to "hope unto the end for the grace that is to be brought unto them at the revelation of Jesus Christ;" not thinking it strange, even though "a fiery trial" should be appointed for them; but rather rejoicing in the prospect of the "glory" in which they are to have their part.

The parallel places in the prophecies of Joel, of Amos, of Micah, and Nahum, are not only metrical and rhythmical in structure, but they are rich in various imagery: magnificence, sublimity, and beauty too, so recommend these protests for righteousness, and these predictions of national woe, that we now read and rest upon these passages with a relish of their excellence as works of genius; and so it is that the Hebrew *Poet* shares the regard of the modern reader with the Hebrew *Prophet*. It is as poetry that these prophecies were adapted to the services of congregational worship; and in this manner were they consigned to the memories of the people. And yet, when we have noted this contrast between the Prophetic and the Apostolic Scriptures, there remains to be noticed another contrast that is more marked, and is full of meaning—

The brief prophecy of Habakkuk—one of those that belong to the earliest era of the Hebrew prophetic time—combines those qualities of style that distinguish his peers and contemporaries; and along with majesty and splendour and vigour of expression, there is the constant protest for truth and justice, and the uniform sublimity of a pure theology, and the scornful rebuke of the folly of the idolater:—"Woe unto him that saith to the wood, Awake; to the dumb stone, Arise, it shall teach! Behold, it is laid over with gold and silver, and there is no breath at all in the midst of it." Then follows an anthem, unequalled in majesty and splendour of language and imagery, and which, in its closing verses, gives expression, in terms the most affecting, to an intense spiritual feeling; and on this ground it so fully embodies these religious sentiments as to satisfy Christian piety, even of the loftiest order. Yet in this respect are these verses the most remarkable that, while there is recognized in them the characteristic Hebrew principle, which gives prominence to earthly welfare, the Prophet, for himself, renounces his part in this—if only he may fully enjoy a consciousness of the Divine favour. Yet this is not all; for he contents himself with these spiritual enjoyments—apart from any thought of the future life and of its hopes; thus does he renounce the present good; and yet he stipulates not for the good of the future! for upon this prophecy—bright as it is in its theistic import, there comes down no ray of the light of the life eternal! Witness these verses—ending the prophet's ministry in the language of hope; but it is a hope very ambiguously worded if at all it takes any hold of immortality:—

Although the fig-tree shall not blossom,
Neither fruit be in the vines;
The labour of the olive shall fail,
And the fields shall yield no meat;
The flock shall be cut off from the fold,
And no herd in the stalls:
Yet I will rejoice in the Lord,
I will joy in the God of my salvation,
The Lord God is my strength:
And He will make my feet like hinds',
And He will make me to walk upon high places.*

* This is an ode to be commended to the care of the chief singer, and to be accompanied by stringed instruments—Neginoth—and adapted (may we not conjecture?) to the movements of the sacred dance, in which the feet—well trained, should give proof of the exultation of the soul—moving "like hinds' feet," even upon the loftiest platform of the temple area. Such should be the gladness of those who took up this ode:—it should be like that of the Psalmist, who would praise God with the psaltery and harp; and praise Him, too, with the timbrel and *dance*, as well as with stringed instruments and organs, and with loud cymbals.

CHAPTER XII.

CULMINATION OF THE HEBREW POETRY AND PROPHECY IN ISAIAH.

Whatever there is of poetry in the roll of the Prophets, whatever of truth and of purity, and of elevation, as to moral principle, and theistic doctrine, and especially whatever there is of catholicity, and of hopefulness for all nations, is preëminently found in the book of the prophecies of Isaiah. These prophecies may well be said to embrace, and to comprehend, and, in a sense, at once to recapitulate, the revelations of all preceding ages, and to foreshow the revelations that were yet to come. The Moral Law is there in the fixedness of its eternal axioms: the spiritual life is there; and the substance of the Gospel is there; for the Redeemer of the world, and the most signal of all events in the world's history, are there; and with the Saviour the brightness of the latest ages of the human family sheds a light upon this prophecy. Revelation culminates in the pages of this Prophet; for the Old and the New Covenants are therein represented.

But how much more than a poet is this Prophet! And yet as a poet he has won for himself the very highest encomiums;—in this sense they are the highest, that they have been uttered by those who, in so warmly commending the Hebrew bard, have been incited by no *religious* partiality or orthodox prejudice; but the contrary. In this instance it would be easy to get released from the task of framing eulogies duly expressive of the admiration to which this poet is entitled; for several German scholars, of the foremost rank as Hebraists, have already so exhausted this theme that it would be difficult to do anything else than to repeat—sentence by sentence, what they have said. Certainly there has been no contrary verdict on this ground;—or none that is deserving of much regard.

If there were now a question concerning the richness and the compass, the wealth, the distinctiveness, the power, and pliability of the Hebrew language, it might well be determined by an appeal to the poetry of Isaiah. With perfect ease, as if conscious of commanding an inexhaustible fund, this Prophet (or now let us call him Poet) moves forward on his path:—terms the most fit and various are in his store:—imagery, in all species, abounds for his use, whatever be the theme, and whether it be terrible, or sombre, or gay and bright. Or if rather the question related to the culture of the Hebrew mind, in that remote age, and to its susceptibility, or to the existence among the people, or many of them, at that time, of a refined spiritual sensibility, these compositions would be vouchers enough of the fact. Let the reader put off for awhile, and let him quite distance himself from, his Bible-reading associations:—let him forget that the book of the son of Amoz is a constituent of the Canon of Scripture; and then, and as thus reading it *afresh*, not only will *the Poet* rise in his view, and take rank as the most sublime, the most rich, the most full-souled of poets, but there will come before him, as if dimly seen, the men of that age—more than a few such—to whom these utterances of the religious life—these words of remonstrance, and of comfort, and of hope, would be reverently listened to, and treasured up, and recited daily. What is it in fact that is clearly implied in the very structure of these compositions? Why are they metrical throughout? Why are they elaborately artificial in their form? It must be for this reason, that the people of that time, and their ecclesiastical rulers, received, with devout regard, the Prophet's deliverance of his testimony, and that, notwithstanding the sharpness of his rebukes, this "burden of the Lord" took its place among the recitatives and the choral services of public worship—to which purposes they are manifestly adapted.

An experiment of this kind would produce its *first* effect, in thus opening to our view at once the preëminence of the Prophet, *as a poet*, and the advanced intellectual and religious condition of his contemporaries. But then an effect speedily to follow this first would be greatly to enhance the conviction that, in this instance, the *Poet*, admirable as he may be, and lofty as was his genius, is far less to be thought of than the *Prophet*. Quickly we feel that he himself thus thinks of his message, and is in this manner conscious of his burden, and that, in his own esteem, he is so absolutely subordinate—he is so purely and passively instrumental, in the delivery of it to the people, that the message, and He from whom it comes, throw into shade whatever is human only, giving undivided prominence to what is Divine. In this manner the reader's religious consciousness so coalesces with the Prophet's consciousness of the same, that, as often as the prophetic formula occurs—"Thus saith the Lord," the solemn truthfulness of this averment commands our assent.

Feelings of the same class, which give the modern reader his sense of the beauty and sublimity of Isaiah, as a poet, carry with them a deep conviction, which no unsophisticated mind can resist, of the seriousness and the truthful steady adherence of the Prophet to his call, as the minister of God. If there be anywhere in the compass of human writings irresistible evidence of genuineness, and of honesty, and of a man's confidence in himself, as the authentic messenger of Heaven, it is here that such indubitable marks of reality are conspicuously present. Truth is consistent, and coherent, and uniform. Truth, beneath all diversities as to the mode of its expression, comes home to every conscience by the unvarying fixedness of the principles on which it takes its stand. And so it is that the utterances of this prince of the prophets, dated as they are through the years of a long life—not fewer than seventy—and called forth by occasions widely dissimilar, are nevertheless perfectly in unison as to the theology on which they are based, and as to the ethical principles which sustain the Prophet's denunciations and rebukes; and, moreover, as to that economy of Grace, toward the humble and obedient, which illumines the first page, and the last page with a ray from the throne of God.

Otherwise thought of than as a message from Him who is unchangeable in His attributes of love, this consistency in announcing the terms of mercy, and this sameness of the style in which the penitent are invited to seek the divine favour, is wholly inconceivable. It does not belong to human nature, with its wayward feelings —it does not belong to human nature, with its constant progression of temper and temperament, shifting from early manhood to the last months of a term of eighty or ninety years, thus to utter the same things, in the same mood, indicative equally of unbroken vigour and of unclouded benignity. Men, however wise and good they may be, will show themselves (as they are) the creatures of their decades:—they will date themselves onward in their style, from their third decade to their eighth or ninth. But this Prophet exhibits no such variations, because, in youth and in age alike, he is delivering a message from Him who abides the same throughout the lapse of years.

If, indeed, there were ground, which there is not, for attributing these prophecies to two authors, with an interval of centuries between them, then we might be content to look only to the thirty-nine chapters of the more ancient Isaiah, the interval between the earliest of *this* portion and the latest being, by the acknowledgment of modern expositors, fifty years. If the Prophet assumed his office as a minister of Jehovah at the earliest date at which he could do so, then he had reached nearly the limit of human life when he uttered the bright presages contained in the thirty-fifth chapter. It was in the heat of manhood that he thus denounces the hypocrisy of the people—their chiefs and their priests:—

> Hear the word of the Lord, ye rulers of Sodom.
> Wash you, make you clean;
> Put away the evil of your doings.

Yet this same bold reprover is not a man who was carried away by his own fiery temperament; for in the same breath he thus opens the path of mercy to whoever may relent:—

Come now, and let us reason together, saith the Lord;
Though your sins be as scarlet, they shall be as white as snow;
Though they be red like crimson, they shall be as wool.

It is the same Isaiah, now in extreme age, and whose duty it had been, throughout these many years, still to denounce the wickedness of the wicked—as thus: (chapter xxxv.)

Woe to Ariel, to Ariel,
The city where David dwelt!
Woe to the rebellious children, saith the Lord!

It is the same ambassador from God—now hoary and tremulous, yet not soured in temper—not sickened by a life-long ministration among a gainsaying people, but benign, as at thirty, and hopeful as always, who sees, in the age to come, "the wilderness and the solitary place made glad, and the desert—the wide world—blossoming as the rose." It is he who says—as at first he had said:—

Strengthen ye the weak hands,
And confirm the feeble knees.
Say to them of a fearful heart,
Be strong, fear not.

. . . .

And the ransomed of the Lord shall return,
And come to Zion with songs,
And everlasting joy upon their heads;
And they shall obtain joy and gladness,
And sorrow and sighing shall flee away.

On every page there is the same protest for truth, justice, and mercy, between man and man: there is the same message of wrath for the oppressor and the cruel, and the same righteous care for the widow, the fatherless, the bondsman, the stranger. On every page there are the same elements of what, at this time, we acknowledge to be a true theology, and which is so *entire* that, after ages of painful cogitation on the part of the most profound and the most exact minds—whether philosophers or divines, whether ancient or modern—nothing that is preferable, nothing that is deeper, or more affecting, nothing which we should do well to accept, and to take to ourselves as of better quality, has been educed and taught, or is, at this moment, extant and patent, in books—classical, or books—recent. This Prophet—if we take him as the chief of his order—is still, after a two thousand seven hundred years, our master in the school of the highest reason.*

This consummation, and this faultless enouncement of theistic principles, in an age so remote, and among a people unacquainted with the methods of abstract thought, is a fact which admits of explication on one ground only—namely, that of the direct impartation of this theology from Heaven. So strongly do those feel this who read the Hebrew Scriptures ingenuously, that the affectation which will be prating about the "sublime and fiery *genius*" of the Prophet becomes offensive and insufferable. Human *genius* soars to no height like this; and as to human *reason*, to find a sure and a straight path for itself on its own level is more than ever it has yet done.

There is, however, another field on which, if we follow this Prophet in his track, from the earliest of his public ministrations to the latest of them, a conviction

* See Note.

of the direct inspiration whence they sprang becomes, if possible, still more firm. These prophesyings—delivered to the people and princes of Jerusalem, on divers occasions, throughout the lapse of seventy or eighty years—contain (might we here use such a phrase) a programme of the Divine purposes toward the human family to the end of time. And this sketch—this foreshowing of a remote futurity, has for its object, or its theme, not humanity in the abstract, not man immortal; but *men in community;* and not a one people only, but the commonwealth of nations. Whatever we intend by the modern phrase—Catholicity, or by the word—Cosmopolitan, whatever we of this age of *breadth* are used to think of when we talk of "the brotherhood of nations," and of the community of races—all these ideas, substantially one, are embraced in that prescience of the future which came to the surface so often during the prophetic ministrations of Isaiah. Let it be noted that what this prescience has in view is a remote *terrestrial* universality of truth, peace, justice, order, wealth, for all dwellers beneath the sun. In a word, this Prophet foresees the accomplishment of that one petition among those commended by Christ to His disciples—"Thy will be done *on earth*, even as it is done in heaven."

What we have to do with in this instance is not just a line or a couplet, here or there, which may have an ambiguous import, and may be startling on account of its coincidence with remote events; for the passages now in view are recurrent—they are ample, and—one might say—they are *leisurely* in the development of their meaning: they open out objects upon which a clear noon-day illumination is steadily resting. The

Seer so speaks as if indeed he saw the things of which he speaks; and he so speaks of them after intervals of time—years perhaps—as if the very same objects, permanent and unchanging in themselves, were by himself recognized afresh as long familiar to his eye. Was it then a man of Judah like others—was it one who paced the streets of Jerusalem, and pressed forward among his countrymen upon the ascents of the temple—was it one gifted only as others may have been gifted, who thus, long before the dawn of historic time (as to other nations) looked right a-head, and afar over and beyond the bounds of thousands of years, and who saw, in that remoteness, not a hazy brightness—an undefined cloud, or a speck of light upon the horizon; but who gazed upon a fair prospect—wide as the inhabited earth, and fair as it is wide, and bright as it is wide, and of as long endurance as the terrestrial destiny of man shall allow? Assuredly the seeing a prospect like this is no natural achievement of genius:—it is nothing less than a prescience which He only may impart who "knoweth the end from the beginning;" and in whose view thousands of ages are as the now-passing moment.

The predictions of Isaiah and the predictions of Daniel are of wholly dissimilar character:—they have a different intention, and they demand exposition on different principles. Those of Daniel are precisely defined, although not opened out in detail;—they are distinctly dated in symbol, they have a limitation also which, in respect of what has the aspect of hope, seems to keep in view a *national* rather than a *cosmopolitan* era of renovation; and then, in exchange for the prospect of good in reserve for all nations, there is in this later-age prophecy a far more distinct doctrine of immortality, and of the resurrection of the dead, than it had hitherto been permitted to the Hebrew prophets to announce.*

The predictions of Isaiah are less distinctly marked—as to their chronology—than are those of Daniel, because they embrace extensive and unlimited eras of the future, and they are unrestricted as to place, because they comprehend all dwellers upon earth. Although localized in respect of the centre whence the universal renovation shall take its rise, these predictions overpass all other bounds:—such as this is the prophet's style:—

In this mountain shall the Lord of Sabaoth make unto all people,
A feast.
And He will destroy in this mountain
The face of the covering covering all people,
And the veil that is spread over all nations.
He will swallow up death in victory.

Placed almost in front of this eighty years' course of prophecy, as if it were the text of whatever is to follow, and as if it were to serve as a caution, or as a counteraction, of any inference that might be drawn from the denunciations that are to occupy so large a space—is, this foreshowing of a high noon of truth and peace for all races and kindreds of the one human family:—

And it shall come to pass in the last days,
The mountain of the house of Jehovah
Shall be established (*constituted*) in the top of the mountains;
And shall be exalted above the hills;
And all nations shall flow unto it.

* Daniel xii. 2. 3. The parallel passage in Isaiah xxvi. 19. should be named as an exceptive instance as to that prophet.

And many peoples shall go and say,
Come ye, and let us go up to the mountain of Jehovah,
And to the house of the God of Jacob;
And He will teach us of His ways, and we will walk in His paths:
For from Zion shall go forth the Law,
And the word of Jehovah from Jerusalem.
And He shall judge among the nations,
And shall rebuke (*convict* or *convince*) many people:
And they shall beat their swords into plowshares,
And their spears into pruning-hooks:
Nation shall not lift up sword against nation,
Neither shall they learn war any more.

These, and eight or ten other passages of similar import, occurring at intervals in the same "roll of the book," if they be read on any other supposition than that of their Divine origin (this understood in the fullest sense) must be regarded as marvels indeed of which we shall never be able to give any solution; and this perplexity has its two aspects—the first is this—that a man of Judah, in that age—let us attribute to him whatever eminence we may, as to intelligence—should *thus* have thought, and should thus have uttered himself, concerning the religious condition of the surrounding nations of that time; and then that, thus thinking, he should have conceived such an idea as that which is conveyed in his anticipation of the conversion of the world, in the last days, to truth in religion. Certain it is that a consciousness of the *spiritual* condition of the nations then neighbouring upon Judæa was the guiding-thought of the Prophet in these passages—as thus:—

Arise! shine! for thy light is come,
And the glory of Jehovah is risen upon thee;
For, behold, darkness shall cover the earth,
And gross darkness the nations;

But Jehovah shall arise upon thee,
And His glory shall be seen upon thee,
And the nations shall walk in thy light,
And kings in the brightness of thy rising.

The language of Isaiah, in thus speaking of the surrounding nations, does not savour of the arrogance of a nation that is insulated by its profession of a purer doctrine than that of others; nor does it betray the irritation or scorn of such a people, maintaining its national existence, from year to year, in a precarious conflict with its powerful neighbours. This language is as calm and as tranquil as it should be—grant it be an utterance from the throne of the eternal God. He who counteth the nations but as "the small dust of the balance" may be expected thus to speak of their delusions: but not so, on any ordinary principles of human nature, the bard of a haughty theistic nation, contemning, and yet dreading, its neighbours, right-hand and left-hand. Conceived of on any such ordinary principles, and if the case is to be judged of on grounds of analogous instances, this simplicity, this dignity, this brevity, are not to be accounted for; what were the facts?—In looking eastward toward the military empires of the great rivers-land, or southward to the manifold and gorgeous idolatries of the people of the Nile, with the profound symbolized doctrine of those worships, the Israelitish bard—the man of glowing imagination, supposing him to be nothing more, would find his faith in a pure theism, and his constancy in adhering to the worship of Jehovah, severely tried. These neighbouring lands, where imperial magnificence surrounded itself with the pomps of a sensual polytheism, and thus gave an air of sparkling joyousness to the cities, palaces, temples

—these lands would naturally be spoken of in terms very unlike these phrases of modest truthfulness: the language which here meets us *we* of this time accept as quite proper to the subject, because we ourselves have come to think of all forms of polytheistic superstition—ancient and modern, in the same manner; to *our* modern Christianized vision nothing can seem more fitting than that the debasing worships of ancient Egypt, or of Assyria, or the foul superstitions of India, should be thus metaphored—as a veil—a thick covering—a gross darkness, spread over the people which still abide under the shadow of paganism. But it was not so to this man of Palestine, three thousand years ago. The Prophet of Judah, in *thus* speaking of the religious condition of Assyria, and of Egypt, and of India, used a style which he could never have imagined—which he would not have employed, if the terms had not been given to him from above. Those will the most readily feel this who are the most accustomed to carry themselves back to remote times, and to realize, in idea, the modes of feeling of the men of countries remote, and of ages now almost forgotten.

So to designate the religious delusions of the nations of antiquity was not the native gift of the son of Amoz:—it was the gift and office of the Prophet of Jehovah; and with a still firmer confidence may we say that the prediction which follows could not be from man, but must have been from God.

The prediction is not of the kind that breathes the mood of national ambition; it is not military, but the very contrary; it is not of the same sort as the Islam fanaticism; it is not in harmony with a fierce propagandism; it was not prompted by the temper of that later age, when the zeal of the Pharisee incited him to "compass sea and land for making one proselyte." This prediction, by the very fact of its employment of figurative language of this material quality—by speaking of the fat things, and the delicacies, and the old wines, proper to a royal banquet, and in associating these figures with those of the gross darkness, and the veil of the covering, precluded any interpretation of a lower species;—for it is manifest that as was the darkness—as was the covering veil—symbolizing religious, moral, and spiritual ignorance and error, so should the feast, and the refreshment, be that of religious nourishment, and of moral renovation, and of spiritual enjoyment. In this instance the apposition of metaphors furnishes a sure guide to the interpretation. And then the history of the nations, from the prophet's age to this, is a continuous comment upon the prophecy. And so does the course of events, at this very moment, give indication of its ultimate entire accomplishment—adverse events and thick clouds of the sky, notwithstanding.

In contradiction of the strenuous endeavours of many at this time to withdraw men's thoughts from the past, and especially so far as the past carries a religious meaning, these Hebrew prophecies—those especially of Micah, and of Isaiah, and of the Psalms,—affirm and attest this vital principle, affecting human destinies—namely, *historic continuity*. It is on *this* ground, as much as upon any other, that the religion of the Scriptures stands opposed to atheistic doctrines of every sort. The Bible holds all ages—past and future—in an indissoluble bond of union, and of causal relationship, and of development, and of progress, and therefore—of hope, animated by a Divine assurance of universal blessings yet to come. Moreover this same historic continuity, this integral vitality, stands connected with a law of geographical centralization. The life and hope of the commonwealth of nations is not a vague hypothesis, which may be realized anywhere, and may spring up spontaneously, breaking forth at intervals from new centres, or startling attention as from the heart of barbarian wildernesses; it is quite otherwise. Even as to the light of civilization and of philosophy, it has shown its constant dependence upon this same law of historic continuity, and of derivation. Much more is it—has it ever been so—as to the light of a pure theology, and of an effective morality.

So did these Hebrew predictions, after a slumber of five hundred years, wake into life among all the nations bordering upon Palestine, when, by the means of the Greek version of the entire body of the Hebrew Scriptures, a true theology, earnestly sought after, and actually found, by the thoughtful in every city of the Roman empire, was silently embraced, and devoutly regarded by thousands of the several races clustered around the Mediterranean Sea, as well as in the remotest East. And so at length were the Prophets of that Elder Revelation honoured in the accomplishment of their words, when the Apostolic preaching—like a sudden blaze from heaven—imparted the light of life to millions of souls throughout those same countries—of Europe, Africa, and Asia.

Every onward movement of the western nations—even those movements which humanity the most condemns—has shown the same tendency to create or to restore, a religious centralization, which, in its degree, has been an accomplishment of these same predictions.

And at this time these shining words of hope and of peace, accepted as they are, and honoured by the one people among the nations whose destiny and whose dispositions carry them far abroad—East and West—are working out their own fulfilment in a manner that is indicative at once of the force that resides in the word of prophecy, and of the Divine power which attends this word, and which shall accomplish it—in every iota of it—in "the last times."

Not yet indeed have the nations ceased to "learn war;" on the contrary, the arts, bearing upon the mechanical destruction of life, and the demolition of defences, would seem to be making such advances as must render the practice of war a day's work only in effecting the extinction of armies, or even the extermination of races. So it may appear. Nevertheless each of those inventions which have had the same apparent tendency have, in the end, availed to shorten the duration of wars, and to diminish the amount of slaughter while they last. Speculations and calculations of this kind are, however, quite beside our purpose. War, when it shall cease to "the ends of the earth," will be excluded by the concurrent operation of influences secular, and influences moral, or religious. Permanent peace will be brought about in the course of the providential overruling of many lower causes, and by the proper operation of causes of a higher quality. This ultimate blessedness shall at once "spring out of the earth, and shall look down from heaven."

What concerns us just now is this—to note in these predictions that which demonstrates the absolute subordination of the poetic genius to the prophetic function of the man. Isaiah—we are told—was a man who should rank high among the men of genius of all ages; and as to his prescience, it was that only which is a characteristic of the poetic inspiration: he was a *prophet* just so far as he was a poet. This hypothesis does not consist with the facts in view. As often as he touches themes that are the most awakening to poetic feeling, Isaiah—and the same is true of his brethren—is brief, and seems in haste to quit the ground on which he has set foot for a moment. It is thus in the passage just above cited, in which the attractive conception of a silver age of peaceful rural life, to which all nations shall joyfully return, presents itself; and again, as in this passage:—

The wilderness and the solitary place shall be glad for them,
And the desert shall rejoice and blossom as the rose.
It shall blossom abundantly,
And rejoice even with singing;
The glory of Lebanon shall be given unto it,
The excellency of Carmel and Sharon;
They shall see the glory of Jehovah,
And the excellency of our God.

The passing forward is immediate to themes of another order:—

Strengthen ye the weak hands,
And confirm the feeble knees.
Say to them of a fearful heart.
Be strong—fear not. . . .

Near is the poet, in these instances, to those primæval conceptions of earthly good which, to the Hebrew people, were fixed elementary ideas. Easy—natural—pleasurable, would have been the transition to the Paradisaical and the Patriarchal morning times of the human family. No such divergence is in any instance allowed; nevertheless the fact remains, whether we duly regard it or not, that the great scheme of the Hebrew prophetic dispensation exhibits, in this instance, as in others, the universality of its intention; or let us rather say—its grasp of all mundane time in this way, that the same bright conditions which had attached to the commencement of the human destinies on earth, are foreseen and foreshown as the ultimate conditions of the human family. As there was a paradisaical morning, so shall there be a high noon to all nations—a noon of *earthy* good, as the proper accompaniment of the triumph and prevalence of religious truth and love.

CHAPTER XIII.

THE LATER PROPHETS, AND THE DISAPPEARANCE OF THE POETIC ELEMENT IN THE HEBREW SCRIPTURES.

A Century onward from the age of Micah and Isaiah, to that of Jeremiah, brings to view the greatness of the change that was to take place in the modes of the one Revelation of the Divine will and purposes. The same principles always, but another style. Let it rather be said—a progressive change was taking place in preparation for that last mode of this teaching from heaven, when the awful realities of the human system, in relation to the future life, were to throw into the shade, as well the bright eras, as the dark times, of this visible mundane economy. Poetry, therefore, which is always a function of this visible economy, gradually disappears from the inspired pages; while the prophetic element assumes, continually, a more definite character, and becomes also prosaic in its tone and style. Nevertheless while, in the prophets of the late age, *Poetry* is in course of subsidence, there does not take place a corresponding relinquishment of metrical forms. An instance of this is presented in the closing portions of the prophecies of Jeremiah—namely, the Lamentations, wherein the artificial metrical structure prevails in a higher degree than in any other part of the Hebrew Scriptures.*

* See Note.

This Prophet—a type of Him who was "acquainted with griefs"—gives evidence at once of the sorrowfulness, the tender sensitiveness of his temperament, and of his want of those loftier gifts which distinguish Isaiah, and which, in the esteem of Biblical critics, entitle him to a high place among men of genius.

The difference between the two Prophets is best seen in comparing those passages in the later prophet which, as to subject and doctrine, are nearly the counterparts of signal passages in the earlier prophet. Such especially are those places in the two in which the majesty of God is affirmed, while the folly and vanity of idol-worship receives a contemptuous rebuke;—such also are those which predict the future kingdom of peace, and the return of the people from their captivity.* A richness of diction, a majestic flow, a compass and accumulation of imagery, belong to the one, which do not appear in the other; but then this later prophet, in some places, approaches that style of definite prediction which was to be carried still further by his successors.

If what already (Chap. IV.) we have said concerning Palestine, as the fit birth-place and home of Poetry be warrantable, as well as the contrary averment con-

* Compare passages in the two Prophets, such as the following: —

JEREMIAH.	ISAIAH.
x. 1—16, and li. 15—19.	xl. 12, to the end. xliv. 6, to the end. xlvi.
xxiii. 5—8. xxix. xxx. 10, 11. xxxi. 1—14.	xxx. 19. 26. xxxv. xlix. 7, to the end. liv. throughout.

cerning the levels of Mesopotamia, then the fact that the Prophets of the Captivity, Ezekiel and Daniel especially, are *prophets* not *poets*, will seem to be, at least, in accordance with a principle, even if it may not be adduced as a proof of it. The captives of Judæa carried with them the Hebrew lyre; but, seated disconsolate by the rivers of Babylon, they refused to attempt to awaken its notes, and themselves lost the power to do so. On the banks of the Chebar (great canal) and on the banks of the mighty Hiddekel, visions of awful magnificence were opened to the seer's eye; and he describes what he saw: but his description is strictly prosaic; nor does the sublimity of the objects that are described at all enkindle the imagination of the reader. The reader, to become conscious of their sublimity, must carry himself into the midst of the scene, and picture its stupendous creations for himself. A passage in Isaiah (chap. vi.) similar to that which opens the prophecy of Ezekiel, produces, by its very brevity, an effect on the imagination which the elaborate description of the later prophet fails to produce.

Along with this subsidence, or disappearance of poetry, there presents itself a more rigorous style of rebuke, and an ethical tone, indicative of the change that was coming upon the national character. The Hebrew man of Palestine—the man of Judah—the citizen of Jerusalem—was, in this late age, represented by the Jew of the Captivity, and this personage has more affinity with the Jew of modern times, than with the Hebrew people of the times of Isaiah. It is true that those of the later prophets who exercised their ministry in Judea—these are Haggai, Zachariah, Malachi—retained the archaic style, if they breathed less of its animation; but it is not so with Ezekiel, or with Daniel: these lead us on toward a dispensation in which poetry should have no part. Objects held forth in vision, for a symbolic purpose, may be stupendous, or they may be magnific, or splendid; but while conveying their import, and demanding explication *as emblems*, they quite fail to stimulate the imagination, or to satisfy the tastes. Not only is it true that allegory is not poetry, for it contradicts, it excludes poetry—it is prosaic emphatically: faculties of another order are appealed to; and when these are in act the tastes, and the consciousness of beauty and sublimity, are neutralized. This sort of antagonism is felt especially in the perusal of the Apocalypse, which, even when the scenery it describes is constituted of objects that are in themselves the most proper for poetic treatment, yet fails entirely to give pleasure on that ground. These exhibitions of celestial splendours, or of infernal terrors, carry with them another intention; and that this intention may be secured, they quell or dissipate those emotions which poetry is always aiming to excite.

An instance presents itself in the chapter (xxxvii.) of Ezekiel in which the Prophet brings into view, with vividness, the scene and circumstance symbolically of a national resurrection. He brings into view the valley of blanched skeletons—the tremors in these heaps of bones—the clustering of limbs—the coming on of muscle and skin to each—and the sudden starting to their feet of an array of warriors.* The painter here

* *Robur, vis, fortitudo, maxime bellica; exercitus.* GESENIUS. This seems the proper force of the Hebrew word. The Greek says only *συναγωγή*: which is less than the meaning.

might be tempted to try his art upon a large canvas, and might do better in such an attempt than the poet could, unless he availed himself of other materials, and put quite out of view the emblematic significance which Ezekiel puts forward, when he says—"These bones are the whole house of Israel." The same principle takes effect in the instance of the vision (chap. viii.) of the chamber of idol-worship, and the worshippers, and the cloud of incense: a fine subject for learned art, much rather so than for poetry.

No vein of poetry, not even a single incidental recollection of the Hebrew imaginative soul, makes its appearance in the book of Daniel. Plainly historical, for the greater part—its prophetic portions—its *revelations*, are of that order which, as we have said, is the extreme antithesis of poetry. The entire class of allusive conveyances of a meaning differing from the obvious or literal meaning of the terms employed, includes allegories, emblems, proverbial phrases, and most varieties of wit; and these, all, are distasteful to those in whom the genuine poetic feeling is in force. True poetry needs no interpreter; for if its figures, its very boldest metaphors, its most startling comparisons, do not interpret themselves *instantaneously*, it must be either because the poet, mistaking his function, has wrapped himself in myths, or because the reader wants the poetic sense.

The seventy years' captivity—the demolition of the Holy City—the breaking up of the Temple service—the ravaging, and the laying waste of the country, and its occupation by a heathen vagabond population—all these events concurred in bringing to an end the Hebrew poetic consciousness: thenceforward the Jewish people

—the gathered survivors of the long expatriation—became prosaic wholly, historic only:—they became, as a nation, such as should render them the fit recipients and teachers of that next coming Revelation which, because it was to demand a hearing from all people, and to invite the submission of the reason, lays a foundation *in the rigid historic mood*, which, though it may admit symbols, rejects Poetry. A glance at the onward progress of this transition, of which the Jewish people were the immediate subjects, may properly be had, at this place, and before we look back upon the Prophetic Period—to take our leave of it.

In following the course of the national religious literature downwards, from the times of the last of the Prophets, it is a wonder to find how rarely—if indeed at all—a sense of the beauty of nature, or any sentiment allied to poetic feeling, comes to the surface in that literature. In truth it would be difficult to find evidence of its existence, or of its survivance, in the Jewish temperament. The books designated as Apocryphal, and which are unknown to the Hebrew Canon, are, some of them, no doubt, of a time not much more than a century later than that of the closing of the Old Testament Scriptures. Nevertheless they are of another order, in a literary sense; and they indicate the supervention of another mood of the national mind. In explanation of the difference (the fact of *Inspiration* is not now before us) it would not suffice to say that the period within which these Apocryphal books appeared was a continuous era of social and political confusion, and of extreme suffering, and therefore unfavourable to the poetic mood, for the same might be affirmed concerning those times in which the Hebrew poetry shone with its brightest lustre.

But another mind had at length come upon the Jewish people, or upon very many of them; the miseries of the captivity had taken due effect upon them, and so the apostolic word had had its exemplification—"No affliction seemeth for the present joyous, but grievous; yet afterwards it yieldeth the peaceable fruits of righteousness to them that are exercised thereby." Idol-worship, in all its vanity and its frightful gorgeousness, had been witnessed in its home, in the broad places of Babylon; and this spectacle had thoroughly sickened the better-taught men of Jerusalem of their own infatuation towards polytheism; it was so that they now loathed and contemned the sensual worships which themselves and their fathers, with a fatal perversity, had hankered after. Not only was idol-worship spurned, but the national sufferings, and the demolition of their city, and the cessation of their own worship, were at length understood in this sense as a Divine chastisement:—the punishment was accepted, the national ruin was meekly submitted to, and thenceforward a new religious life was inaugurated among them, and for a length of time it was nobly maintained.

The national repentance, if not universal, had, no doubt, been real in more than a few instances. Evidence of this renovated religious feeling is found in that book (Baruch) which, among the Apocryphal writings, comes the nearest to a style that might substantiate its claim to be included in the Canon. A bright monument is this book of a people's mood while enduring, in exile, the contempts and the oppressions of barbarian tyranny:—penitent—submissive to the tyrant who was regarded as the instrument of the Divine Justice; and while submissive, yet hopeful.* The return of the afflicted Jewish people to its duty and to its office, as witness among the nations for truth in Religion, was a preparation for that coming time when, with heroic constancy, they contended for their national and religious existence against the two neighbouring monarchies—the Syrian especially. But this season of doubtful conflict was a time of stern earnestness among the people, and would not be favourable to a *spontaneous* development of the Poetic feeling; besides, the men of the captivity found, on their return to their country, that they had sustained an irretrievable loss—the loss of their language. Instead of it, a dialect had come into use which was incapable of giving utterance to thought and feeling of this order: it was itself of heterogeneous composition:—it had been the product, not of a nation's mind, but of its calamities:—in all its deviations from the ancient forms it bore testimony to the facts of subjugation, expatriation, and of the influx of corrupt populations; besides that in itself

* The book of Baruch stands alone among the books of the Apocrypha, and should be read—religiously, and read historically; and in this sense especially the appended Epistle of Jeremiah, which, genuine or not so, has a graphic distinctness in its exposure of the folly of the Babylonian worships, exceeding what is found in the parallel passages in Isaiah. The writer undoubtedly had *seen* the things of which he speaks: he so speaks as those among ourselves are wont to speak who, with English religious feeling, walk about in the towns and cities of southern Europe. With a homely contempt, and vivacious satire, the writer of this Epistle says—what now might find a place in a Protestant journal of a tour in Italy or Spain:—"For as a scarecrow in a garden of cucumbers keepeth nothing, so are their gods of wood, and laid over with silver and gold . . . they light them candles, yea more than for themselves, whereof they (these gods) cannot see one . . . . their faces are black through the smoke that cometh out of the temple."

it was harsh, unmelodious, defective; it was the vernacular of the busy population of vast plains, and of crowded cities.

During the same periods not only had the rich and copious and metonymic Hebrew given way to the rugged Aramaic (not more poetic as related to Hebrew than the Dutch language is as related to the English), but another inroad was rapidly taking its course—as throughout western Asia, so not less in Palestine than around it—namely, that of the Greek language: at first prevalent as an upper class or governing tongue, and at length, in the apostolic age, as the ordinary popular medium of discourse. But then this importation of the *language* of Greece by no means brought with it the taste or the poetry of Greece, any more than, in any genuine sense, it brought its philosophy. Greek, as the language of literature, came in upon the Jewish mind, not to *enlarge* it, not to *enrich* it, but as a sophistication. Evidence to this effect is largely before us in the extant compositions of that time—in the Apocryphal books, and in the pages of Philo and Josephus. The Jewish mind of that time had weaned itself from the Hebrew breast, and it was imbibing, instead, a nutriment which, to itself, could never be a "sincere milk," easily assimilated, and promoting its growth. The Greek philosophy did not make Jewish Rabbis philosophers, any more than Homer and Sophocles had made them poets. Thus it was that, between the Aramaic barbarism which poetry and philosophy alike would resent, and the Grecian high culture, which the Jewish mind was not prepared to admit, poetry entirely disappeared from the literature of the people: and as to philosophy, it lodged itself upon the upper surface—like houseleek upon the tiles of a building, into which it can strike no roots, and which lives and grows where it lodges, fattened upon no other soil than that supplied by its own decayed foliage.

The meditative Jewish mood—such as it exhibits itself in the book of the "Wisdom of the Son of Sirach" —not wanting in ethical value, or in epigrammatic force, is yet only a groping wisdom. The sage sees not more than a glimmer of light upon earth; and he barely lifts his eyes aloft toward the heavens;—the light of immortality does not send down one cheering beam upon those dim pages; and it must have been from other sources than from these quaint indeterminate compositions that the strenuous martyrs of the time of Antiochus Epiphanes drew their courage in contending to the death for the faith and hope of the nation.

In the course of not more years than those which divide ourselves from the era of the Reformation, the Jewish mind had quite fallen away from what might be called its Poetic Mood. No writings of that order— that we know—had been produced in Judæa. The Rabbis only—and probably it was a few only of these —were familiarly conversant with the archaic national language. A cumbrous, circuitous, and often a sophisticative mode of commenting upon the Prophets, and of darkening their meaning, had taken the place of what might have been a nutritious popular instruction. In so far—and there is reason to think it was very far—as the Greek version had come to be used instead of the Hebrew Scriptures, in the weekly service of the Synagogue, such a substitution would have the effect of removing, to a remote distance, thatpoetic consciousness to which the Inspired Prophets had been used to make their appeal.* The version of the Seventy is bald, prosaic, and wanting in rhythm, as well as majesty. It had, indeed, carried a substantial knowledge of truth far and wide among the nations; but it had so carried these elements as if, while leaving behind the graces of the Hebrew Poetry, and failing to take up the graces of the Greek Poetry, it would commend the grave principles of Theistic doctrine to the Gentile world, stripped of all attractions except those of a severe reality.

Such was the preparation that had been made, in Judæa itself, and throughout the surrounding countries, for the advent of ONE whose ministry was to be of another order—a fulfilment indeed of all prophecy; but an awakening of the nations to a Revelation which must utter itself in terms the most concise, and the freest from ambiguity—in terms which, statute-like, shall not only easily find their equivalents in all tongues—barbarian or cultured, and not only maintain their intelligible quality to the end of time, but, more than this—such as shall reappear with luminous force in the courts of the unseen world, when and where all men are appointed to render their final account. There can be no *Poetry* in the Statute-Book of Universal and Eternal Right! The Hebrew Poetry had been the free medium of the Divine communications during ages while the future unseen destinies of the human family, if not undetermined, were not to be proclaimed. Earth's own voices, earth's harmonies and graces, were mute, and had long been mute, when He should appear who is "from above," and whose mission it was to institute

* See Note.

a new life—the life eternal—the life in attestation of which multitudes were, ere long, to welcome death on the rack—in the amphitheatre, and in the fire.

The extant memorials of the early Church—the martyr-Church—exhibit few, if indeed there be any, indications of the revival of that consciousness of the sublime and beautiful in Nature which had been so long in abeyance. The period of preparation for Christianity, and the subsequent martyr ages, must be reckoned to include a space of nearly seven hundred years. It was not until long after the conclusion of the martyr time that this consciousness reappears at all within the field of Christian literature. When therefore it is attempted to show the derivation of our modern poetic feeling from the Hebrew Scriptures, the attempt would be hopeless to establish an "unbroken succession," as if the flow had been continuous. That river, the streams whereof, making glad the city of God, sparkled up from the Holy Hill, disappears at the time when the prophetic dispensation comes to its close; and these waters of Siloam then found for themselves an underground conduit alongside of the lapse of many centuries; nor do they come again into day until near our modern times.

Assuredly the Rabbinical writers did not so drink of those waters as to receive thence a poetic inspiration! These grave, learned, laborious, and whimsical doctors, had so used themselves to converse with whatever is less important, and nugatory, and frivolous, that they had become incapable of apprehending whatever, in Nature, or in life, or in Holy Scripture, is great—beautiful—sublime: in all things that which was factitious or arbitrary had fixed the eye of the Rabbi, who had become blind to the majesty of the creation. The Prophets were men who lived abroad—breathing the air of the hills and plains, of the forests and of the gardens of Palestine; but their commentators—the Talmudists—were men of the cloister, the light of which was dim, and its atmosphere dust-burdened and sultry. Imagination of a sort the Rabbi might boast; but it was prolific of monstrous chimeras, and chose rather the prodigious than the true. Astute more than wise, the Jewish masters of thought groped along a path abounding in thorns, and scanty in fruits.*

As to the Christian community—in the East and the West alike—eager theological controversies came in the place of sufferings. Heresy, instead of Paganism, showed itself, even more than imprisonments and tortures, to be out of accordance with the spirit of Poetry. Christian men—orthodox and heterodox alike—had passed through that vast intellectual and moral revolution which had brought with it the consciousness of Truth in Belief, as a personal concernment—incalculably momentous. With this feeling of individual relationship to God, on terms to which an abstract scheme of theology was to give its sanction, the dialectic Reason came to be invoked, and was brought into play continually; and the style of this controversial reason is always strenuous, harsh, and unmelodious. The controversial mood, full of disquietudes, and of evil surmisings, and of angry imputations, is the very opposite of the discursive, imaginative, poetic temper. No condition of the human mind shows a front so repulsive

* See Note.

to taste and feeling as does the logical mood, with its formal egotism, and its intolerance. This temper of earnest wrangling (albeit for the right) is death to imaginative, as well as to the moral, sensibility. For centuries it seemed as if men, in contending for the Truth of God, had quite ceased to see or to know that the world we live in is beautiful, and that the universe is great.

There was a season in the growth of the Ascetic Institute—dating its rise in the Decian persecution—in the lapse of which there may be traced much of the spirit of Romance, and something of the spirit of Poetry. A conception of romance, if not of poetry, one might believe to have inspired, even the crabbed and dogmatic Jerome, when he put together, for popular use, the prodigious legends concerning the ascetic heroes—St. Paul the Monk, St. Hilarion, and St. Malchus, and others of the sort. It is certain, as to Palladius, and the compilers of the Lausiac Memoirs, that they had caught a feeling of the sublime, if not of the beautiful, in Nature; and the terms in which they speak of the horrors of the bladeless wilderness suggest the idea that the complementary conception of what is gay and beautiful, from the neighbourhood of which the heroic anchoret fled far, was not quite absent from their thoughts. These writers, in their encomiums of what might be called—spirituality run savage, betray their own consciousness, and that of their heroes, of those decorations of the material world upon which they dared not look: whatever was fair, bright, gay, joyous, in creation was contraband in the ascetic philosophy; nevertheless some of those who signalized their zeal in denouncing these graces of Nature gave evidence, obliquely, of the strength of their own forbidden feeling towards them.

In many instances the Christian solitary was a man of culture, who, in sincerity, had fled from the abounding corruptions of cities, with their Christianized paganism—and who, when he had well nestled himself in his cavern, and had learned a lesson, not extremely difficult, in a warm climate, how to exist and be content in the destitution of the appliances of artificial life, and had come to draw spiritual nutriment from every misery, would return to his early tastes, and would follow that leading of pious meditation which finds its path from the worship of God, the Creator, to the manifestation of the Divine attributes in the Creation. No wilderness in which man may exist is absolutely bladeless: no solitude can be wanting in the elements of sublimity, if it be skirted by purple and jagged rocks, which outline themselves sharply against a cloudless azure by day, and against the curtain of stars by night. When once the genuine relish of natural beauty has been engendered, the rule will be—or often it will be—the fewer the objects on which it feeds, the more intense, the more concentrated, will be the feeling they excite. The shrivelled grass—the thorny shrub—the scanty rush, will prove themselves to be fraught with all poetry; and then fertile devout meditation will feast itself upon these crumbs of the beautiful—even as the life-long tenant of a dungeon learns to satisfy the social instincts of humanity in tending a spider.

Far more of what, with our modern tastes, we should admit to be true poetic feeling, here and there makes its appearance upon the rugged surface of the ancient asceticism, than we can find in the factitious versification of some of the great Church-writers of the same time—eastern or western. Such spontaneous adornments of the ascetic life, if compared with the laboured poetry—so called, of Gregory Nazianzen or of Ambrose, might suggest a comparison between the rich mosses, with a hundred hues—that embossed the rocks around the hermit's cavern—and the dazzle and the glare of the marbles and jewellery of the basilicas of the imperial city.

Grotesque, more than poetic, are those romances in the composition of which Jerome (as we have said) beguiled his leisure at Bethlehem, and abused the credulity of his contemporaries. But another style meets us when we look into the correspondence of the accomplished and spiritually voluptuous Basil—an ascetic indeed who, while maintaining his repute as a saint—not falsely, but factitiously—knew how, in his retreat on the banks of the Iris, to surround himself with rural enjoyments which might have been envied by the younger Pliny, in his villa on the margin of the lake of Como.*

It does not appear—or the evidence to that effect is not at hand, showing—how far the Psalms of David, rich as they are in poetic feeling, availed to nourish a kindred feeling within the monastic communities. Through the lapse of a thousand years—dating back from the time of the revival of literature in Italy—the Psalter had so been rolled over the lips of monks, morning, noon, and night, in inane repetitions, as must have deprived these odes of almost all meaning—spiritual or intellectual. Let the modern reader imagine

* See Note.

what would be the effect upon himself of repeating the hundred and fifty Psalms, entire—round the year, fifty times or more!

But the waking hour of the European mind came on; our modern consciousness toward Nature, as well as Art, sprang into existence; and along with this renovation of the Tastes, as well as of the Reason of the western nations, there came the diffusion, and the restored influence of the Inspired writings. Thenceforward this mighty influence, which was at once a *force* and a *guidance*, took its way alongside of the recovered classical literature; and the two powers—the sacred and the profane—went on commingling their energies in those various portions which have given nationality to the literature, distinctively, of Italy, of England, of France, and of Germany.*

* See Note.

CHAPTER XIV.

THE MILLENNIUM OF THE HEBREW POETRY, AND THE PRINCIPLE WHICH PERVADES IT.

There is presupposed in the phrase which has been used as the title of this volume, an idea of unity or continuity, as belonging to the Hebrew Poetry. We speak of the *Spirit* of the Hebrew Poetry, and in thus speaking a meaning is conveyed to this effect—that there is a oneness of intention, or a constant principle, or a prominent characteristic, which may be recognized throughout, and which attaches, more or less decisively to each writer, in a long series—connecting the whole, and imparting to the mass a high degree of consistency and of homogeneousness. The Hebrew Poetry, from its earliest era to its last day, stands in view as a One Poetry.

This averment in its behalf means something more than this—which might as well be affirmed of the Poetry of Greece, or of that of Persia, or of Rome—that it is the literature of one people or race, and of a people strongly marked with the peculiarities of their national mood of mind, and of their habits, and their religious notions and usages. More than this must be intended to be affirmed when we so speak of the literature of the Hebrews, and we must mean what would best be made intelligible by the hypothesis that, in the midst of these many and diverse voices—each uttering itself after its own fashion, and following each other through the lapse of more than a thousand years—there is heard the mind and feeling of ONE, who is unchangeable in disposition and principle—the same yesterday, and to-day, and in all time. This, undoubtedly, *is* the hypothesis on the ground of which we accept the books of the Canonical Scriptures, as given by the Inspiration of God—in a sense peculiar to themselves. But just now let this hypothesis (unquestionably true as it is) be set apart, or removed from our view. That which remains, after this abeyance of the belief of Inspiration has been effected, is a congeries of facts of such a kind that they must compel an immediate return to that belief, apart from which these facts can receive no solution whatever.

So familiar are the topics involved in this argument that the reader who is well used to his Bible may believe that he fully apprehends them: and it may be so; and yet it is not so with many who, following the daily routine of Scripture lessons in the track of the misadjusted order (which in a chronological sense is *disorder*) of the Old Testament books, fail to perceive, or fail to recollect, that, in passing from one Psalm to the next, or from one Prophet to the next, they may have spanned a five hundred, or even a thousand years; and moreover that they have made this leap in a retrograde direction:—as, for instance, when an ode later dated than the Captivity, is followed by one which is earlier dated than the Exodus. These anachronisms of our modern Bibles take possession of our minds in a disadvantageous manner, and stand in the way of clear and firmly held convictions concerning the historic reality of the series of events. If the English language, in a thousand years, had undergone as little change as did the Hebrew language in that time, and if we were to read, in constant mislocation, passages of Cowper and of Chaucer, or of Milman and Bede, it would demand a very frequent reference to the dates of our literature to dispel the chronological confusions that would beset us.

The degree of uniformity or homogeneousness in the literature of a people, which might easily be regarded as probable, on common principles, would be of this kind—first, there is the same language throughout, with diversities of dialect only; and there might be the same metrical or rhythmical system; then we should find the same figurative material—related as this would be to the climate and the country; and we might also find the same theology and ethics—or nearly the same —as well as allusions to nearly the same political and social institutions. Prevalent as these characteristics might be, and enduring as might be their influence, it is not to be imagined that a series of writers, representing the national history through so long a term as more than a thousand years, should fail to exhibit great diver sities on such grounds as these, namely—(1) The indi vidual disposition and intellectual disparities of the writers (this must be even if they were all nearly contemporaries and fellow-citizens). (2) The varying position of these writers, as belonging to, or as representing the several orders and interests in the commonwealth. (3) The influence upon each writer of those marked changes in the habits and dispositions of a people from which no people, hitherto, has been exempt—or not exempt if many centuries of their history are to be included. In these senses uniform, and in these senses also diverse, the literature—or say, the poetry—of a one people may be accepted as the product of causes the operation of which is intelligible.

The Hebrew writers do in fact exhibit much diversity in the several respects above named:—individually they differ—each has his manner:—differences also are perceptible among them arising from their social position, as of the sacerdotal class, or of other classes:—differences also there are the distinctness of which is sufficient, in several instances, to support an inference as to the place in the national history to which each writer belongs. Yet in this last-named respect the differences are far from being such as, on ordinary principles, might seem likely to arise from the greatness of those changes through which the Hebrew race had passed in this lapse of time. These changes embrace the most extreme and peculiar conditions under which a people may at all conserve its continuous identity; for the fortunes of this people went the round of national well-doing and of disaster. Not to go back to the patriarchal age, although then this poetry had had its commencement, the Hebrew lyre gave evidence of a long and well-skilled practice at the very moment when the race, in tumultuous excitement, stood, ransomed and astounded, upon the eastern margin of the Red Sea. The training of the people who, with their Leader, there sang the song of triumph unto Jehovah (Exodus xv.) had been such a schooling in music, and in recitative worship, as might be carried on in the house of bondage, and while the tribes, in severest servitude, were labouring under the sun in the brickfields of Pharaoh. Yet it was then and there that this peculiar function of the Israelitish race made its bold essay of power. This lyre, attuned on the banks of the Nile, did its office until the moment of sadness came—a thousand years later, for leaving it to sigh in the winds by the rivers of Babylon. Frequent notes of this same lyre give proof that the tent-life of the terrible wilderness had not put it to silence; and at the time when these wanderings were to cease, strains burst anew from its wires of surpassing majesty (Deut. xxxiii.) It might seem as if rhythm, and music, and bold imagery, so floated in the air far around the camp of God, that even the false-hearted prophet, when he looked down upon it from "the high places of Baal," caught the same rhythm and the same fire.*

Throughout the precarions times of the Judges—a three centuries or more—when everywhere within the borders of Israel, often—

the highways were deserted,
And the travellers walked through by-ways:
The villages ceased—they ceased in Israel;

—even through those dark years of almost national extinction, the energies of sacred song did not decline. The ruddy youth of Bethlehem found poetry and music—one divine art—ready for his hand, and for his voice, and for his soul; and his Psalms are vouchers for a fact so well deserving notice, that neither the sweetness of these tones, nor their depth, nor their grandeur, were in any manner affected, for the worse, by the changeful fortunes of the man. It is the same soul, graceful and ten-

* It belongs to another line of argument to note the fact that Balaam's reluctant prophecy was—"The word put into his mouth by God," (Numbers xxiii.)

der, even when it is the most impassioned, which utters itself, whether the poet be the leader of a band of outlaws in the rugged wilderness, or the anointed of the Lord, with tens of thousands of warriors at his side.

The Israelitish monarchy, through another long era—a five hundred years—underwent seasons of fiery trial in its alternations of power and splendour, and of decay and subjugation, and almost of extinction; and these revolutions in the political and social condition of the people were enough—were more than enough—under ordinary conditions, to bring about an absolute loss, or final disappearance of the poetic feeling—the poetic habitude, and even of the rhythmical art—the metrical *practice*, among a people. The people of Greece lost the soul of poetry within as short a time, and under conditions much less severe.

But there was a vitality in the Hebrew Poetry which preserved it from decay through these eleven centuries of national fortunes and reverses. There was a principle within it which resisted every influence that might have wrought upon it, either to abate its tone, or to alter and vitiate its moral and religious import. Not only did this poetry last out its destined millennium, but, with a robust persistence—with a fixed and resolute consistency—it continued to vindicate the same moral axioms, and to denounce, in the same terms of inexorable rebuke, the vices of mankind at large, and the corruptions of the one people in particular. Amidst the varying moods of a passionate people, this millennial utterance does not vary by a shade from its pristine theology, or its pristine ethics. Do we please to call this theology "unphilosophic?"—if it was so in its earliest forms, it continued to be such in its latest forms—notwithstanding the tendency of religious thought, always and everywhere, to sophisticate its notions, and to complicate its phraseology, in the direction, on the one hand, toward mysticism; on the other hand, toward vague, fruitless, and negative abstractions. Or do we please to say that this Hebrew morality was severe and uncompromising? If it was so at its birth in the glooms of the wilderness of Sinai—such also was it in that day of sadness when the triumphant idolater carried "of the vessels of the house of the Lord to Babylon, and put them in his temple at Babylon." Or if we say—and this is far nearer to the truth—that the Hebrew religious system rested, peacefully, upon an assured belief of the graciousness and clemency of Jehovah; such it was at the first, when the Eternal proclaimed Himself—"the Lord—the Lord God, merciful and gracious, long-suffering, and abundant in goodness and truth;" so was it in that later age when the terms of the divine economy towards man were to be repeated in form—"What now doth the Lord require of thee, but to do justly, and to love mercy, and to walk humbly with thy God."

This consistency—this exemption from the variableness that attaches always, and everywhere else, to whatever is human—is utterly inconceivable until, for its explanation, we bring in the one truth that, whoever might be the Prophet that challenges the people to a hearing, the SPEAKER is ever the same—the same in mind and in purpose through a thousand generations.

That first principle of true Religion—the Personality of God (insufficient and unpleasing are all phrases of this order!)—this principle always taught and affirmed in the Hebrew Scriptures, is also insensibly conveyed in that mode which—rather than, and far better than, any formal affirmation—gives us our consciousness of the individuality—the separate independent personality of those around us. Whence is it, in fact, that, in our every-day converse with those who make up our homes and social circles, we unconsciously acquire our conception of the disposition, the moods, the tastes, the constitutional faults and virtues, and the mental bulk of each and all? A knowledge of character—a knowledge so important to every one's own conduct—is a slowly derived induction; it is an accretion from day to day, built up out of each person's casual utterances and incidental discourse, as every one is moved or provoked by the occurrences of the passing hour. If we only hear what has been said on any occasion, we know who has said it:—the utterance is index of the person; or if a single utterance be not sufficient for this recognition, a few, taken at hazard, will not fail to remove any doubt as to the speaker. It is the same as to our feeling of the individuality of the prominent persons of history. If memoirs sufficient are extant—if there are records sufficient, of the sayings and the doings of noted persons, we come to know *the person*, thenceforward, even with a distinctness that approaches the vivacity of actual acquaintance.

If, then, we accept it as an axiom of Biblical science that a main purpose of the Old Testament Scriptures was this—to ingrain upon the minds of men this vivid conception of God—the one Living and Ever-present Creator, Ruler, Father—then it is seen that this purpose has been secured in that one method in which alone it could be effected—namely, by the record of utterances, each related to some occasion of the time, on the part of Him who is *thus* to be made known. The Speaker—

unchanging in disposition and in His principles of conduct—utters His mind by a direct conveyance of it in the form—"Thus saith the Lord." Century after century, through all the shiftings of a people's weal, and of their correspondence with their neighbours, God, their God, thus utters His mind. Nothing approaching to this vivid revelation, this bringing the conception of the PERSON home to the consciousness of men, has elsewhere ever taken place: it is the peculiarity of the Hebrew Scriptures.

Why should the Hebrew testimony concerning the true and living God—why should it have been thrown into the poetic mould?—why should this theology have been made to flow as a river through the levels of time, reflecting, as it passes, the objects on its banks? One might speculate to little purpose in attempting an answer to this question. Meantime the fact is before us—the Hebrew Poetic Prophecy is a revealing of God, carried on through a millennium, in all which course of time, just as the thunder of heaven is even-toned, and is always like itself in awful grandeur, and is unlike other sounds of earth, so did the voice of the Eternal continuously peal over-head of the chosen people, and thus did it take firm possession of the human mind—which never, thenceforward, lost its consciousness toward God, as a MIND—a WILL—a HEART, and a concentrated RESOLVE, in a right knowledge of whom stands our well-being—present and future.

If there be among those that actually read the Old Testament Scriptures any who are wavering in their belief of the proper inspiration of the prophetic books, such persons might be advised to put to themselves a question which, perhaps, hitherto they have never propounded, or even thought of, namely, this—Whether, in the habitual perusal of these books, there has not formed itself in their minds what might be called a *consciousness* of the Divine Being as—A Person of History—a feeling or cognition, much more sharply defined than an abstraction can ever be? And then this well-defined historic conception is consistent with itself in all its elements:—every particle of which this one Idea is constituted is characteristic, and is in harmony with the whole. If it be so—

Then comes a second question, which may be thus worded—Is it conceivable that an Idea of this order—a conception so majestic, and so vivid and real, and so truthfully historic, should, even if once it had been formed, have floated itself onwards, unbroken, through the waywardness of so many uncontrolled human minds? Onwards, unbroken, it has come, even from the remote age of its first expression, down to the latest age of its last utterance. Nothing that is incredible and inconceivable can be more inconceivable than is a supposition of this kind. With a healthful confidence in the sureness of the instincts of truth, *a mind in health* returns to its belief that it is indeed the voice of God which has given consistence and authority to the millennium of the Hebrew Scriptures.

It is a trite theme with Biblical expositors to insist upon that doctrinal and ethical consistency which imparts its character of oneness to the Canonical writings. Argumentation on this ground is perfectly valid; yet what now we have in view differs from that argument, as well in its substance, as in the use that may be made of it. Difficult it is, and must be, to give distinct expression to a conception of this kind, involving as it does, the most sacred elements, and in doing so to avoid apparent improprieties; so to write as shall offend no religious decorum, and yet so as shall be sufficient for bringing into view, with distinctness, an occult analogy. If, however, a writer's *intention* is well understood, indulgence may well be granted him on any single occasion when he bespeaks it.

If the Hebrew Poetry, regarded as a whole, be a national literature, and if it carries upon its surface, very distinctly, its nationality, and not less distinctly the individuality of each writer in the series—it carries with it *also*—and it does so with a bright distinctness (let us speak with all reverence) the *Individuality* of the INFINITE, the ETERNAL, the JUST, the GOOD, and WISE, who is the AUTHOR of this Hebrew literature in a higher sense.

The Bible reader—if his consciousness has not already been damaged by his converse with petulant and negatory criticism—is here challenged to pursue the suggestion that has been put before him. The more he gives himself to this line of thought—following it out in a new perusal of the prophetic Scriptures, from first to last—the more convincing will be the inference, and the more irresistible the impression, that these Scriptures are everywhere marked with an Individuality which is not that of the people, and which is not that of the men—the prophets in series—but is that of HIM "who spake by the prophets."

An argument resting on this ground may easily be put aside by those who may be inclined to escape from a foreseen inference; for an appeal is made to a sense—to a feeling—to a moral and a literary taste which all men have not, and which some who once had it have lost, and of which any one may choose to profess himself destitute. We now address ourselves to those whose mental and moral condition is of that kind which readily coalesces with Truth, and not the less so when it is found beneath the surface. We say—found beneath the surface in this sense:—the individuality of each of the inspired writers presents itself to view, *on the surface:* the theology and the moral system of all—as *one religion*, is conspicuous *on the surface* of the Scriptures; but what we here venture to speak of in terms of reverence—namely, the Personal Character or Individuality of the Divine Being—is a fact—distinct indeed, but occult, and needing therefore to be sought for.

CHAPTER XV.

THE HEBREW LITERATURE, AND OTHER LITERATURES.

Much might easily be written, pertinently perhaps, and ingeniously, no doubt, and learnedly too, with the intention of instituting a comparison between the Hebrew Scriptures and other national literatures, which must be those of China, of India, in its two fields, and of Persia, and of Greece. Comparative criticisms on this ground may be instituted either with an intention hostile to the claims of the Hebrew literature, or with an intention favourable—not so much to those claims, as to the assumed literary repute, and the supposed genius and intelligence of the several writers.

Comparisons of this kind, and it is the same whether the intention of those who institute them be hostile or apologetic, we hold to be founded altogether upon an erroneous hypothesis; and in fact they never fail to exhaust, quickly, any small substance of reason that there may be in them, and to spend themselves in disquisitions that are nugatory, impertinent, and pedantic. The reader soon becomes sick of any such attenuated criticisms, in the course of which the writer swelters away to no end—for he has set out on a path that leads to nothing. If now putting out of view the Oriental literatures, with which the mass of readers can have none but a third-hand acquaintance, and which must be fragmentary and insufficient for any purposes of intelligent adjudication

—and if we were to bring into view that only ancient literature with which educated persons are more or less familiar—the literature of Greece—its Philosophy, its History, its Poetry—lyric, dramatic, and epic, then might any proposed comparison with the Hebrew books be peremptorily rejected, on this ground, that the dissimilarities—the contrasts—the contrarieties, are so great and striking as to throw absurdity upon the attempt to establish any ground of analogy—whether for purposes of encomium or of disparagement.

The Greek literature, in each of its species—not less than its inimitable sculptures—is a product of art; it is an elaborate combination of the poet's or of the artist's individual genius and practised skill, with the highly-cultured taste, and the large requirements of the men of his time. But, as we have said, again and again, the Hebrew writers are never artists. Two or three books of the Canon excepted, if indeed these should be excepted, then it must be affirmed that everything within this circle is unartistic in a literary sense, and unlaboured. Certain metrical usages are complied with by the poet; and so he complies with the grammatical usages of his language: but his course of thought obeys an influence of another, and of a higher order. It would not be enough to affirm—That the manner of the Hebrew writers is that of simple-hearted men, who naturally fall into an inartificial and fragmentary mode of expressing themselves; for this affirmation does not satisfy the requirements of the instance before us. Their manner is not an artless innocence; it is not the rudeness of a pristine era; for, from the first to the last, it has the force and the firm purpose proper to a deep intention. Moreover the constant course of things in the development of a people's mind is this—that a literature which is inartificial in its dawn, goes through a process of elaboration in its noon-tide; nor ever fails, in its decline, to become false in taste, and wanting in soul.

No process of this sort gives evidence of its presence in the passage of the Hebrew Poetry from age to age; and yet its presence becomes manifest enough at the very moment after the sealing of the prophetic economy: thenceforward Jewish literature shows its grey hairs. Within the compass of the Psalms there are odes which belong to the extreme points of the national history—if we take its commencement at the time of the Exodus, and date its conclusion a century later than the return of the remnant of the people to their City, and the restoration of their worship. We here embrace more than a thousand years; yet, on the ground of the natural progress of Poetry, from its earliest to its latest style, this difference of date would not be detected, and it is indicated only by references to events in the people's history.

The Hebrew literature differs absolutely, and it differs in a manner that sets at nought all attempted comparisons between itself and that of Greece. It does so, for instance, in the department of history; for even if we take up that of Greece, not as we find it in Thucydides, but as it pleasantly flows on as a devious river in the pages of Herodotus, we should do no service to the Hebrew chroniclers by attempting to show that, if *they* had written of Assyria, and of Babylon, and of Egypt, discursively, we might have found in our Bibles a match for the Clio or the Melpomene. With these narrators of single lines of events there was no ability of the same order; there were no literary habits of the same order.

Even less tolerable would be an attempt to match David or Isaiah with Æschylus, or Sophocles, or even with Hesiod or Pindar. It is not so much that we might not find in the Greek writers—Plato, for instance, or Æschylus—the rudiments of a theology—true and great, so far as it goes; but in no Greek writer, in none anterior to the diffusion of the Gospel, are there to be found any rudiments whatever—any mere fragments, however small—of that Life of the soul toward God, and of that Divine correspondence with man which, in every Psalm, in every page of the Prophets, shines—burns—rules, with force—overrules Poetry—drives from its area the feeble resources of human art, and brings down upon earth those powers and those profound emotions which bespeak the nearness of the Infinite and Eternal, when God holds communion with those that seek to live in the light of His favour.

There is, however, a ground—not indeed of comparison, but of intelligible contrast, which it is well to pursue; for it is here that the proper claims of the Hebrew Scriptures come into a position where there neither is, nor can be, any sort of rivalry.

Let it just now be granted (for a moment) that, within the circle of the Greek literature—including its history, its poetry, and its philosophy—there might be found a *sufficient* theology, and a *sufficient* system of morals—a belief toward God, and a practice of the virtues—personal and social—justice, temperance, mercy, or benevolence; and let those who would risk such a paradox affirm that, on the whole, the Greek theology and ethics are as commendable, and as eligible, as are the theology and the ethics of the Hebrews: yet is there this difference—if there were no other—that the one religious scheme has thrown itself into a form to which a direct authentication, as from Heaven, could never be made to apply; while, on the contrary, the Hebrew theology, and its ethical system, exist in a form to which the voucher from above may be made to attach; and therefore that this scheme may meet the requirements of mankind—as an authenticated Religion, which may be taken up and used as the rule and warrant of the religious life. Briefly to open up this contrast will be proper; and two or three instances, selected from different quarters, will be enough to show what it is that is intended.

The question is not—Which, in any two samples, is the preferable one, on abstract grounds, as more true, or of better tendency than the other?—but this—To which of the two—when placed side by side—it would be possible (or, if possible, useful) to attach the seal of Heaven, as our warrant for accepting it as the source of belief in religion? Nor does it at all concern us to inquire whether, in Plato, the theology and the philosophy be his own, or be that of his master—whether it is Socrates who speaks, or Plato, for himself and his master; in either case it is the same flow of human thought throughout these Dialogues—deep—sincere—ingenuous—a depth which has secured for them, and must ever give them, an immortality among cultured nations, to the world's end. And this is an immortality which perhaps may brighten so much the more, when, in the onward course of religious opinion, Christianity—or let us better say, the Religion of Holy Scripture, at length accepted, rejoiced in by all men, shall draw all things that are the most excellent into its wake—no one thenceforward unwisely attempting to bring the two upon a level, as if both alike were Revelations—both alike inspired. The one is sterling, excellent, admirable, weighty, and of inestimable value: —the other is Divine—it is more than human:—God has sealed it as His own, and the two stand before us, distinguished, not only in this way, that the one bears on it a stamp which the other has not;—nor only in this way, that the doctrine of the one, as compared with the doctrine of the other, is preferable, and is more true, and is more conspicuously Divine—but in this way, that the one body of religious thought which actually carries the seal, presents itself under conditions adapted to so peculiar a purpose and to so special a service as that of receiving this mark from Heaven, and of going forth into all the world—to rule the human mind, and to make valid every hope and every dread that can strengthen virtue.

Poor and narrow indeed is that jealousy, pretended to be felt for the honour of our Christianity, which prompts some to lay bare the ambiguous speculations of the PHÆDO—pointing the finger at its tremulous places, and vaunting its dimness, and ending with the triumphant interjection—"See what was the darkness of heathenism!" Nay, this dimness was crepuscular; it was not a shadow of the eventide. This dimness, regarded in its bearing upon the progress of the human mind, bespoke the morning at hand; and why should we doubt it, or why be backward to give utterance to our confidence, that, to these illustrious minds—this Creed—"wherefore we hold it to be true that the soul is immortal and imperishable"—was, to him who so spoke, a presage of day? The dying sage, who said, γὰρ τὸ ἆθλον καὶ ἡ ἐλπὶς μεγάλη, shall he not find that, within the Hades, on the threshold of which his foot then calmly rested, there was, in due time, to be opened, a door of hope?

"To stay oneself," says this teacher, "with absolute confidence, or to utter with assurance, as certain, the things we have thus discoursed about, would not become a wise man." Nevertheless, the argument on this side was of such strength that, as he says, a man might well live, and practise every virtue, on the faith of it. The reasoning of Socrates, if translated into the terms of modern philosophy—if put into its equivalents in French, German, or English, would not carry conviction to many minds; and the less so because reasons, drawn from the instincts of the moral life, which with ourselves must have the greatest force, are not, in this instance, adduced. Nor is the faith of Socrates (Plato) in any proper sense a *theological* faith. God is not the reason of the immortality of man; nor is He the Granter of it; nor is the favour of God spoken of as the light of that life future.

But even if the argument of the PHÆDO were more complete than it is, in a theological sense, it is, at the best, nothing better than the opening out of a hypothesis:—the reasoner disposes of certain objections; he fortifies his position on this side, and that side. Human thought is here evolving itself, after its manner, on ground over which no road has been laid down, and on which no sure light shines. In what way, then, or to what purpose, might this, or, indeed, the entire body of Plato's writings, receive a warranty from Heaven, and so come into a place of authority, in matters of belief? To no such purpose as this are they adapted. Looking now to the APOLOGY, and to the PHÆDO, as related to the same great question of a future life, the attractive quality of both is that modesty, that calm philosophic balance of the mind, professing its choice of a belief that is favourable to virtue, and enheartening especially to those who bear testimony for wisdom and goodness among the enemies of both; the Martyr-teacher will yet do no more than declare his own faith, and make profession of a hope, the reality of which, or its futility, none among the living knows, or can know:—it is known, he says, to God alone.*

Taking the Platonic belief—just as it stands in these Dialogues, and in the Apology, the *substance* to which, in any way whatever, the seal of God might come to be attached is—not, that belief itself; but only—the dialectic conditions under which it may be entertained, as a probable hypothesis, by a wise and good man. The voucher could reach this extent only—that it is *allowable* so to believe concerning the future of the human soul. If beyond this we should say—the Socratic belief might have received an *explicit* approval, this could only be by appending to the Platonic text a supplementary text—a page or paragraph, which, in fact, is not there. What we have to do with is—Plato, as the existing manuscripts have put him into our hands.

Then there would be a further difficulty in affixing the seal of Heaven to the Socratic, or the Platonic creed—namely, this—that the belief of the immortality and future blessedness of good men is not in any way made to take its rise in a theology, or even in an ethical

* If the last words of the Apology may seem ambiguous, the inference we are here concerned with will be the same:—the doctrine of immortality, as professed by Socrates, was not more than a choice among contrary hypotheses. See Note.

scheme. Although Plato is not himself an atheist, his doctrine of immortality is absolutely atheistical. How then shall He in whom is the life of the future life authenticate a creed in which the Divine Attributes find no place, and are not once named?

In search of a belief which might thus be made available as a Religion—authenticated by God, we must look elsewhere. The rareness and the brevity of those passages in the Hebrew Scriptures which relate to the future life we are all used to speak of, and also to conjecture the probable reasons of this reserve. Yet few as such passages may be, and brief as they are—this characteristic attaches to each of them—namely, that the language of each is peremptory, and assured. Great is the difference—on this ground—between a copious discursive disquisition—with its probable conclusions—laboriously reached—and a ten words sharply uttered, in the natural tone of one who is reporting things of which he has a direct and infallible knowledge. This sort of determinate averment—inviting no discussion, and supposing no question or contradiction—possesses, let it be clearly understood, that logical form which it should have, in adaptation to the purpose of receiving the seal of God.

In turning from the recorded hope of Socrates, to the recorded hope of David, the contrast we are here concerned with is not that of *quality;* nor is it that of the *quantity of illumination* which is shed upon the two respectively, but this—which arises from a distinct affirmation, resting upon knowledge in the one case, compared with the avowal of an opinion, on grounds of probable reasoning, in the other case. Where Socrates professes his hope of a happy release from the pains and labours of life, and an admittance into the society of the heroes of past time, who, he says, are inhabitants of Hades *for ever*, David thus gives the upshot of his nightly meditations, and thus, as we might say, does he open the roll of the book, in readiness for its receiving the seal of Heaven, by bringing in the Lord—the First Party in this compact, even as if visibly present for the purpose :—

I have set the Lord always before me;
Because He is at my right hand I shall not be moved:
Therefore my heart is glad, and my glory rejoiceth:
My flesh also shall rest in hope;
For thou wilt not leave my soul in Hades,
Neither wilt thou suffer thine Holy One to see corruption.
Thou wilt show me the path of life:
In thy presence is fulness of joy,
At thy right hand are pleasures for evermore. *

As is the difference between the first doubtful streak of light in the eastern sky, and the blaze of noon in the tropics, such is the difference in quantity of illumination between the hopeful belief of Socrates, and the firm belief of David. Equally great also is the difference as to the *quality* of that light in each instance—might one say—as to the *actinic force*—the germinative energy of each.

Yet if we allege that the Platonic philosophy, because it is hypothetic and indeterminate, could not be given forth to the world as a Divine Revelation (even if it were of much better religious quality than it is) should we not be led to seek for what might serve such a pur-

* The Messianic meaning of this Psalm has no bearing upon our argument in this instance.

pose in those products of the Greek mind, the very characteristic of which is a determinative and categorical declaration of principles? Shall we not find in Aristotle that which Plato will not yield? With this purpose in view, it is natural to turn to the Nicomachean Ethics:--a book of sharply cut definitions and distinctions, within the circuit of which nearly every term belonging to the glossary of common discourse, as well as of philosophical discussion, finds its due place, in and between its contraries, and its cognates, and its synonyms. Exact, discriminative, unquestionable, for the most part, are these refined collocations of ethical terms. How far such a book might be made to subserve the purposes of a Treatise on Morals is not a question that concerns us in this place: it might, in a sense, serve this purpose, and so might a Lexicon, if cut in pieces, and put up anew in logical order, instead of the alphabetical order.

It is clear that what might be said of a treatise like the Nicomachean Ethics, might be affirmed also of Euclid's Elements of Geometry. Both profess to be demonstrative: or otherwise to state the case, Aristotle and Euclid, alike, so deal with the matter in hand, at each step of their progress, as to exhaust all supposable contrary affirmations. In each instance any hypothetic contradiction is overthrown, or is driven off the field. On the ground of formal logical demonstration no place is left for *authentication*, as if it might be superadded to the process of reasoning. If the reasoning, in any single instance, were faulty or fallacious, then it could gain nothing by the seal which a higher authority might give it: but if the reasoning be valid, and if we may examine it, in every link, then a voucher for its truth is quite superfluous:—nothing is added to our faith in the relations of extension to be told, from on high, that the three angles of a triangle are equal to two right angles —or to 180 degrees. The definitions of this treatise —the Ethics—accord, or they do not accord, with the notions we may have entertained of the usages and proprieties of the Greek language, in the class of terms which it embraces. Rarely, or to a very limited extent only, does Aristotle dip into the depths of the moral consciousness: for, as he is wanting in a theology—if theology be more than a naked abstraction—so he wants soul, nor could he ever be thought of as the Prophet of great truths; or as one who was "sent of Heaven." Whither else, then, on the field of Greek literature, shall we turn in search of any such embodiment of religious and moral principles as might be fit for receiving an authentication, so that it might be accepted and trusted to by men everywhere? The Poets of the earlier era—Hesiod and Homer—may be thought to give expression, in some undefined sense, to a religious and moral system; but this system, if thus it may be spoken of, everywhere so commingles itself with, and weaves itself into, the texture of a polytheistic tissue, that no voucher for great truths could be attached to the mass, so as not to complicate itself with the fables that thicken around it, on every page. Nor does an extrication of the true from the fabulous become at all more easy when we reach times of higher refinement, and of a more elaborate art, as it is found in the tragedians—Æschylus, Sophocles, or Euripides.

Much has been said and written of late in behalf of what professes to be a benevolent and catholic doctrine concerning the religious schooling of the human family:

—all tribes of earth, it is said, have been alike cared for, and have been led forward in company toward the true and the good; and among those who have thus been providentially disciplined, the Hebrew people is not forgotten. Yet to each and to all *alike* an unauthenticated Revelation has been granted. China has had its Bible—the Buddhist millions have had their Bible—and so have the people of Persia and of Greece; and so of Palestine: all men cared for alike! (a good belief, indeed,) and all, not only cared for alike, but dealt with in the same manner; for among each people there has been raised up a prophet, or a series of prophets—men of soul and of fire, who, either as philosophers or as poets, have quickened the inert masses around them, and have left on record their testimony on behalf of virtue.

Hold we then to this catholic modern doctrine until we see what it involves. There is assumed in this creed a providential interposition in human affairs; and there is supposed a beneficent purpose, which is the guiding reason of this interposition. Then, if it be so, this peculiarity of the Hebrew literature, and of its body of poetry especially, is brought into prominence; for it is this literature, and it is this alone among the literatures that are extant, which, from its earliest samples to its last, adheres to that form of peremptory affirmation which fits it to receive a supernatural attestation; and thus to become an authoritative source of religious belief, beyond the circuit of its birthplace:—that is, to men everywhere to the world's end. If the teaching of Buddha was from Heaven, and if Homer, Hesiod, Plato, Aristotle, were ministers of Heaven, and if Moses also, and David, and Isaiah, were such, then were these last-named teachers so overruled in the delivery of their teaching as to do it—not hypothetically—not ambiguously—not scientifically—not as if *uncertain*—in ignorance; and yet not as if *certain* in the way of demonstration; but authoritatively, and in a tone, and in terms, which imply, and suppose, and are proper to, a continuously given supernatural attestation.

CHAPTER XVI.

THE HEBREW POETRY, AND THE DIVINE LEGATION OF THE PROPHETS.

GREAT, substantial, and of the highest value are the achievements of modern criticism, in its laborious explorations of the Hebrew Scriptures; nor can it be doubted that more will yet be done on this field when the time shall come—and it is sure to come, though we may wait long for it—that the same learning (or more learning) and the same industry, and the same liberty (or even greater liberty) shall be employed on the same path of philological and historical elucidation, wholly free, which it is not yet, on the one hand, from the sinister purposes of infidelity, and on the other hand, from those groundless alarms which take their rise in indeterminate convictions of the Divine Legation of the Prophets, and so, in a precarious religious belief.

It is not on the pathway of criticism, whether philological or historical, that a determinate conviction to this effect will ever be attained. Individual men will not, nor do they in fact, become believers in this method: religious communities—that is to say, the masses of professedly Christian people—with their teachers, as a body, do not, in the pursuit of studies of this order, rid themselves of that wavering, anxious, unquiet, half-compromising, tone and style which indicate a deep-seated perplexity—a root of unbelief, ready always to shoot up and put forth leaves on the surface.

But take the question of the Divine Legation of the Hebrew Prophets to an upper, and this is its proper, ground—namely, the ground of the greater question, concerning the truth and reality of a Spiritual System —even of the life of the soul toward God, and there, and on that ground, a Faith shall be attained in possession of which no peril can be incurred on the side of even the freest criticism.

Did the Hebrew Prophets speak "as they were moved by the Holy Ghost?" Did they so speak as no men but they, and the Apostles, have ever spoken or written? We should seek a reply to this question in the answer that must be given to another question—Is there a life divine—is there a life of the soul toward God?—Is there a communion of the finite spirit with the INFINITE, on terms of intimate correspondence, in which the deepest and the most powerful affections of human nature are drawn forth toward, and centred upon, the Perfections of the INFINITE BEING? If there be—and there is—a life of the soul toward God—a life not mystical, not vague and abstractive—then we find our reply to the *included* question concerning the Hebrew Prophetic Scriptures; for it is in these, and it is nowhere else—no not to the extent of a line—a fragment—it is within this range that the Spiritual Life is embodied, and is expanded, and is uttered in a distinct and articulate manner. It is within the compass of the Hebrew Poetic and Prophetic Scriptures that all moods and occasions—all trials and exercises—all griefs and perplexities—all triumphs and all consolations—all joys, hopes, and exultations—all motives of patience, and all animated expectations of the future, find their aliment, and their warrant also. In a word, if there be a life of the soul toward God, and if this life be real, as toward God—then are the Hebrew writers true men of God;—then is it certain that they were instructed and empowered—each of them in his time—to set it forth, for the use of all men, to the end of the world.

Thus have believed and thus have felt, millions of the human family—even "a great multitude which no man can number," gathered from among the nations, throughout the ages past.

But there is now, and there has long been, a contradiction of the Divine origination and authority of the Old Testament Scriptures, which has been identical, or nearly so, with a denial of that life of the soul toward God of which these Scriptures are the exposition. This is the natural course of things; for to those who themselves have no experience or consciousness of the spiritual life, the Hebrew Scriptures can be indeed only a dead letter—unintelligible, flat, vapid, and unattractive, and therefore open to that hostile and disparaging criticism which has so much abounded of late. We say the two denials have been nearly identical; and yet not absolutely so; for a strenuous endeavour has been made of late to affirm a sort of spirituality, while the claim of the Old Testament Scriptures to Divine origination has been resentfully rejected. Those who make this endeavour do not allow themselves to inquire whence it is that they themselves have derived those notions (defective indeed) of the spiritual life which they profess:—the derivation cannot have been from oriental sources, which yield nothing, at the best, but a pantheistic mysticism:—nor can it have been from the Greek classical literature, for in this literature no element whatever—no, not a stray spark—not the remotest indication of the affectionate communion of the human soul with God—God, near at hand and personal—is to be found, either in the poets, or in the philosophers. Nor has this vague spirituality derived itself from the writings of the Evangelists and Apostles, for in these the spiritual life—the *devotional* life, is *assumed*, and it is vouched for as real; but it is not expanded or expounded. Those, in fact, who profess a sort of spirituality, and who, in doing so, reject the claims of the Hebrew Scriptures, have stolen what they profess:—or they have snatched it up, not caring to know whence it has come into their hands.

Happily, as to a thousand to one of devout Christian people, well assured as they are of the reality of the spiritual life—conscious as they are of it, and finding therein their solace—their peace—their anticipation of its fulness in the future life—these religious persons have remained uninformed of the exceptive pleadings of modern criticism; and thus they hear and read their Bibles in the tranquil confidence of faith;—and it is a *warrantable* confidence in which they live, and in which they die—ignorant of gainsaying: or it may be that some rumours of these nugatory contradictions come, once and again, to the knowledge of such persons, giving them a momentary uneasiness:—a rude assault—repelled, at the moment, is presently forgotten! Well that it should be so!

But an injury more serious—a damage less transient, is sustained—at this time—by many among those who, partakers as they are of the spiritual life, have been brought, by their education, and by their social habitudes, within range of the modern exceptive criticism;—especially of that portion of it which bears upon the Hebrew Scriptures; and which also has a malignant intention. From this cognizance of adverse criticism much trouble of mind springs up; and this is perhaps more often enhanced or deepened, than assuaged or dispersed, by listening to the well-intentioned explanations, and extenuations, and glozings, and evasions of Christian teachers. The disturbed mental condition—the damaged spiritual health of this large class of religious persons is, at this time, the problem of Christian Instructors. Authenticated and well-informed instructors—themselves perplexed, and themselves inwardly unquiet—do their best, honestly, for the help of their people; but they do it with little satisfaction to themselves or others.

It is not perhaps many, even of these well-informed Christian teachers, who well perceive—if they perceive at all—that the epidemic trouble is altogether the consequence of modes of religious thinking that are quite recent: too recent are they to have been provided for in our schemes of religious teaching. The remedy will come in its time; and the life of the soul toward God—relieved from this temporary oppression, will regain its healthful condition with renewed power.

Nevertheless, this renovation will not take place apart from some severe and painful procedures in demolishing cherished prepossessions. If we have coveted, and have actually possessed ourselves of the privileges and the triumphs of knowledge, *it is inevitable* that we should endure the pains consequent upon that acquisition: these pains are as infallibly sure to come on, as if they were enacted by statute. We must not fondly think it possible to retain the comforts of ignorance (which are many and *real*) while we are in the fruition of the better blessings of knowledge. The present trouble of the religious body may be interpreted as premonitive of a renewed life which shall ere long be granted to the Christian community, from on High.

It is not enough to say—the modern mind, for we must say—the *Northern* modern mind, has passed into a mood which, as yet, has not got itself adjusted to a rightful acceptance of a Revelation attested as such by supernatural interventions. In the nature of things a Revelation, attested as from God, by supernatural interventions, can never adjust itself to *generalizations* of any kind; for a Revelation which might be dealt with —either as to its mode of reaching us, or as to the substance of the matters so conveyed—as open to *generalizations*, must cease to be what it declares itself to be—a unique Revelation :—it must at once be, and not be—an instance that has no parallel.

On this ground there is a lesson yet to be learned by the thoughtful men of this present time :—these, or the sons of these, shall look back and wonder that this lesson was found to be so hard ; and in truth we of this time may come to think of it as less difficult if we duly considered the fact that a problem, equally perplexing, was solved, and that a lesson equally revolting was learned, so recently as two centuries ago, or a little more, by our intellectual ancestors—even by the great guild of mind at the challenge (mainly) of Bacon.

This problem, upon the solution of which our modern philosophy now broadly takes its rest, bears more than a remote resemblance to the problem in the solution of which the Christian body, throughout the world, shall at length rejoice, and shall take its rest.

It had been believed "by them of old time"—it had been held as a first truth, beyond the range of doubt, that the material universe—the visible Kosmos, *must be*, and is, in conformity with a scheme of logical generalizations, and that phenomena, of all kinds, should be interpretable on the ground, and by the means of, those generalizations, which did office in philosophy as its *organon*. But the time came for the proclamation of a *Novum Organon*, and at that proclamation old things passed away, as a dream, and all things became new. Fatal to the universe—according to logic—were those words of doom—*Homo naturæ minister et interpres.*

Some real progress has been made of late in winning the assent of the Christian community to the parallel axiom, which puts the words "Holy Scripture" in the place of the word "Nature" in Bacon's aphorism. So far as this it is admitted, in regard to the substance of truth conveyed in the Inspired writings, that—The best theologian is the best interpreter; or, otherwise worded—The best theology is that which is an undamaged product of a free and genuine interpretation of the sacred text. This now assented-to axiom stands opposed, on the one hand, to all logic-made theologies; and, on the other hand, to that theology which pays little or no regard to Scripture, and which—putting contempt upon the Bible—takes at pleasure out of it just so much, or as little of doctrine as may suit every man's notions of what it is fitting to believe.

Thus far a conclusion has slowly grown upon the Christian mind—among ourselves at least; but the axiom has a further application, which still awaits the assent and approval of the same Christian mind. The perplexities of the present time, regarding the authority and the constitution of the Inspired Scriptures, are the indications of an unsettled or undetermined belief on this ground. The assailants of the proper inspiration of the Scriptures think themselves strong in their position, and reckon themselves sure of a triumph, not distant: —they believe they shall so make good their array of Bible-faults as shall compel their perplexed opponents to acknowledge an overthrow, and so to leave the Bible to its fate. This overweening and unwise confidence is indeed a demonstration of the vanity and the presumption of those who entertain it, and of their own want of (or loss of) those greater qualities of mind which should have secured them against so slender an infatuation.

But then, on the believing—or, as we say, on the orthodox side, there are indications, not to be mistaken, of indecisiveness, and of the anxieties which attend a transition-period in matters of faith. So it is that we find expressions of this kind abounding on the pages of orthodox apologists—Ought we not to expect *difficulties*, even serious difficulties, in Holy Scripture?—As to most of the objections urged by infidel writers, they are susceptible of a reasonable answer;—and as to such as remain, at present, unsolved, we are to regard them as left where they are for the trial of our faith. And thus again—The Scriptures were not given to teach us natural science; and we ought not to look into them for a philosophy which the human mind is to work out for itself.

These, and such-like exculpatory and palliative averments, are true and proper, so far as they go; but they do not avail, and never can avail (every one feels it) to the extent that is just now required for allaying the prevalent uneasiness. Not at all do such explanations suffice for substantiating the modern (Reformation era) notion of verbal inspiration. How can that notion hold its ground in front of the long catalogue of the results of genuine modern criticism? This cannot be; and the adherents of a theory so inconsiderately framed await, in alarm, the moment of an unconditional surrender.

Intermediate, or compromising theories, many and various, have been propounded. Yet a question has barely been considered of this sort—Whether the need, at all, of a theory of inspiration is not quite imaginary, taking its rise in a natural prejudice of which we should rid ourselves? It is inevitable (nor blameworthy) that, if we think much of God, and of His ways, we should run off into theories—should assume much, in our purblind way, concerning the attributes of God, and His ways of governing the universe, and of dealing with men at large, and especially of His providential treatment of those who love and fear and serve Him. So it comes about, on frequent occasions, that we give oblique utterance to these unwarranted surmises, and acknowledge the breaking-up of some theory when, in painful and distracting instances, we speak of—a *dark* Providence—a *mysterious* Providence! The ways of God are not what we had supposed they *ought* to be:—they run counter to all our notions of what is wise and good; we are therefore perplexed and offended.

A similar perplexity and a similar offence come in to trouble us when Biblical criticism puts in its plea for a hearing. The ground of this perplexity, or, let us say, the history of its rise, might thus be rudely put into words—If I imagine myself possessed of all knowledge—natural, historical, and spiritual, and if I am sincere, and if my intentions are in every sense wise and good, and if, being thus *qualified*, and thus *disposed*, I sit down to write a book—that book shall be faultless *in every sense*:—not only shall it be *true* throughout, but it shall be the best book that ever has been written, as to its taste, its style, its literary execution: in a word the book will be such as may defy criticism, on every ground.

But the Bible *is* the Book of God;—or, according to the modern phrase—the Bible has God for its Author. Most true indeed is this;—but it is not true in the sense in which the modern Church has understood its own saying. If the Bible has God for its Author, why is it not such a book as I would have written, if I were qualified, as above stated? Clearly it is not such a book; and we are staggered in our faith.

In the day when the Church—the Christian community—shall have come fully to know (and they must acquire this knowledge by aid of criticism) what sort of book the Bible *is*, then will they have come to know also, what sort of book the Bible ought to be. It is, we may be sure, such a book as shall, in the most complete and absolute manner, accomplish and bring about, in the world at large, and in the souls of men individually, the purposes for which it was sent: but the accomplishment of those inscrutable purposes is wholly irrespective of those points of perfection which, to the human apprehension, seem of primary importance. In this sense how true is it that "the things which are highly esteemed among men" are in *no esteem* with God:—it may be they are in His sight deserving of reprobation. The Bible is not—AS A BOOK—the book we should have made it; nor is it the book we should now make it, if the Canon were submitted to our revising wisdom. But it *is* the book of Him who has thus commended it to our acceptance:—

"For as the rain cometh down, and the snow from heaven,
And returneth not thither,
But watereth the earth,
And maketh it to bring forth and bud,
That it may give seed to the sower, and bread to the eater;
So shall my word be that goeth forth out of my mouth:
It shall not return unto me void,
But it shall accomplish that which I please,
And it shall prosper whereto I sent it."

So indeed has it prospered in every age since its first promulgation, and in every land to which, according to the Divine purpose, it has been sent. Thus has it prospered in quickening to life millions of souls—in nourishing the Divine life within these souls. So has it prospered in ruling the life, in strengthening the purposes, in giving heart to the courage of martyrs; and patience and contentment, and a bright hope, to the individual spirits of that great multitude which is gathering into the kingdom of heaven. Well, therefore, may we spare ourselves the labour of inquiring, according to our small critical manner, whether the books of Scripture are well adapted to subserve the purposes for which they profess to be given—namely, the religious and moral instruction of the nations. These purposes they have subserved—they are now subserving—and they shall continue to subserve, to the end of time; and, in a time not remote, shall they carry light and life, even to every land which hitherto they have not visited.*

After so large, and so long-continued an induction, demonstrative of the efficiency and of the sufficiency of the Scriptures for imparting life to the souls of men, and for nourishing that life, what more do we need? Nothing, if only we will be wise and ingenuous—as befits us—discarding an hypothesis which, natural as it is, has no foundation in reason; but which, so long as it is adhered to, gives abundant occasion to infidelity, and spreads disquietude among ourselves. There is no need of a new theory of inspiration, or of a new principle of Biblical interpretation; but this only is needed, that every hypothesis and theory—better or worse—should be put out of view—should be laid aside—should be forgotten. The mode of that commingling of the Divine and the human in Scripture, upon which these theories profess to shed a light, will never be known to us, any more than the commingling of the worlds of mind and of matter in the scheme of animal life will become known to us:—both are inscrutable. Yet we are well assured of the actuality of both Mind and Matter in the animal system, and in the human system especially. We know each—distinctly and infallibly, when we regard each as it is seen from its own ground; but each becomes a problem insoluble—a perplexity distracting, when it is looked at from the ground of the other. In the desperate endeavour to solve this problem, and to be fairly rid of this perplexity, we first look in upon mind, as seen from the ground of the animal structure, and we say—mind is

* See Note.

—nothing but a function of the nervous substance. Yet this easy conclusion plunges us soon into perplexities that are still more hopeless. If this will not do, then we shift our ground, and looking out of the window upon matter—upon the material universe entire, we say—matter is a nihility—it is nothing but a condition of thought; or if there *were* a real world beyond us, we could never know it. Thus far the good bishop of Cloyne. But it will not do; and at the hearing of this paradox there ensues a riot on the highways of the common world, and a doctrine so whimsical is hooted off as intolerable. The lynch-law of common sense is brought to bear upon it, and then we are left where we were—mind and matter—each resolutely holding its own as before—philosophers notwithstanding. What is needed here is not a new theory of the universe, but humility enough to cease asking for one.

Very near to a strictly parallel instance, or real analogy, comes the instance of the commingling of the Divine and the human in Holy Scripture. It is quite true of the human structure—*in a sense*, that it is all mind; and it is quite true of the same structure—*in a sense*, that it is all material organization; and if it be an error to affirm that man is organization, and *nothing else*, or to affirm, on the other side, that he is mind, and *nothing else*—a greater error, and an error crammed with confusion, would it be to say of human nature—*this* part of it is mind, and *that* part is matter; thus partitioning the members, and dividing the substance.

Take the case, then, of Holy Scripture—assuming that the analogy we here introduce has some ground of reality. Three doctrines, as in the above instance, stand before us:—

1. That the Inspired Scriptures are wholly Divine, and *nothing else*. There are few at this time who will roundly profess this doctrine, in unqualified terms; but there are many who greatly desire to do so, and who would do it, if they dared: but in so far as they do it, they stand condemned, and speechless, before the body of evidence, which shows in score of instances in proof of the contrary. Infidelity triumphs in its antagonism to this doctrine; and it makes the more noise on this ground because it can triumph on no other ground. Above this field the eagles and the vultures are soaring, for here is—"the carcase."

Or we may say (2) that the Scriptures (canonical inspired) are wholly human, and nothing more;—or, to state this hypothesis in mitigated terms, that these excellent writings are inspired just as all other good and useful books are inspired. This doctrine, the simplicity and facility of which tempt shallow thinkers to adopt it, leaves unaccounted for the great facts of Scripture; namely, its theological, its ethical, and its historical portions. To those who think more coherently, the problem of the Bible, considered apart from its supernatural origination, is a problem that confounds all reasoning, and that renders hopeless—indeed impossible—any induction on the ground of history.

Or (3) it may be affirmed that, within the compass of the Canonical Scriptures, there are certain portions that are Divine, and other portions that are merely human, and that it is the office of criticism to segregate these intermingled elements. A difficult, as well as a perilous labour this must be! Well we might ask—and yet despair of receiving an answer to the question—Who is sufficient for this work? Not a person—not an

Ecumenical Synod—and a Royal Commission; we dis- us that school of learned incompetence—we put the individual Bible reader for himself. There must be a second inspiration then to elicit inspiration from its incompleteness. This is a case of that kind in which one of two claimants to a property is sure, in the end, to lay his hand upon the whole; because the plea which is admitted to be valid in relation to the smallest fragment, may be urged, with equal reason, bit by bit, in relation to every separate part. On the other side, the claimant who urges an unfounded plea will be compelled to surrender his ground at each step when he is pushed on do so.

But if we reject each of these three suppositions, and if we take instead of them our confidence in the Scriptures—theories of inspiration put out of view—shall we not surround ourselves with perplexities? Probably it will be so if we are hypochondriacs in religion: it will be so if the principle of religious faith has suffered paralysis from contact with sophistry.

The man who is in the enjoyment of health of body, and soundness of mind, will know that he has a body; and he knows also that he has a soul; and he knows that human nature is thus constituted of two diverse elements, to deny the reality of either of which is to plunge into an abyss of unmitigated contradictions. Yet no man of sound mind attempts to draw a line of demarcation between body and soul, or to distinguish between mind and matter in the working of human nature; nor will he affirm of any one part or function of the one that it has absolutely no dependence upon the other. But, while unconscious of these distinctions, he well knows that he is in possession of a nature which is available for every purpose of thought and of action. This knowledge is enough, for, from the conscious possession of a sound mind and a healthy body there arises a responsibility to think rightly, and to act rightly in all the relations of life. This compound human nature, blending, as it does, a spiritual and an animal structure, carries with it an *authority* which the man disregards at his peril.

And so it is in regard to the authority of Holy Scripture. If there be indeed a moral consciousness—if there be a spiritual sense, we then feel and know, with the certainty of an infallible perception, that, in these writings—wholly unlike as they are to any other writings—we are hearing the voice of God:—while listening to these writers we are in communication with the Father of spirits. When we thus read, and while we thus listen, the soul *in health* does not stay to put the futile and peevish question, Is this text—is this passage, human or Divine? It is the patient who is "grievously tormented with palsy" that puts this question to those about him, and to himself, and gets no reply.

There are many questions which may be fit for exercising the ingenuity of casuists, a proper reply to which is this—that, the giving a reply at all may well be postponed to a time when some instance of the sort shall actually present itself. So as to questions of this kind—What are we to do if a revelation, credibly attested by miracles, propounds for our belief, or for our practice, what *must* be rejected? What should be done in such a case shall be duly considered when the occurrence of an instance of that kind has indeed been established.

Yet there is a class of instances to which more or less of difficulty attaches from a cause already referred to—

namely, an assumption—gratuitous and unwarranted—concerning the Divine attributes, or concerning the modes of the Divine intervention in human affairs. Instances of this sort attach mainly to the Old Testament Scriptures. The feeling which prompts these assumptions is, for the most part, a modern feeling; it is a refinement; it is a sentimentalism; it is valetudinary; it is fastidious. It is a feeling which receives its correction, not merely from a larger knowledge of national usages—ancient and modern; but from a broader aspect of human nature. This breadth—this freedom—this boldness, is indeed a characteristic of the Scriptures—Old and New Testament equally so. If the fastidious modern reader of the Bible is himself unconscious of this freedom and boldness, it is because, by frequency of perusal, he has fallen into a sort of Biblical *hypnotism*, or artificial slumber, under the influence of which the actual meaning of words and phrases fails to rouse attention. This dozing habit may be well in its way, and it is well if it saves offence; but no offence will be taken by those who—profoundly conscious of the awful voice of God in the Scriptures, and immoveably firm in their belief to this extent—are animated by the courage which is proper to a fervent and enlightened piety; and who, in the daily perusal of the Prophetical books and the Psalms, rejoice in, and fully relish, that fearless dealing with human nature, and with its incidents, which at once vouches for the historic reality of the record, and is evidence of a power more than human pervading the whole. Just as the material world and the animal economy has each far more of strenuous force in it than we moderns—if we had been consulted, would have allowed it; so is the Bible—bold—broad—strong, in a degree which makes the reading of it a trial and a grievance to our pale-faced sensibilities, and to our pampered tastes. The remedy is to be found at once in a more robust mental health, and a more thorough spiritual health.

This more robust mental health, combined with a deeper spiritual health, shall show itself in a liberty of thought which indeed is—free thinking. The attendant upon this free thinking will be a free criticism; and the two shall put to shame as well, the spurious freedom of unbelief, as the spurious criticism which feeds itself upon husks, and has no appetite for nutritions food. When we yield assent to the Scriptures, as an authenticated Revelation, this assent and this consent of the reason, and of the soul, bring with them an exemption from disquietudes of every kind. There are no alarms where the ALMIGHTY is present to save and to bless.

CHAPTER XVII.

CONTINUANCE OF THE HEBREW POETRY AND PROPHECY TO THE WORLD'S END.

THE history of nations furnishes so many instances of the extinction of intelligence and civilization, and so few —if indeed any—of its *permanence* in any one region, or as to any one race or people, that the decay and gradual extinction of the light of mind seems to be the rule, and its continuance anywhere, beyond the reach of a few centuries, the exception;—and hitherto this is not an established exception.

This decay, and almost extinction, has had place in the instance of each of the Oriental races. The people of China, and of Thibet, and of India, and of Ceylon, and of Persia, and of Mesopotamia, occupied, in remote times, a position in philosophy, and in the arts, and in social habits, and in populousness, and in political power, and wealth, which is very feebly, or is not at all, reflected in the condition of the modern occupants of the same regions. The same must be affirmed of Egypt, and Nubia, and Abyssinia. The same also of the people of every country upon which the Macedonian kingdoms once so splendidly flourished. The same, moreover, of the countries which were the birth-fields of the Arabian race.

But it is believed, or it is customarily taken for certain, that our modern European civilization rests upon

12*

a basis as immoveable as that of the pyramids of Gizeh. It is thought that the marvels of the mechanic arts, and the ready means which these arts afford for the instantaneous interchange of knowledge, and the consequent breadth of intelligence among the masses of the people, are guarantee sufficient against the prevalence of brute despotisms, as well as against the insensible encroachments of those sordid, sensual, and brutalizing tendencies which are inherent in human nature. Gladly should we all think this: nevertheless there are forebodings of another cast which might easily find support in the actual course of events at this very moment, and as well in the new world, as in the old world. Might not then the question of the permanence of our European civilization be regarded as a problem that is in suspense, between opposite probabilities?

The prevailing belief on the bright side of this problem rests, for the most part, no doubt, upon grounds of secular calculation. It is imagined to be inconceivable that our actual civilization, based as it is on a broad political framework, and sustained as it is by its philosophy, and its arts, and aided as it is by its printing-press, and its railways, and its telegraphic wires, should ever fall out of repair, so as to become lumber upon the field of the European and the American populations.

Yet there is a faith in the world's future—a bright faith also, albeit it is less sharply defined, and is of more depth, subsisting among us; and this faith may easily be traced to its rise in the Hebrew Scriptures. This subject has already been brought forward in these pages (Chap. XI.) The Hebrew Prophet, we have said, is the man of hope. The Hebrew Prophets and the

Psalmists are the authors of hope in regard to this present mundane economy; and it is they, rather than CHRIST and His Apostles, that, looking on to the remoteness of the existence of nations, see, in that distance—terrestrial good; they see—truth—peace—love; and they foretell a social system at rest. A last utterance of the *ancient* prediction was heard overhead of Bethlehem when the coming in of the new dispensation was announced by a "multitude of the heavenly host." But in the end—in the furthest distance—the two economies shall coincide, and *then* there shall be great joy to all nations—"Glory to God in the highest, *and on earth peace*, good-will toward men." In the ages intervening—it is "not peace, but a sword."

The Hebrew Prophets (Poets) represent the mundane religious economy; and they vouch for its ultimate realization in universal peace. Evangelists and Apostles represent the economy of the unseen and the future; and they vouch for that immortality in Christ, for which the painful discipline of the present life is the necessary preparation. But this discipline, and this life hereafter, must come to its bearing always upon the individual human spirit; for it takes no account of races—of nations—of communities. (Gal. iii. 28; Coloss. iii. 11; 1 Cor. xii. 13.)

Nevertheless the two economies are not at variance; for the two tend in the same direction, and they shall, in the end, coalesce. They do so *now*, inasmuch as the *individual spiritual life* has received its exemplification, and its ample development, within the compass of the poetical books—the Prophets and the Psalms; nor shall the individual spiritual life ever seek to alienate itself from, or become indifferent to, those liturgies, and those litanies of the soul, in its communion with God. Never shall those forms of praise—prayer—penitence—exultation—those deep expressions of the emotions of the quickened soul, cease to be—what hitherto they have been—the genuine promptings of love, fear, and hope, toward God. Futile have been all endeavours—so often repeated in modern times, to dissociate the two Revelations, or to take up a Christianity, divorced from the Old Testament. In each instance the attempt has given evidence of the absence of that spiritual consciousness apart from which there remains nothing in Christianity itself that is much to be cared for; or which may not be found in Epictetus and Marcus Aurelius, in nearly as acceptable a form.

So far as the two economies go abreast on different paths, and so far as they have different objects in front of them, they may seem to be *divergent;* but, in contradiction of this apparent divergence, there occur, in each, what might be termed—nodes of intersection, or points, where the two are coincident. Such a point of junction may be found in that signal Messianic prediction—the seventy-second Psalm; if this be taken in connection with the second Psalm, and with the forty-fifth, and with the hundred and tenth. These odes, which are susceptible of none but the most vapid interpretation, if their Messianic import be rejected, point in the same direction, but not in the same manner. They agree in foreseeing a mundane empire, administered from a centre—an empire wielding irresistible material force, which shall be coæval, for a period, with adverse forces; but which shall trample upon all, and at length be recognized by all. In the second Psalm, and in the hundred and tenth, and, in part, in the forty-fifth, the imagery has the aspect of vindictive force—force, not softened, or only a little softened, by intimations of clemency. Yet this martial energy has, for its end, right and truth, and the establishment of order. In *these* odes there occur no distinct points of accordance with the rules, the purer precepts, or the moral intention of the Christian dispensation. Right and power shall be in conjunction, and the two which, hitherto, have so usually been sundered, shall then—according to these predictions—walk the earth hand in hand, for the terror and extermination of every wrongful tyranny. This then is the world's future—according to the Hebrew Prophets; and who are they that do not exult in the prospect?

The seventy-second Psalm allies itself with the Psalms above mentioned, as in the fourth, the ninth, and the fourteenth verses. Force, employed in the maintenance of right, and for the deliverance of the oppressed, is still present:—the minister of wrath is still at hand. As the Primus Lictor, with the formidable fasces on his shoulder, stood at the elbow of the Roman magistrate, prompt to inflict death—*animadvertere*—upon any that should dare resist the power, so, in this prediction, there are notices of contemporary wrong; but then there is deliverance at hand, and the *time* that is indicated in this instance is some way onward in the course of events—for, as to the adverse powers, they have either "learned wisdom," or they have fallen to rise no more.

The Sovereign Right has now become a genial influence—which is gratefully accepted—even as are "the showers of heaven that water the earth." Everywhere shall this administration of justice and mercy have come to be commended (ver. 15.) All races, all nations, shall at last feel and acknowledge the blessings of this rule—

> All shall be blessed in Him:
> All nations shall call Him blessed.

Not only from this realm of right shall violence and wrong be excluded; but the hitherto perplexing problem of the equilibrium of orders shall at length have found its solution; for it is said of the upper class that— "like Lebanon"—it shall be great and fruitful; and as to the lower class—even the dense millions of cities—it also "shall flourish like grass of the earth"—room enough shall be found for it; nor shall its greenness be grudged.

Upon all these images of mundane wealth we here catch the mild effulgence of the Gospel. It is now our Christianity—it is now that doctrine of love to establish which the army of martyrs bled at the first (and often since) and to maintain which the preachers of truth, through long centuries, have prophesied in sackcloth: —it is this "everlasting Gospel" that at length—like a sun, rising in a stormy morning—has climbed the heavens, has hushed the winds, has scattered the thick clouds of the sky, and thenceforward it rules the azure in the burning brightness of an endless noon.

The Hebrew Scriptures—every way secure of their immortality in a literary sense—are secure of it also as they are the expansion, and the authentic expression, of the spiritual life—a liturgy of the communion of souls with God:—secure moreover, as they are the foreshadowing of the Gospel, and of the coming of the Saviour of the world; yet this is not all, for, embedded in these writings—confided to the Hebrew Poetry—

are those hopes of a mundane future—peaceful and benign—which the best men in every age have clung to, and which they have used, as the ground and reason of their sacrifices, while they have believed that, not for themselves, but for the men of a distant time, they have spent life, and have laid it down.

Effective philanthropy has always taken its spring from the ground of a religious faith in a bright future, of that sort for which the Hebrew Scriptures are our sole authority. And as to this effective, laborious, self-sacrificing benevolence, it combines whatever is peculiar to the Old, with whatever is peculiar to the New Testament—taking from the one source its expectation of mundane national welfare, and from the other source drawing those powerful motives which prevail over all motives, inasmuch as they draw their force from a belief of the life eternal.

Thus it is that the controversy of the present time, between those who hold fast their confidence in the historic revelation contained in the Scriptures, and those who reject it, and who would rid themselves of their own misgivings on its behalf, is brought to an issue on this ground. There is a question concerning the human destinies—The human family has it had a known commencement? and has it a known middle period of development and progress? and has it in prospect a known—a predicted—ultimate era of good? Is there in front of the nations an ἀνάπαυσις—is there a σαββατισμὸς—is there a time of refreshment, a season of rest—a year of release—a redemption, an end of the reign of evil, and a beginning of the kingdom of God, on earth? If not, then the thick veil of barbaric ignorance, violence, sensuality, and cruelty, shall be drawn anew over the nations, and the world must return to its night of horrors.

The positions affirmed in these pages in behalf of the Hebrew Scriptures (those of them especially that are poetic in their style and structure) are briefly these seven:—

That the poetry of these writings everywhere appears as a means to a higher end; or otherwise stated—that the poet, whatever may be his quality or his genius, is always the Prophet of God, more than he is the poet.

That whatever may be the individual characteristics of each of these writers, as a poet, they teach always the same theology, and they insist always upon the same moral principles.

That although, for the most part, they boldly denounce the errors and immoralities of their contemporaries, they employed a medium, as to the *structure* of their writings, which implies a reverential acceptance, and use of them, on the part of the people, and of their rulers.

That amidst, and notwithstanding, all diversities of temper and style in the men, and all changes in the national condition, there prevails, from the first in the series to the last, an occult consistency which is expressive of what we have ventured to speak of as—the Historic Personality of God.

That within the compass of the Hebrew Poetic Scriptures there exists—(and in these writings alone)—a Liturgy, and a Litany, of the spiritual life—the life of the soul toward God; this Liturgy being inclusive of the forms of congregational worship.

That the Hebrew Poets and Prophets—besides the special predictions which they utter relating to the destinies of surrounding nations, and besides the preparation which they make for the advent of Him who should be the Saviour of the world—give a testimony which is the ground, and which is the only warrant, of the hopeful anticipation we entertain of the issue of events in times that are yet future.

That it is thus, while predicting a bright age to come, that they bring into combination those higher motives and purer principles which the Gospel furnishes, and in the universal prevalence of which that bright prospect shall be realized.

NOTES.

Note to page 43.

MANY pages would be required for giving even a very scanty sample of those secular variations of the religious mind, which are indicated by the style and the feeling of commentators, on selected passages of Scripture. To collect such a sample, if sufficient to answer any valuable purpose, would indeed be a heavy task; and, to present it in a useful manner—a task from which I must shrink. Instead of attempting this, I must be content to direct the attention of any reader who may have leisure and opportunity to act upon the suggestion, to the class of facts which should be kept in view on this ground.

The varying style and feeling of commentators upon Scripture may be regarded, for example, as it is exhibited in the instance—first, of the Church writers of the Greek, and then of the Latin Churches—then in those of the African Church, and in these compared with the Rabbinical commentators. These variations would bring to view the changes that are taking place, from one age to another, in consequence of insensible mutations of the human mind; and also, as indicative of the effect of what, to borrow a phrase from geology, might be called—the catastrophes of religious history. Such revolutions, namely, as that of the Lutheran Reformation; or such as the sudden rise and spread of Methodism in England; or as that of the German Rationalism in the last century. Any reader to whom the patristic volumes are accessible may, if he so please, turn to the places indicated below, as *samples* only of what is here intended. Let then the sample be the manner in which Christian commentators have met the difficulty which presents itself in that imprecatory Psalm, the 136th—"Happy shall he be," &c. ORIGEN brings this passage forwards as an instance, among several others, proving the necessity of that rule of spiritual interpretation which understands the Old Testament histories always, and only, in a symbolical sense:—If not (vol. I. p. 41. Benedictine) what shall we say to the polygamy of the patriarchs, and to other similar instances, or to that of the vindictive utterances of that Psalm, which would seem to recommend or sanction the indulgence of vindictive passions—"Filia Babylonis misera: beatus qui retribuet tibi, &c.?" In like manner does he argue with Celsus (vol. I. p. 710)—he says:—The "little ones" of Babylon—the "babes," are those new-born urchins of evil in our own hearts, which good men will be prompt to destroy:—this offspring of Babylon—confusion—the heads of which, while young, must be dashed against the stones! The same ingenious mode of exposition—clearing a difficulty at a leap—is enlarged upon in another place (vol. II. p. 348):—The baby concupiscences meet their fate when their little brains are dashed out against the rock—"Petra autem est Christus." The same occurs in several different places:—it is, in this Father's view, the undoubted meaning of the Psalm: (so again, vol. II. p. 433; and vol. III. p. 313.) In nearly the same strain writes St. Augustine (Exposition of this Psalm); yet with a difference marking the feeling of the Church toward its late enemies—persecutors and heretics:—In any case the "Rock," upon which either infant carnal suggestions or Babylonish errors are to meet their end, is, CHRIST. In a sounder style St. Chrysostom (Exposition of this Psalm) contends with the apparent difficulty fairly, and he alleges what may be accepted as a sufficient explanation in clearing it up: he says—πολλὰ γὰρ οἱ προφῆται οὐκ οἴκοθεν φθέγγονται, ἀλλὰ τὰ ἑτέρων πάθη διηγούμενοι, καὶ εἰς μέσον φέροντες: but, he adds, If instead of the passionate utterances of the captives at Babylon—whose language of exasperation the Psalmist only *reports*—you would know what is his own inner mind, you have it in those words (Ps. vii.)—"If I have rewarded evil, &c." In a passage which has frequently been quoted, of late, in which St. Jerome confesses the anguish of his soul, so often endured in the parched wilderness, arising from the inroads of worldly and luxurious recollections (Epist. ad Eustochium) he gives, like Origen, the symbolic interpretation to the vindictive passage in this Psalm; and so this strange conceit continued to be in favour with the ascetics to a late age. The babes of Babylon are, this Father says, "the ever new-born desires of the flesh—and the rock upon which they are to be dashed is CHRIST." And thus also Cassian

(p. 144):—"Exurgentes primùm cogitationes carnales illico repellendas esse . . . et dum adhuc parvuli sunt, allidere filios Babylonis ad petram." So it will be everywhere and always, where and when Biblical exposition takes its course, *unchecked by criticism.* Easy would it be to furnish illustrations of this fact drawn from sources not so remote as the patristic times, or the middle ages. The properly religious and spiritual use of Holy Scripture needs a near-at-hand counteractive or corrective criticism, apart from which the most dangerous species of perversion or even of sacrilege does not fail to be fallen into. The religious Bible-reader may well invite criticism to do its office; but it must be *religious* criticism; not that of those who appear to be wholly destitute of faith and piety.

Note to page 75.

Why did not Herodotus describe to us the Al-Kuds—the Holy City, which he visited? The supposition that the Cadytus of Herodotus was Jerusalem has been generally admitted as probable; but it has recently been called in question, as by others, so by Dr. Rawlinson (Herodotus, vol. II p. 246.) A discussion of this question, in relation to which no direct evidence can be adduced on either side, would be out of place in these notes. I wish only to state that I am aware of a contrary opinion, especially of that of so competent a writer as Dr. Rawlinson, who thinks that it was Gaza, not Jerusalem, which Herodotus intends.

Note to page 93.

The comparative copiousness of languages—the Hebrew especially. A language which would deserve to be called scanty or poor in its vocabulary, especially in the class of words denoting the objects of nature, will give evidence of this poverty in translations from itself into a more copious language: it will do so in one of these two modes, namely, either the translation would itself be as bald and poor as the original; or, if itself rich and copious, it will be found to have employed many more words than are found in the original:—that is to say, where in the original the same word occurs, five times or more, on similar occasions, because the writer had no better choice, the translator into a copious language, who has a better choice, is able easily to improve upon his author, and to give to his version an opulence which he did not find in his original. Tried on this principle, it will not appear that the Hebrew language, as compared with the Latin, or with the Greek, or with the English, or with other modern languages, gives any indication of this deficiency of words. In this note I can attempt nothing more than, as mentioned in the text, to indicate one method among others, in which an inquiry of this kind might be pursued.

Take as an instance the 65th Psalm, which is a rich descriptive ode. It will be recollected that, in ascertaining the number of words occurring in any one composition, or, as we say, the *glossary of that single composition*, the Hebrew *affixes* and *suffixes* give rise to a difficulty, which however is not insurmountable; yet it is sufficient to be adduced in explanation of what might seem an erroneous reckoning, to some small extent. In the Hebrew text of this Psalm there occur —including affixed prepositions, and suffixed pronouns—137 words: but the absolute words—particles put out of view—are 118. In the Latin of the Vulgate, rejecting particles corresponding to those rejected in reckoning the Hebrew, about ninety words are employed, as equivalents for the 118 of the original If we now turn to the Greek of the Septuagint, reckoned in a similar manner, there occur eighty-two words, which stand as the representatives of the Hebrew, as above said. Consequently, several of these Greek words must have done service for two, three, or more distinctive Hebrew words: —as we find three English words (mentioned in the text, p. 92) representing eight or ten in the Hebrew. Whether the Greek translators might not have given a better choice of words, in this instance, is not now the question; probably they might; but at least the presumption is, that the Hebrew, as compared with the Greek language, in the class of *descriptive* words, does not fall far short of the Greek as to its copiousness.

The authorized English version of this Psalm employs, as does the Hebrew, 137 words, from which number, throwing off, as above, particles, expletives, and the like, the words substantive (*i. e.* nouns substantive, nouns adjective, and verbs) may be reckoned as ninety; this number standing for the 118 of the original. We should not therefore be warranted in affirming that the Hebrew language is poor, as compared with our own: an inference of another kind is warrantable —namely, this, that this language, if we were in possession of a complete *Copia Verborum*—an absolute Hebrew Lexicon—as we are of the Greek and Latin, would well stand comparison with either of them, at least in respect of those classes of words of which poets have occasion to avail themselves. The Hebrew would no doubt appear to be deficient in abstract philosophic terms, in those technical phrases which indicate artificial modes of life, and the practice of the arts; and in the entire class, so large as it is, of words modified—extended—contracted, or intensified, by the prefixed prepositions.

Any one who may be so inclined, might, with little labour, carry out the above-suggested mode of comparison, in the instance of the several European versions of the Psalms. Instead of the 65th Psalm, take the 50th, which has 252 words in the Hebrew—reckoned at 140; or the 91st, which has 170—reckoned at 97; or the 38th chapter of Job, including 402 words—its absolute glossary, say—205.

Note to page 130.

The book of Ecclesiastes may seem to be an exception to what is here affirmed; and it is so, in so far as the great controversy concerning the wisdom that is earthly, and the wisdom that is heavenly, is argued, as if on even ground, between the advocates of each. The problem is stated, and it is discussed, for some time, as if it were undeterminable. "There is a vanity which is done upon the earth; that there be just men, unto whom it happeneth according to the work of the wicked; again, there be wicked men, to whom it happeneth according to the work of the righteous: I said that this also is vanity." This apparent misdirection of events, as men must judge of them, is a vanity—it is a confusion—it is a whirl, which makes meditation giddy. Nevertheless, evenly balanced as this argument may seem, it is not left in an undetermined state at the last:—the disputants are not allowed, both of them, to boast a judgment in his favour. Most decisively is the disputation brought to its close on the side of piety in the last sentences:—"Let us hear the conclusion of the whole matter." It is the same in that other remarkable instance—the 73rd Psalm, in which the perplexed and discomforted writer confesses, with mingled grief and shame, the prevalence, too long, of his rankling meditations. But he had already recovered his footing; and thus he *prefixes* his *conclusion*:—"Truly (notwithstanding any appearance to the contrary) truly God is good to Israel, even to such as are of a clean heart."

If in this instance there may have been a debated question, it is a question already answered; and the answer has been assented to. In Ezekiel this same argument—it is mainly the same—is determined in another manner (chap. xxxiii.) and the grounds of donbt are different. There is here a peremptory affirmation of the rectitude of the Divine government, if its *final* adjudications are taken into the account. Of the same import is the expostulation which occupies the eighteenth chapter; and in this course of reasoning—this Theodicæa—the awards of a future judgment are undoubtedly understood; and so in a similar passage—Malachi iii. 13–18.

Note to page 156.

Asks a sacrifice of the body and of the soul. "If ye be reproached for the name of Christ, happy are ye. . . . If any suffer as a Christian, let him not be ashamed" (on that account). As to those "that suffer according to the will of God, let them commit the keeping of their souls, as to a faithful Creator, in well doing." Thus speaks St. Peter; and thus the author of the Epistle to the Hebrews, in recounting the martyrdoms of earlier times, says of the martyrs that they "died *in faith*," in faith of "a better resurrection." And so Christ, in preparing His people for the fiery trial that was in prospect, says—"Fear not them that kill the body, but after that have nothing more that they can do." It was on this ground that the martyrdoms of the early centuries, and those of later times as well, were nobly endured. And it was thus that "the hope set before us in the Gospel" was at the first confirmed:—thus was it sent forward to all times ensuing; and thus again must it be, if ever again Christian men and women, *as such*, shall be called to bear testimony, on the rack and in the flames—to their hope in Christ. But no such value as this, which it actually bears, could have attached to Christian martyrdom, if it did not stand out as *an exceptive instance*, broadly distinguishable from all other instances of suffering, inflicted by others. In respect of such sufferings, or such occasions of mortal antagonism between man and man—or between nations, the powerful instincts of human nature take their course, needing to be ruled always, and curbed and repressed, by those Christian principles which forbid revenge. and forbid especially the *harbouring* of resentments, or the cherishing, as a sweet morsel, some vindictive purpose. Christianity deals in *a special manner* with the case of suffering *for the truth*—for the word of Christ; but it deals *universally*, by its law of love, and of self-denial, with those impulses that are properly natural, and apart from which neither the life of individuals, nor the existence of communities, could be secured. The Christian man will not attempt to *exscind* the irascible emotions; but he will strive to master them, in like manner as he governs the animal appetites.

As to the presence and operation of these vindictive emotions during the præ-Christian ages, a freer scope was then allowed them, and men who were virtuous and wise spoke and acted in a manner which we of this time have learned greatly to modify; we have so learned this better lesson—*partly* in consequence of the broad Christianization that has had place throughout the European nations; and *partly* also by a not reprehensible confounding of the *martyr-doctrine* of Christ with the universal Christian principle of self-restraint and moderation. A confusion of this sort, natural as it is, and especially so in the case of highly sensitive Christian persons, has taken effect in rendering the martial tone of some of the Psalms, and the vindictive language of others of them, a sore trial to peace-loving, gentle-hearted modern Bible readers. The trial is the more severe, because those modes of evading the difficulty which the patristic expositors had recourse to, would not, at this time, seem to us tolerable.

Few indeed among us would accept, as good and true, the symbolic expositions of Origen, or those of Augustine, of which a sample has been given in a preceding note. If a caution were needed against fanciful interpretations of this order, we might adduce this last-named Father's exposition of the 149th Psalm. It fills several pages, and no doubt it exhibits much ingenuity, as well as a right Christian feeling:—"Jam, fratres, videtis sanctos armatos: adtendite strages; adtendite gloriosa prælia, ... Quid fecerunt isti habentes in manibus frameas bis acutas? Ad faciendam vindictam in gentibus. . . . . Quomodo, inquies, pagani occiduntur? Quomodo, nisi cum Christiani fiunt? Quæro paganum? non invenio, Christianus est! Ergo mortuus est paganus. . . . Unde ipse Saulus occisus est persecutor, et Paulus erectus est prædicator? Quæro Saulum persecutorem, et non invenio; occisus est." Much is there to the same purpose in this, and in the parallel places; but this method could not now be accepted. Let it be granted that, in such instances, there is indeed a spiritual meaning—a meaning hidden and *intended:* but no doubt there was a primary meaning; and it is this primary meaning which the modern expositor should hold himself bound to place in its true historic light. He will then be at liberty to adduce, at his best discretion, the ulterior meaning of the passage.

Note to page 170.

Sicilian cattle-keepers. I have already affirmed my belief (Chapter XV.) that comparisons attempted between the Hebrew poets, and those of Greece, can scarcely in any case be valid or available in a critical sense; for besides other grounds of difference, which are many and obvious, there is this one, which should at once preclude any such endeavours to ascertain the relative merits of the two literatures:—in the one an artistic excellence is aimed at, and the poet did his best to secure an award of admiration from his contemporaries; the Hebrew poets give proof of a lofty indifference to everything resembling literary fame. The reference to Theocritus has this meaning, that this poet's literal, graphic, *unideal*, exhibitions of rude Sicilian life, throughout which a sense of the beauty of Nature, and of the sweetness of country life, barely appears, would place him in a position of disadvantage by the side of the Canticle of Solomon, the charm of which is the vividness of this feeling toward Nature; and beside this, there is the warmth, the softness, the delicacy, the fondness of those feelings—properly conjugal, which come up in each strophe. Moreover, the erotic idyls of Theocritus—like those of his imitator—are damaged by a *putrid stain* from which—let it be noted—the Hebrew poetry—universally—as well as this Canticle, is absolutely and wholly free.

Note to page 172.

. . . . *a passage cited from the book of Ecclesiastes.* Neither in these pages, nor in any other of my writings, have I professed myself competent to enter upon discussions relating to the date or authorship of the separate books included in the Canon. Disclaiming any such qualifications, I am shielded from blame, as toward the Canon, in offering an opinion of that casual sort which any attentive reader of the Scriptures may well think himself at liberty to propound. The date and authorship, and consequently the strict canonicity of the book of Ecclesiastes, I leave to be discussed among those whose professional learning fits them to engage in an argument of that sort. At a first glance the passage cited—"I gat me men-singers, and women-singers, and the delights of the sons of men—musical instruments, and that of all sorts," suggests the idea of a time much later in Jewish life than the age of Solomon. It is not that the practice of music—vocal and instrumental—had not reached a stage of great advancement in that age; for we must believe that it had; but there does not appear evidence in support of the opinion that music had been *secularized* at so early a time; or that *concerts* had come to hold a place in the routine of the amusements of the harem. If a passage in Ezekiel (xxxiii. 32) might be understood as implying a practice of music, not sacred or liturgical, this evidence touches upon a time as late as the Captivity.

Note to page 200.

Isaiah . . . . our master in the school of the highest reason.

This is a broad affirmation which is likely to be rejected and resented. But whoever does so reject and resent what is here affirmed in behalf of the Hebrew prophet, should be prepared, not merely with a naked contradiction of the averment, but with a list of names from among which we might easily find another and a better teacher, in the school of divine philosophy. The production of any such list may be a more difficult task than those imagine who would be prompt to profess that it might be accomplished in a moment.

There is a preliminary work to be done on this ground; for among the names that will instantly occur to every one who is conversant with the history of philosophy many must be excluded from any such catalogue on a ground of exception that is quite valid; as thus—when we are in search of those who might fairly dispute with the Hebrew prophet his place at the head of theistic thought, we must not name, *as if they were his rivals*, any of those who, in fact, have sat at his feet, and who achieved whatever they may have achieved by building upon the Hebrew foundation. In abstract philosophy the advantage is incalculably great of starting in a right direction; whether or no the best path over the ground be afterwards followed. This ground of exception will at once reduce our liberty of choice to a very few names. The long series of theologians—philosophical or biblical—who have received their early training within the pale of either

Jewish or Christian institutions, have set out—capital in hand: as well intellectually, as morally, they have been provided with the materials and the terms of theistic speculation; and not only so, for every habitude of mental labour has been acquired and matured under, and amidst, Bible influences. Those primary elements of religious speculation which include the idea and the belief of the Personality of God, and of His moral government, and of the emotional relationship of the human spirit to God—the Father of spirits, and the Hearer of prayer—all these elements are, in the most exclusive sense —*Hebrew elements:* it is in these writings that they *first* occur: and it is within these writings that they have received an *expression* and an *expansion* beyond which no advance has since been made, anywhere, within the range of literature—ancient or modern. Moreover, these primary elements of theology and of piety are of such force in themselves, and they so hold their sway over the human intellect and feelings, when once they have been admitted, that to disengage the mind from their grasp is exceedingly difficult—it is a wrenching effort to which very few have been equal, even among the most resolute and robust of modern sophists.

Those therefore who might be named as our masters in theology, or a philosophy which might supplant theology, must be such as have either lived and taught far remote from any glimmer of Biblical light, or they must be those, if indeed there be any such, who, living within the circle of that light, have freed themselves entirely from its influence. How difficult it has been to do so is shown by the extravagance—by that style of paradox—by the hyperbolic endlessness in speculation, which have marked the course of modern atheistic philosophy in Germany, France, and England. It has not been otherwise than as by a convulsive out-leap from the ground of Biblical belief, that men like Feuerbach, or Hegel, or Auguste Compte, or Holyoake, or Geo. Combe, have landed themselves upon the howling wilderness of baseless abstractions—or "free thought."

The atheistic thinkers of classical antiquity are comparatively mild in mood; they are for the most part free from acrimony: they stop short of nihilism, and they retain some ground of confidence in the foundations of knowledge. The ancient Pyrrhonists stand in a light of great advantage, as to temper and style, when placed by the side of the modern professors of atheism. In fact, this comparison suggests the need of another term which modern languages do not supply; for the word *atheist* has acquired an ill sense from the malign mood of those who would declare themselves at one with the non-theists, or with the universal sceptics, of antiquity. Whence has come this opprobrious or sinister meaning of the word? It may be said it has come from the contumelious style, and the ill temper of their opponents, namely—Christian theists. In part it may be so; but not wholly, nor chiefly, for the opprobrium has been *earned* by those to whose names it has come to be attached: a savour of virulence has become the characteristic of writers of this class; and if we ask why it should be so, the reason is not far to seek—modern *non-theists* have not been able to distance themselves far enough from the true theology—the Biblical theology, to relieve themselves from an uneasy consciousness of its presence. So it has been that the simple negation of belief has taken to itself the temper of a growling hatred. The classic fathers of the same philosophy were tormented in no such manner as this; and therefore they conserved their philosophic equanimity. It was not until the time when the easy-tempered atheism of antiquity came into conflict with Christianity, as in Porphyry (if we may accept the evidence of his opponents) that it acquired its *animus*—its sharp arrogance, and its resentful dogmatism.

When it is affirmed, as it has been affirmed once and again in these pages, that the Hebrew theology is the only theology which might be propounded to mankind as—*a religion*, an appeal in support of this averment may be made, on the one hand, to the unvarying issue of all philosophical speculation which opposes itself to the Biblical theism: this issue has been Pantheism, or avowed Atheism; or, on the other hand, we might appeal to the many attempts that have been made to establish, or to *demonstrate* a theism of abstractions, on the side of Biblical belief, or in supposed confirmation of it. A sufficient instance of what may be looked for on this ground is the noted *Demonstration of the Being and the Attributes of God.* We need not cite the acknowledgments of several strong-minded Christian theists who have avowed their dissatisfaction with Clarke's line of abstract reasoning. It is enough to say that, although reasonings of this order may help the belief of a few believers—much as sea-breezes and sea-bathing enhance the health of those who *are* in health—this *Demonstration* avails little or nothing with any but the few whose minds are so constituted as to find rest on metaphysic ground. Certain it is that a *Religion* for mankind never has been set a-going upon the stilts of metaphysical logic: who then shall be enthusiast enough, in future, to attempt an enterprise of this order? There never has been—there never will be, A RELIGION—no, nor a theology—of abstractions, There will be no other religious theism than that of which the Hebrew Scriptures are the source. Thus it is therefore—taking a distinguished individual of a class as its representative, that even now in this nineteenth century we claim for Isaiah the position due to him as our master in the school of the highest reason.

Note to page 212.

Metrical structure of the Lamentations. In part the highly artificial structure of these poems is conspicuous even in the English version (or indeed in any other version). Each verse has two, three, or four members, or sentences, in apposition; which together constitute the one meaning or sense, of the verse, irrespectively, often, of the meaning of the preceding, or of the next following verse. Where, as in several places, the meaning is continuous, from triplet to triplet, yet there presents itself a break, or change, more or less manifest. Thus far the metrical structure gives evidence of itself in a translation; but not so the acrostic or alliterative rule, which of course can be seen only in the Hebrew. Throughout the poetical books, generally, the modern division of chapters is arbitrary or accidental, and it is often disregardful of the sense and connection of passages; but in the Lamentations this division into five portions, or independent poems, rests upon the alphabetic structure of each portion; unless it might be said that the third chapter, with its sixty-six verses, would better have been divided into three. The first chapter, with its twenty-two verses, corresponding to the letters of the Hebrew alphabet, each letter taking its turn to stand first in the verse. So the second chapter. The third has its three alphabetic series—sixty-six in all. The fourth, twenty-two; the fifth, twenty-two. As well the regularity of this structure, as the few instances of departure from it, convey a meaning which may be noted; but the probable reasons, in each instance, whether arising from the requirements of the *alphabetic* rule, or from the higher requirements of the *subject-matter*, could not be set forth otherwise than in adducing the Hebrew text, and in following a track of probable conjecture as to what might have been the choice of words, or the *no-choice*, in each instance in which a departure from the exact metrical rule occurs. In the instance of the 119th Psalm—the structure of which is quite different—the want of a *sufficient* choice of words, *suitable* for the initial word of eight verses, is indicated by the *recurrence of the same word*, two, three, or four times, in each compartment, or strophe. An accomplished Hebraist, whose ready recollection of the *copia verborum* of the language might enable him to do so, would not, perhaps, find it very difficult to trace what we may allowably call the *verbal reasons*, or even the glossary necessities, which had been followed, or yielded to, in several of these instances; and this, as well where the metrical rule has been adhered to, as where a deviation from it has been admitted.

Leaving unattempted any such critical analysis of the metrical Hebrew poems as is here imagined, we may very safely assume, as probable, a reason why a structure so artificial as that of the Lamentations, or of the 119th, and other Psalms, should have been employed in the constitution of the Canon of Scripture. Generally, the reasons which supply our answer to the questions—Why should the Inspired writings adopt the poetic style, and why, to so large an extent as they do? and why should they in this manner submit the *thought* to the arbitrary sway of *metrical rules?*—apply in full force to any minor question, relating to cases in which certain rules of structure, which are *in an extreme degree artificial*, are complied with by the inspired writers. The obvious advantages of the poetic style, and of a metrical structure, are—the adaptation of both to the tastes and culture of the people; and especially the adaptation of the latter to the purpose of storing these compositions in the memory, from infancy upward. Thus it was that the minds of this—indeed favoured, though afflicted—people, were richly furnished with religious and moral sentiments; and thus was meditative thought nourished, and suggested, and directed, and was made conducive to the momentous purposes of the individual, and of the domestic spiritual life. Too little do we now take account, in our Biblical readings and criticisms, of this deep-going purpose of the Hebrew poetic Scriptures, which, through centuries of national weal and woe, have nourished millions and millions of souls—" unto life eternal." Thus it was that those who, in the lapse of ages, should be "more in number than the stars of heaven," were trained for their gathering, one by one, into the "bosom of Abraham."

As to the Lamentations, and the highly artificial structure which distinguishes them, as being the most artificial portions of the entire Hebrew Canon, a peculiar, and a very deep historic meaning is suggested by this very peculiarity. Through long—long tracts of time, this one immortal people has been left, as if forsaken of God, to weep in exile. The man who found a grave in any strange land, but a home in none, took up this word—"Thy testimonies have been my songs in the house of my pilgrimage." In the scatterings and wanderings of families, and in lonely journeyings—in deserts and in cities, where no synagogue-service could be enjoyed, the metrical Scriptures—infixed as they were in the memory, by the very means of these artificial devices of versets, and of alphabetic order, and of alliteration—became food to the soul. Thus was the religious constancy of the people, and its brave endurance of injury and insult, sustained and animated. Thus was it that, seated in some dismal lurking place of a suburb, disconsolate where all around him was life, the Jew uttered his disregarded plaint:—

> Is it nothing to you, all ye that pass by?
> Behold, and see if there be any sorrow like unto my sorrow, which is done unto me,
> Wherewith the Lord hath afflicted me in the day of His fierce anger.

The purpose which has been kept in sight in these pages may here again be adverted to. The one inference that is derivable from the fact of the artificial, or arbitrary metrical structure of the Hebrew poetic Scriptures is, as I think, this—that the high intention of the Inspired writings is secured—*over* the conditions and the requirements, and the necessities, of language:—this high intention is secured *beneath* these conditions and requirements and necessities; and it is secured *in* and *among* them. Where these requirements seem most to rule the course of thought, and where most the tyranny of the medium appears to triumph over the sovereign purpose—that purpose nevertheless comes off undamaged and entire. In witnessing what we might regard as a conflict between the medium, and the mind, of Scripture, the mind saves itself, and the medium prevails, only in appearance.

Note to page 222.

The Greek version of the Hebrew Scriptures. A large subject, abounding in facts that invite, and that would repay, learned industry, is the diffusion of the Septuagint translation during the pre-Apostolic era, and its actual influence in preparing a people, gathered from among the heathen, for the promulgation of the Gospel. The facts belonging to this subject would need to be collected at the cost of some labour, from the earliest of the Christian writers—especially the apologists, such as Tatian, Athenagoras, Clement of Alexandria, and Origen. Much, of course, from Philo and Josephus. More than a little also might be gleaned from the writings of Plutarch, Seneca, Athenæus, Horace, Juvenal, Lucian; and much from the two treasures of antiquity—the "Evangelic Demonstration," and the "Preparation," of Eusebius. Among those instances of providential interposition which favoured the spread and triumph of Christianity, none are more signal, or more worthy of regard, than is this of the early and wide diffusion of the Old Testament Scriptures by the means of the Alexandrian version. Whatever may be its faults, or failures—and on this ground more is often alleged than could be proved—undoubtedly it truthfully conveys the theologic purport of the Hebrew Scriptures; and in so doing, at the first, that is to say, from about B. C. 140 to, and beyond, the Apostolic age, it had "made ready a people for the Lord" in almost every city wherein the Greek language was spoken. Wherever the Apostles came "preaching the word," they found among the frequenters of the Sabbath services in the Jewish Synagogue not only *listeners*, as they might also among remoter barbarians, but *learners*, who already were well conversant with the phraseology of a true theology, and of a pure devotional service. In most cities there were a few of the philosophic class (this may fairly be assumed) who were used to drop in to the synagogue and listen to the reading of Moses and the Prophets. No doubt, among the "honorable women" of those places there were *many*—very many—Sabbath worshippers who had found, in the Jewish Synagogue, that liturgy of the soul which woman's nature more quickly discerns, and more truly appreciates, than does man's nature, or than his pride will allow him to accept, or care for. Thus it was that by means of the Greek Scriptures, road-ways had been made for the conveyance of the Gospel—north, south, east, and west; and thus that word had been fulfilled—"Prepare ye the way of the Lord, make His paths straight."

It was, we say, the *truth* in theology that had thus been carried forth throughout the Greek-speaking world: it could not be the *poetry* of the prophets; it was their theism and their ethics. To Greek minds of the cultured class, the strange idioms, and the allusive phrases which abound in the version of the Seventy, must have had the effect of quite dispelling or offending those tastes which, otherwise, the Hebrew poetry might have awakened. Readers of Greek poetry could not but distaste the Psalmists and the Prophets—if thought of as poets. Such readers accepted them only in their higher character as teachers of piety.

Note to page 224.

The Rabbinical mood. The Rabbis of a later age appear to have followed in the track of their masters—the Scribes of the Apostolic age; and, serviceable as these Jewish versionists and commentators no doubt are—for they were ministers in the providential scheme which has secured the safe transmission of the Inspired writings to later times—it was not their function to concern themselves with the soul and spirit—with the fire—of the national literature; but only with the letter. Thus writes a competent critic:—"Nihil nisi traditiones Scribæ docuerunt, quid sc. hic aut ille Doctor, aut Synedrium quondam docuerit aut determinarit; quid Hillel, Shammai, Baba ben Buta, Rabban Simeon, aut Gamaliel, aut alii eruditi, asseverint, aut negarint; aut qui hanc aut illamve quæstionem proposuerint, aut qui hoc aut illud determinarint . . . Doctrina omnis Scribarum circa externa maximè versabatur, vulgares scilicet communesque ritus ac cærimonias, ut in Codice Thalmudico ubique apparet. . . . Vix quidquam præter carnalia Thalmud continet, ut legenti patebit." LIGHTFOOT, vol. I. p. 504.

Note to page 227.

Basil's description of his delicious retreat, on the banks of the Iris, I have had occasion to adduce at length in another place. The passage has also been cited more than once or twice by modern writers, and I need not repeat the quotation here, where, in fact, it could bear upon the subject of this volume only in an indirect manner. It is enough here to point out the characteristic difference, distinguishing the ascetic tastes and style of the Eastern, and of the Western monachism: a poetic feeling, a mildness, a sense of the beautiful, may be traced in the one, contrasted with the rigour and murkiness that belong to the other. It is true that *abstemiousness* was carried to a greater extent by the Greek ascetics; but *severity* in modes of living was the boast of the monks of the West. Fasting was comparatively easy in the sultry East, and in Egypt—appetite was terribly clamorous in Gaul. So says Sulpitius Severus:—"Nam edacitas in Græcis, gula est, in Gallis, natura." Dialog. I.

Note to page 228.

The influence of the Inspired writings upon national literatures.

It cannot be said that the Hebrew poetry has given *a poetry* to any modern literature. Its influence has been rather to give poetry—to give depth, force, animation, feeling, to the prose, and to the political and common life of those modern nations among whom the Scriptures—the Old Testament especially—have been the most freely diffused. Hitherto no attempt to idealize, or to *heroize*, or to transmute into the dramatic form, the persons, or the events, or the conceptions of the Bible, has been anything better than a failure: the instances that might be named as exceptions, might better be named as examples confirmatory of this broad assertion. What are Racine's Esther or Athalia? What is Klopstock's Messiah? What is Milton's Paradise Regained? What are these ill-judged enterprises better than Mrs. Hannah More's Sacred Dramas?—vapid, wearisome, ineffective, either for edification, or for entertainment! Paradise Lost is not an exceptive instance; for it is a mere germ—an almost nothing—in this great poem that is properly *Biblical:* it is a realization of conceptions that have had quite another source, or other sources; modern, much rather than ancient, and in which Moses and the Prophets make much less appearance than do Dante, Michael Angelo, and some of the German and middle-age painters. In a *Christian* sense, it must be acknowledged that the paganized orthodoxy (is it orthodoxy?) of Paradise Lost offends, much more than it satisfies, Christian belief. Whatever in Milton is purely terrestrial and *human*, reaches at once the sublime; but whatever is celestial, whatever is transacted on an upper stage, barely saves itself from the bathos: or if among the supernals the true sublime is attained, it is in hell, not in heaven, that this success has been achieved.

There is room for a parallel affirmation in regard to the poetry of ancient Greece, which has not given *a poetry* to any modern literature; but instead of this, it has been Greece, in its *history*, in its philosophy, in its politics, that has given *a poetry*—a depth, a force, an animation, to the prose—to the public life of (free) modern nations. A repetition, or an attempt to put forth in modern guise the classical poetry, barely reaches the faint evanescent colours of the reflected arch in a double rainbow: such repetitions are exercises for schoolboys. Yet is it true that modern public life, in free communities, has breathed a spirit which has drawn the power and fire of poetry from classic *prose*. It is neither Homer's heroes, nor those of Æschylus, that have made the great men of modern states what they were: but it is the real men of the best times of Athens: it has been *this* influence, mainly, that has thrown a poetic glow upon selfish ambition. So far then as what is here affirmed may be true, we shall look for the "mighty influence" of the Scriptures when it has displayed itself in national literatures, not in the *poetry* directly, but in the prose, and in the life of each people; and so it will be that the Bible-reading nations of modern Europe have displayed, in the most decisive manner, that richness as well as quaintness—that soul-force, that intensity of the social affections—that moral energy of the irascible emotions, which declare their source to have been the Hebrew Scriptures. The England and the Scotland of the seventeenth century were rich in men of force, whose behaviour and language, whose courage, and humanity too, breathed a Bible inspiration, raised above vulgarity or barbarism by the training of Bible history and poetry.

Note to page 248.

The Apology of Socrates. The closing words of the Apology, as reported by Plato, may be open to a question, as to the precise meaning which they carry—or which they carried in the mind of the master, or of his disciple: they are these (often cited)—'Αλλὰ *γὰρ ἤδη ἀπιέναι ἐμοὶ μὲν ἀποθανουμένῳ, ὑμῖν δὲ βιωσομένοις· ὁπότεροι δὲ ἡμῶν ἔρχονται ἐπὶ ἄμεινον πρᾶγμα, ἄδηλον παντὶ ἢ τῷ Θεῷ.* There might be room to ask—In thus speaking was Socrates thinking of the life and the world he was leaving, or of the world—the hidden future, the Hades—upon which he was about to enter? If of the former, then his meaning would be—God only knows whether it be not a better thing to die, as I am about to die, under an unmerited sentence—to die, an innocent man, than to live—as you, my inequitable judges, will live, condemned now by your own consciences, and soon to be followed by the execrations of the Athenian people. But even if the philosopher, as we may well suppose, had his eye fixed upon the future—the unseen world, there are still two senses between which a choice might be made; for he might intend to say—God only knows whether the happiness which I have in prospect is not such as greatly to outweigh all those pleasures of the present life which you, my judges, may yet live to enjoy. Or, on this *second* supposition, the other sense may be this—God only knows to which of us—whether to me, or to you—the happier lot shall be assigned, when, at length, *you and I together* shall come to meet our dues, severally, in Hades, according to the award of inexorable and impartial justice. This last meaning of the words may find support in some passages of the Phædo: but perhaps it draws its chief support in our minds, from our own Christian beliefs. The version of the phrase which Cicero gives (Tusc. Quest. I. 44) does not determine the sense—"Utrum autem sit melius." Lactantius (Instit. VII. 2) in repeating this passage from Cicero, adduces it in illustration of his argument, touching the uncertainty of all philosophical speculations—"Quare necesse est omnes philosophiæ sectas, alienas esse à veritate; quia homines errant, qui eas constituerunt; nec ullum fundamentum, aut firmitatem possunt habere quæ nullis divinarum vocum fulciuntur oraculis."

Whatever the meaning of the martyr-philosopher in this instance, or in other instances, might be, it is certain that he, and his profound disciple, laboured to their best, in the mine of thought; or, changing the figure—that, with sincere purpose, they toiled along that rugged thorny path that leadeth upward from the sordid and sensual levels of the world, toward a world of light, truth, goodness, upon which upward, rugged, thorny path, none shall walk and lose his way—none, if indeed the modesty and the sincerity of Socrates be in them, for it is these qualities that give the soul its aptitude to receive guidance from above, where it may be had. Socrates, and Plato too, in professing their consciousness of the need of a heavenly leading on this path, approached very near to an expression of David's better confidence:—

Thou wilt not leave (*abandon*, οὐκ ἐγκαταλείψεις) my soul in Hades;
Thou wilt show me the path of life:
In Thy presence is fulness of joy;
At Thy right hand are pleasures for evermore.

Note to page 266.

The mission of the Scriptures. A subject too large, as well as too deep to find room for itself in a note; but it is a subject which might well engage the meditations of those who will, and who can, calmly think of the course of things at this moment. There is a stage of intellectual and literary sophistication, commingling fastidious tastes and the sardonic frivolity of luxurious modes of life, which will never consist with the feelings, the tastes, the moral habitudes, that belong to a devout reading, study, relish, and home-use of the Bible. Whoever has had near acquaintance with leisurely cultured life, in this, its advanced stage of refinement, and whoever has felt the potent influence of such an atmosphere upon himself for a length of time, and has learned to relish the ironies, the mockeries, the spiritualisms of the region, with its soft intellectuality, and its epicureanism, will think that a thousand leagues of interval are not too many to intervene between such a region and a home where there is feeling and truth, and within which the Scriptures—Prophets and Apostles—might be listened to, and where those ministers of God might make their appeal to the deeper principles of human nature. Is it that the canonical writings have been proved untrue? Is it that Revelation has lately been tried, and found wanting? It is not so; but those who spend life in the precincts of well-bred affectations find that they have come into a mood which renders the Bible, in its wonted place—on the table, at home—an unwelcome object. There is felt to be a sacrilege, even, in opening the book while the fancy is revelling in whatever is frivolously intellectual and artistically sensuous. To produce this effect, there need be nothing gross or licentious in the converse of our intimates, whose converse, nevertheless, does not consist, never will consist, with Bible-reading habitudes: the two influences are irreconcilably repellant, the one of the other.

In every highly-cultured community there is an upper stage, or privileged enclosure, within which this sophistication bears sway, and is always in progress; but so long as its circuit is limited, and so long as it includes none but either the wealthy, and the parasites of wealth, and a few intruders, the masses of the people may retain the native force of their feelings—their genuineness, their serious beliefs, and their consciousness of the strenuous realities of life. Among such a people the Bible may retain, and may exert its proper influence. But there is a tendency, which, from day to day, is enlarging the circle of upper-class sophistication, and which therefore, in the same proportion, is driving in the boundaries of the more robust national moral consciousness. Narrowed continually it is, moreover, by all those well-intended devices of recent invention, the purpose of which is to bring the luxuries of art, in all lines, and the fine things of literature, within reach of the middle, and of the labouring classes.

Should we then step forward, and, in gloomy mood, attempt to arrest this course of things? This may not be; nor would any endeavours of this sort avail for the purpose intended. Nevertheless the issue is inevitable; or it is so unless, within the upper classes, and especially within and among the ministers of religion, a decisive renovation of religious convictions should take place. Let this be, and then the Scriptures will retain their place of power; but if not, then our institutions, however stable they may seem, will crumble into dust, wrought upon daily, as they are, by the dry-rot of sophisticated intellectuality, and epicurean tastes. This is the course of things in England; and such has long been the actual condition of our nearest continental neighbours.

At this moment the spread of infidelity, especially in the educated classes, is spoken of with alarm. Yet the unbelief of educated Englishmen is not a product of reason: it is not the ascertained upshot of an argument: it is not the result of a controversy which may have been unskilfully managed on the side of belief. This infidelity, or this pantheism, or this atheism, which walks the streets with a noiseless camel-tread—breathing in the ear from behind—this rife infidelity, is the natural out-speak of intellectual and literary sophistication, and of that relish for frivolous pleasures, the operation of which is to render the tastes factitious, and to lull the moral consciousness, and to falsify the social affections; and which so perverts the reasoning faculty that evidence produces an effect in an inverse ratio to its actual force.

Meantime the Scriptures are fulfilling their mission. Among ourselves, and abroad, the Bible goes on its way, and it prospers *to the end whereto He that thus sends it, sent it.* The Scriptures take effect upon men—singly, and in communities—among whom what is real in human nature, what is strong and great, still subsist: the Scriptures come where they come, as the dew; or as the rain from heaven; or they come as the tempest:—the word is gentle, and germinating; or it is a force irresistible: and it does its office, here or there, as the need may be, where human nature, as to its moral elements, is still in a culturable state, and is still reclaimable: as to those, and at this time they are many, who, in respect of the moral elements of human nature, have passed beyond this range by the deadly influence of luxurious refinements—the message from Heaven leaves them where they are, and goes forward. It is thus that individual men, and that communities, may lose their part in God's Revelation. At this time, and among ourselves, so false and fatal a condition is that of a class only; but it is the class which, by its culture, and its intelligence, possesses the means and the opportunity to speak for itself; and it is thus that an estimate of its numbers, and of its mental and moral importance—greatly exaggerated, is made by itself, on the one side; and by those who speak of it in tones of vivid alarm, on the other side.

THE END.

BIOGRAPHICAL SKETCH.*

Isaac Taylor was the son of the late Rev. Isaac Taylor, a dissenting minister at Ongar, in Essex, and brother of Jane Taylor, whose "Contributions of Q. Q." are well known. He was born about the close of the last century, and, we believe, educated privately under the immediate superintendence of his father. He was originally destined for the dissenting pulpit, and commenced a course of preparatory study; but he soon relinquished the idea of becoming a minister, and turned his thoughts to the bar. His connexion with the legal profession was not of long duration. He betook himself to literature, and for many years lived in retirement at Stanford Rivers—a beautiful rural retreat in the immediate vicinity of his native place. In this secluded spot he wrote and published anonymously "The Natural History of Enthusiasm," and other works, some of which have had a fair share of popular favour, more especially among the enlightened and thoughtful of the various dissenting communities. His other principal works are "Ancient Christianity," published periodically, and manifesting an intimate acquaintance with the writings of the early fathers—an attempt to meet the Tractarians on their own ground, and to prove that some of these ancient writers were not so immaculate, either in doctrine or morals, as to entitle them to the blind adherence claimed for them by their modern eulo-

* From "Men of the Time." Kent & Co. London. 1859.

gists—"Elements of Thought," a small treatise which is used as a sort of *vade mecum* by students entering upon their philosophical studies in dissenting colleges—"The Physical Theory of Another Life," in which he indulges in speculations respecting the material condition of man and other created beings in a future state. The mental characteristics displayed in this and his other works gave rise to a highly amusing and interesting article from the pen of Sir James Stephen, in the "Edinburgh Review." Mr. Taylor, however, was comparatively little appreciated as a writer until it became known that he was the author of "The Natural History of Enthusiasm." He had been for some time before the public *in propriâ personâ*, but failed to elicit that attention to his writings which their intrinsic merits deserved. His circuitous style and Coleridgean manner of viewing the various subjects on which he wrote proved a great barrier to his popularity. His classical learning, his philosophical acuteness, and his general culture, were never called in question; but the laboured obscurity of style, and his indefinite mode of expression, proved substantial obstacles to his literary fame. "The Natural History of Enthusiasm," however, was very differently received by the religious public. It was fortunate in the time of its appearance. It was issued when the excitement and enthusiasm connected with Row and Irving were at their height. Mr. Taylor's philosophico-religious turn of mind, his previous studies, and even his peculiarities of style, enabled him to treat this subject in a manner agreeable to all professors of religion, of whatever sect or denomination. Young men preparing for the ministry began to imitate the idiosyncrasies of its style, and some with greater success to imbibe its unsectarian spirit. His other works on kindred subjects, "Fanaticism," "Spiritual Despotism," "Loyola and Jesuitism," "Wesley and Methodism;" the series of sacred meditations entitled "Saturday Evening," and "Home Education;" have all been well received, although their popularity has been by no means equal to that which "The Natural History of Enthusiasm" has all along maintained. In addition to his gifts as an author, Mr. Taylor possesses a certain amount of mechanical genius, which, we believe, he has turned to some profitable account in originating various designs of a useful and ornamental character. It may not be uninteresting to add that his habits are simple and methodical; although a "recluse," as he somewhere in his writings styles himself, he is said to be an expert and eager angler, and fond of healthy and manly sports. He spends his Saturday mornings in directing the games of his children, while his Saturday evenings are devoted to meditations of a religious character, similar to those which appear in the work under that name; and on Sundays he occasionally preaches, although a layman, to the great delight of those who are fortunate enough to hear him. His books have all, or nearly all, been republished in America, and have had an extensive circulation in the States as well as in Canada.

A CATALOGUE

OF THE

WRITINGS OF ISAAC TAYLOR.

Ancient Christianity,

And the Doctrines of the Oxford Tracts for the Times. Fourth Edition, with Supplement, Index, and Tables. 2 vols. 8vo., pp. 550 and 700. London, 1844.

Ancient Christianity,

And the Doctrines of the Oxford Tracts for the Times. Supplement, including Index, Tables, &c. 8vo., pp. 142. London, 1844

Spiritual Despotism.

Second Edition. 8vo., pp. 504. London, 1835.

Fanaticism. 8vo.

Natural History of Enthusiasm.

Eighth Edition. 8vo. London.

Saturday Evening.

Sixth Edition. 8vo. London. 12mo., pp. 379.

Home Education.

Crown 8vo. London, 1838.

Physical Theory of Another Life. 8vo.

Four Lectures on Spiritual Christianity,

Delivered in the Hanover-Square Rooms, London, March, 1841. 12mo., pp. 203. London, 1841.

Elements of Thought;

Or, Concise Explanations, Alphabetically Arranged, of the Principal Terms Employed in the Different Branches of Intellectual Philosophy. Seventh Edition. 12mo. London.

An Essay,

Introductory to a New Edition of Pascal's Thoughts. 12mo.

Transmission of Ancient Books

To Modern Times. 8vo.

Essay

On the Application of Abstract Reasoning in the Christian Doctrine. Originally published as an Introduction to Edwards on the Will. 12mo., pp. 163. Boston, 1832.

Wesleyan Methodist;

A Review, published in the Edinburgh Review.

Introductory Essay

To a Translation of Pfizer's Life of Luther.

Loyola and Jesuitism

In its Rudiments. 12mo., pp. 416. London, 1850.

Process of Historical Proof. 8vo.

Balance of Criminality,

Or Mental Error. 12mo.

Jane Taylor's Works.

A New Edition. With a Life and Notes. 5 vols. 12mo.

Wesley and Methodism.

Josephus, The Works of.

A New Translation, by the Rev. Robert Traill, with Notes, Explanatory Essays, and Pictorial Illustrations. Edited by *Isaac Taylor.* Royal 8vo. London, 1847.

Restoration of Belief.

The Restoration of Belief. 12mo., pp. 381. Cambridge, 1855.

World of Mind.

The World of Mind, an Elementary Book. 12mo. London, 1858

Logic of Theology.

Logic of Theology and other Essays. 12mo., pp. 384. London, 1859.

Ultimate Civilization.

Ultimate Civilization, and other Essays. By Isaac Taylor London, 1860.

Hebrew Poetry.

The Spirit of the Hebrew Poetry. 8vo., pp. 363. London, 1861.

www.ingramcontent.com/pod-product-compliance
Lightning Source LLC
Chambersburg PA
CBHW022055230426
43672CB00008B/1180